PRAISE FOR *FREE*

"If mass incarceration is one of the great moral crises of our time, then how we treat those who are recently freed is just as much of a travesty. The stories Lauren Kessler shares in *Free* show how prison changes people and fails to set them up for success on the outside. Lauren integrates data with compelling vignettes to illustrate a better way forward for those who will be released from prison."

—Eric Garcia, author of *We're Not Broken: Changing the Autism Conversation*

"*Free* is an important contribution to the body of incarceration literature. It is also a captivating read: each chapter and each story makes you eager to read the next."

—Laura Bates, author of *Shakespeare Saved My Life: Ten Years in Solitary with the Bard*

"With tenderness and empathy, Lauren Kessler speaks to how and where we fail the thousands of individuals coming out of prison every year. Kessler asks us to get to know these six men and women and to come to understand and celebrate their remarkable journeys. I love the writing in this important and timely book. These moving stories will stay with you."

—Alex Kotlowitz, bestselling author of *There Are No Children Here*

"It is nothing short of phenomenal to read these stories of people who move from prison to freedom. Lauren Kessler's immersion journalism gives us a place from which to witness the world we've made and how people who make mistakes must learn to navigate through it against impossible odds."

—Lidia Yuknavitch, bestselling author of *The Book of Joan* and *The Chronology of Water*

ALSO BY LAUREN KESSLER

A Grip of Time: When Prison Is Your Life

The Write Path: Essays on the Art of
Writing and the Joy of Reading

Raising the Barre: Big Dreams, False Starts, and
My Midlife Quest to Dance the Nutcracker

Counterclockwise: My Year of Hypnosis, Hormones, Dark
Chocolate, and Other Adventures in the World of Anti-Aging

My Teenage Werewolf: A Mother, a Daughter, a
Journey Through the Thicket of Adolescence

Dancing with Rose: Finding Life in the Land of Alzheimer's

Clever Girl: Elizabeth Bentley, the Spy Who
Ushered in the McCarthy Era

The Happy Bottom Riding Club: The Life
and Times of Pancho Barnes

Full Court Press: A Season in the Life of a Winning
Basketball Team and the Women Who Made It Happen

Stubborn Twig: Three Generations in the
Life of a Japanese American Family

After All These Years: Sixties Ideals in a Different World

FREE

TWO YEARS, SIX LIVES, *and*

THE LONG JOURNEY HOME

LAUREN KESSLER

Published by Sourcebooks
P.O. Box 4410, Naperville, Illinois 60567-4410
(630) 961-3900
sourcebooks.com

Library of Congress Cataloging-in-Publication Data

Names: Kessler, Lauren, author.
Title: Free : two years, six lives, and the long journey home / Lauren Kessler.
Description: Naperville, Illinois : Sourcebooks, [2022] | Includes
    bibliographical references.
Identifiers: LCCN 2021052691 (print) | LCCN 2021052692 (ebook) |
Subjects: LCSH: Ex-convicts--Social conditions. | Ex-convicts--Services
    for. | Prisoners--Deinstitutionalization.
Classification: LCC HV9281 .K47 2022 (print) | LCC HV9281 (ebook) | DDC
    364.8--dc23/eng/20211105
LC record available at https://lccn.loc.gov/2021052691
LC ebook record available at https://lccn.loc.gov/2021052692

Printed and bound in the United States of America.
VP 10 9 8 7 6 5 4 3 2 1

For Cheryl, Karen, and Karuna

Hope is like the sun,
which, as we journey toward it,
casts the shadow of our burden behind us

SAMUEL SMILES

AUTHOR'S NOTE

This is a work of nonfiction.

Because the line between fact and fiction has recently become blurred in ways many of us could never have imagined, I want to be clear: All the people in this book are real. None are inventions or fabrications. There are no composite characters. I have not knowingly changed any facts or details about them or their lives, with the following exception: I did change the names of the characters I call Vicki (as well as her partner and children) and Dave. Unlike the others whose reentries are chronicled here, these two lead private lives, and I chose to protect that privacy.

All the events you will read about are real. All the conversations are real. I have chronicled these as faithfully as I know how. Many I directly heard and witnessed or participated in. Some are the products of multiple in-depth interviews. A few were gleaned from audio, video, or text records kept by others.

Any liberties I have taken are liberties not of fact but of interpretation. I saw these people, these events, through my own eyes and filtered them, as all nonfiction writers do, through my own sensibilities. I mean to respect these people who let me into their lives. I mean to shed a light on their journey. I mean to tell truths both factual and emotional.

PROLOGUE

When she was eighteen, Belinda was convicted of stabbing her pimp. She hadn't meant to kill him, just hurt him. She'd been on the streets since she was fourteen, when her mother stopped the car and told her to get out, and she had learned to take care of herself. Or at least stay alive. She spent the next twenty-two years behind bars. The day she was released from the Coffee Creek Correctional Facility, it was raining. She was wearing sweatpants a size too large and a cheap nylon jacket, clothes brought in by a friend the day before. She was lit up, like a girl rushing out to meet her prom date. There was no prom date. There was a clutch of late-middle-aged women from a faith-based group that had connected with her in prison. There was a dog. It was one of the dogs she had helped train as part of a prison-run canine companions program. She briefly hugged the women then got down on one knee and nuzzled the dog for a long moment. The dog remembered her.

The ladies knew exactly where Belinda wanted to go. In two cars, they caravanned to the nearest Starbucks, less than two minutes away. She'd heard about this Starbucks from someone inside, a woman who'd come to prison more than a decade after Belinda. Belinda hesitated at the door. Two of the ladies walked in. A third stood next to her, waiting, silent. Then she gently laid a palm on Belinda's back and ushered her in. They found a table. They ordered for her. She wanted a caramel Frappuccino. Someone had told her about caramel Frappuccinos. When she took that first sip, she closed her eyes.

———————

A month later, Belinda and I sit in a booth at a chain steak house. She had allowed me to witness her release that day because we had connected while she was still inside. I had interviewed her about her experiences with the prison's hospice unit, where inmate volunteers sat with the dying as their lives ended behind bars. It was part of my research on incarcerated life that became my first book about life inside prison, A Grip of Time. I liked Belinda. She was tough. She had to be. But the hospice work had, I thought, touched a place inside her that maybe had not been touched before. I wanted her to do well on the outside. I thought I owed her at least a dinner for the time she spent answering my questions, for her honesty. And so I had proposed this get-together.

Now, sitting across from her, I take note that she has ordered the most expensive item on the menu plus three extra sides. The food on the plates in front of her could feed a family of four. Belinda hardly touches it. She has not looked up from her phone since we sat down. A month ago she had never held a smartphone in her hand. Now she is nonstop texting with her thumbs. She had gotten the phone three weeks before. She had acquired a boyfriend a week later.

She was in the throes of what sociologists call "asynchronicity." While Belinda was in prison, her age cohort moved on. Inside, time was frozen. Outside, other young women acquired (and dumped) boyfriends or girlfriends, went to concerts, got (and lost) jobs, maybe went to college. On the outside, other young women moved to new apartments, new towns, new countries, had adventures, changed their look, had career aspirations that worked out or didn't. On the outside, other young women grew into their thirties, found their place, lost it, reinvented themselves, settled in. They had children. Inside, Belinda had experienced a lot, but none of this. At forty, she was still in many ways a teenager. She was a teenager with a new phone texting a new boyfriend.

I watch her. Her hair is dyed matte black. Her eyes are thickly rimmed with black eyeliner. I can see a light etching of crow's feet in the corners of her eyes. She has that hard look women have when they've spent a lot of time in prison. She looks her age, maybe older. Prison does that to you. But she acts like a high schooler. I wonder what this disconnect might mean for her reentry. That night I offer to mentor her, be a sounding board, listen to her stories, take her out to lunch or dinner every few weeks. She agrees.

It didn't happen. Belinda was consumed with this boyfriend. And then with the one after that. With the miracle of the smartphone. With social media. With Frappuccinos at Starbucks.

She stopped texting me back. She didn't answer my calls. I never found out what kind of life she made for herself, and that not knowing haunted me.

CHAPTER 1

He walked across the control floor, the big, bare windowless space that sat at the center of the prison. The air was stale and damp. It smelled of concrete, iron, and sweat, like a basement locker room. There was a guard on his right, a guard on his left. It was maybe thirty feet across the worn linoleum to the first check point and the first barred iron gate. The guard sitting in a little room behind the bulletproof glass studied the screen in front of him, pressed a button, and the gate inched across steel tracks to open a doorway to a long corridor. This was an old prison, the oldest in the state. The gates were old. They creaked and clanged. The cell blocks—there were four of them—were old. They were Sing Sing-style "cages within cages" that looked like the setting of every grim prison movie ever made: parallel rows of barred cells, forty cells long, five tiers high, narrow metal walkways, nothing but concrete and steel. He had lived in this place for nineteen years. He was thirty-seven. Today he was getting out.

When the gate finally opened, he walked down the long,

narrow corridor, careful to keep close to the right-side wall so the cameras could see him. At the end of the corridor was another gate. He stood there waiting for another guard who was sitting, invisible, in another little room behind bulletproof glass. The guard looked at his screen and pressed a button. The second iron gate inched open. Now he stood in a small room waiting for the same guard to open the third and final gate.

He had taken care of himself during his long years inside, not just this almost two-decade stretch in a maximum security penitentiary but the two and a half years before that when he was confined to a youth detention facility. He was strong and athletic looking but without that aggressive, pectoral-amped, I-pumped-iron-on-the-yard-for-years physique so common to inmates. His head was shaved, but the tough look was softened by his rectangular glasses, which made him look both studious and smart, which he was. He had strong cheekbones, a square jaw, and when he let it happen, a wide smile. His skin, half-way between copper and olive, was the smooth, unblemished skin of a man who had not spent much time outdoors. Today, a midsummer day, he was dressed in a spotless white T-shirt and baggy black gym shorts. It was the first time in nineteen years that he did not have to wear prison blues. He stood, shoulders back, head up, facing that last gate that separated him from the life he would try to live as a free man. His name was Arnoldo.

He was poised, that summer morning, to reenter a community he barely knew. He was poised to reenter the circle of a family that had grown and changed without him. They were waiting for him on the other side of that third gate. It inched open. He walked up a short ramp through one doorway and then another, this last one bracketed with metal detectors. And then he was out, in the visitors' waiting room, leaning over to hug his mother.

The top of her head rested under his chin. She couldn't stop crying. He hugged his brother. Then he got down on one knee to embrace first one, then the other of his two young nieces. He might have felt the tears coming, but he kept his emotions in check. That's what you learned to do in prison. Still, he wanted to be swept up by the moment. He wanted it to last. But he had something to do, a promise to keep, before he could say goodbye to his incarcerated life. He forced himself to break off the reunion. He would have time for his family later. He headed out the front entrance of the prison, down the worn concrete steps, past the sentry tower, and out to the street.

On State Street, a few yards from the driveway that curved into the prison's ten-acre compound, sat a municipal fire hydrant. The city of Salem, Oregon's sleepy capital and home to four of its fourteen prisons, a youth correction facility, and a county jail, had years ago mounted a community volunteer project to paint all its hydrants a bright canary yellow. Several years ago, when they were first becoming friends, Sterling had pointed out the hydrant to Arnoldo. Sterling was a lifer who had been inside since he was sixteen. Long before, he couldn't remember just how long, he had noticed the hydrant when he was standing at one of the barred windows on the fourth floor of the prison, the floor that housed the chapel, its library, and its meeting rooms. From there you could see over the twenty-five-foot perimeter wall across a swath of weedy grass, across a small creek and another patch of grass to the main road. That's where the hydrant was. During the long, gray rainy season that was western Oregon for five or six months a year, the hydrant was a spot of color. It was a long way off, but once you saw it, your eyes were drawn to it every time you looked out the window. At least Sterling's were. And later, Arnoldo's.

Few inside the prison noticed the hydrant. You had to be on the fourth floor to be able to see over the walls, and some of the prison's more than two thousand men had never been on the fourth floor. And even if you attended services or meetings or events in that corner of the floor, even if you made your way to the chapel's library, you had to *want* to look out. Some men who'd been inside for many decades had stopped looking out the window years ago. They had to. Prison was their life and always would be. Looking over the walls led to imagining a life beyond the walls. That was unbearable, so they turned their backs.

Sterling spent most of his days on the fourth floor where, since 2014, he had worked as the chapel clerk, managing the calendar of chapel-sponsored events, supporting volunteers with room reservations and setup, spreading the word about programs, helping to communicate with security about inmate attendance. Everyone who was able to work had a prison job. Arnoldo—when he wasn't serving time in the hole for infractions big and small, for fighting, for being in the wrong place at the wrong time, for his gang connections—worked in the prison's laundry. It was the state's second-largest commercial laundry, a moneymaker, a huge, deafening facility that handled soiled linens trucked in from dozens of hospitals and other institutions. It was considered a good job inside because of the possibility of overtime (wages in the so-called prison industries in the state were reported to be, at most, forty-seven cents an hour) and because even when the prison was on lockdown, the laundry still had to operate. That meant you could get out of your cell for work when no one else could leave, not for chow hall, not for showers, not for pill line, not for any reason other than keeping the laundry operating.

Sterling and Arnoldo had met out on the yard back in 2012,

when they had both volunteered to work on a crew to prep the softball fields for summer games. It was hard work and it was unpaid, but it was outdoor work, which meant more yard time. Inmates were allotted only so much time outside. If you had a history of what was called "pro-social behavior" and made it to the top level of the prison's nonmonetary incentive system you had the privilege of spending up to three hours a day seven days a week out in the yard. Those on the bottom tier were allowed an hour and a half five days a week. Those were precious hours, especially in the spring.

Working side by side, weeding, pushing wheelbarrows, grooming the baseball diamonds, the two men made an unlikely pair. Sterling, who sometimes referred to himself as a "marvelous mulatto," was half African American, half Italian, a tall, lanky, loose-limbed man with a dusting of freckles and impressive dreadlocks that reached down his back. Arnoldo, shorter, stockier, bald, was Mexican American. Inside, Black and Latino prisoners rarely mixed, eating at different tables in chow hall and congregating in different sections of the yard. Each group had its own club—Uhuru Sasa for African American inmates, the Latino Club for Hispanic inmates—and each had its own gang, affiliations that followed the inmates in from the outside. Gang hostility from the outside sometimes erupted into fights on the inside. The fights sometimes escalated into yard brawls. A brawl could, and sometimes did, turn into a riot. There would be multiday lockdowns and months of punishment in segregation cells for those on both sides. Arnoldo belonged to a gang. He was, in fact, a gang leader.

As unusual as it was for men of different races to establish relationships, it was almost as unusual for lifers and nonlifers to be friends. Lifers were in for what inmates called "a grip," a sentence that might be for the entirety of their life—life without parole (LWOP)—or a life with parole (LWP) sentence that meant twenty-five, thirty, thirty-five, or more years as they pled their case, often many times, before rehabilitation panels and parole boards. LWP often meant the *possibility* of parole, with no guarantees. Lifers had their own club inside—it was the biggest and oldest club in the prison—with events and fundraisers, even an annual banquet. They had their own newsletter. Their unending or close-to-unending sentences created a special bond between them. The longer they spent behind bars, the looser their ties were to the outside world. Parents died. Siblings and friends moved on to live their own lives. What remained, after thirty years, was the guy on your cell block who had been around just as long as you had. Lifers were hesitant to invest the time in getting to know and trust and care about a man who might be gone in a "dime" (ten years). Losing that hard-earned friendship would be just one more loss in a life full of losses. So lifers stuck with lifers. Sterling was a lifer. Arnoldo was not. He had a "flat" sentence, a firm release date. Once inside he'd gotten two extra years tacked on to that sentence for assault, but he knew that on July 18, 2017, he'd be walking out the door.

Sterling's case was a lot more complicated. It was, in fact, one of the most complicated cases in the state's history. It would have been different had he originally been sentenced to life *without* parole for the murder he'd committed as a sixteen-year-old. Ironically, if that draconian sentence had been imposed back in 1994, he might not be behind bars right now. Or he would be anticipating a release date in the near future. That's because in 2012, the U.S. Supreme Court had ruled that a mandatory life without parole sentence for juvenile offenders was unconstitutional. It was, the justices agreed in *Miller v. Alabama*, cruel and unusual punishment that violated the Eighth Amendment. Juvenile offenders who'd received LWOP would have those sentences reversed. Depending on how long they had already been imprisoned, some would be freed immediately; others would await timely parole dates. But what Sterling had was a de facto LWOP sentence. He had two LWP sentences to be served consecutively, which added up to a lifetime. But because his official sentence was not LWOP, *Miller* did not apply to him. When Arnoldo walked out of prison that day, Sterling was about to begin his twenty-fourth year behind bars, entangled in what appeared to be an endless legal battle for the right to have his case reviewed.

Although close in age—Sterling was just three years older than Arnoldo—the two were temperamental opposites. Sterling was spark; Arnoldo was banked fire. Sterling was bold, verbal, witty. There was a spontaneity about him. He was a gifted spoken word poet, a natural performer. Arnoldo was understated, reflective, deeply cautious. He was a serious man who held himself tightly. But as they worked side by side they talked, and the longer they talked, the more they found they had in common. They had both come into the system as juveniles after childhoods scarred by abuse. Sterling's mother had given birth to him while shackled to a hospital bed. She was serving eighteen months in prison for forging checks. A loving grandmother raised him until she died. Then he was shuffled to the home of a wife-beating grandfather and his alcoholic second wife and later, at age thirteen, to the house of a drug-dealing uncle barely out of his teens himself. Sterling slept on the couch or in the cab of a truck in the driveway. When he realized no one knew or cared where he was or what he did, he took to the streets. He stole cars, vandalized, took drugs, bullied, scammed, learned that the riskier your exploits, the greater your street cred. He learned how to be a "player."

Arnoldo's early home life was dominated by an alcoholic father. He was a man who, when sober, could be (as Arnoldo later told himself) "just the kind of father you wanted to have." He was also a violent, abusive drunk who tried to drown his young son, a man who would later be sentenced to fifty years in prison for murder. Arnoldo's mother, protecting herself and her children, ran away from the marriage, leaving the culturally comfortable Texas border town of Arnoldo's childhood to make a hardscrabble life more than two thousand miles north as an agricultural worker in the alfalfa and potato fields of eastern Oregon. This is where Arnoldo felt the sting of prejudice for the first time in life, where he remembered a teacher telling him he would never amount to anything and would probably spend his life in jail, where he joined a gang of equally displaced Mexican American kids whose parents worked in the fields, where he started using drugs, where he started carrying a gun. And using it.

The two men had grown up and come of age in prison— Arnoldo remanded to juvie at fifteen, Sterling sentenced to an adult penitentiary at sixteen. And by the time they met and had become friends out on the yard, both had spent all of their twenties and most of their thirties behind bars. They had also both served hard time, spending a succession of months-long stretches that accumulated into years, and then more years in solitary confinement in what was known officially in this prison as the Intensive Management Unit (IMU) but what the inmates called "the hole." That kind of time could break you. But neither of them broke. They hadn't let the system harden them either or make them paralyzingly or self-destructively angry, as it did for so many others. Neither had they let themselves be tamed.

They had, in defiance of the system, managed to keep a part of themselves whole. "Choosing hope / fuels spiritual fires / in cold chaos," Sterling wrote once. He admired what he recognized as Arnoldo's warrior spirit. He had the same spirit, the same tenacity. They were stubborn, independent men with a sense of their own power that kept them both sane and in trouble. They clicked.

When Sterling started working up in the chapel, he began inviting Arnoldo to events. One event was a talk by an American criminologist named Howard Zehr, a pioneer in the field of restorative justice (RJ). This was not a new subject to Sterling. He had taken a restorative justice course offered inside the prison by Nathaline Frener, then a University of Oregon law professor. Through that class, he had learned that RJ, a progressive movement launched back in the mid-1970s, focused on bringing together victims and perpetrators. Rather than defining "justice" as solely the administration of punishment, RJ proposed notions of accountability, empathy, and making amends. Mediation and reconciliation were the key concepts. RJ was a way for those who did harm to take moral responsibility for that harm and to face the consequences their actions had on their victims, their families, and their communities—not just by going to prison but by opening themselves up to the emotional and psychological chaos they had caused others. As it evolved, RJ worked to provide a de-escalated space outside the heat of a courtroom or the glare of media attention for the victims to tell those who harmed them how they had been harmed. Some believed the process opened the door to forgiveness, or at least a kind of closure that a prison sentence often did not give to those whose lives were forever altered by crime. RJ was focused on victims and offenders, but it might also be applied to prison culture, to warring gangs, to men who reacted aggressively, often violently, without considering harm or consequence.

Zehr had also talked about trauma. Trauma was the leitmotif of so many prisoners' lives, both pre-incarceration and later, for years, often decades, sometimes a lifetime. The products of toxic home and street environments, they were now confined to the toxic environment of prison, where showing emotion was showing weakness, where empathy was an invitation to exploitation, where "healing" was not something real men needed to do. Wounds scarred over. They toughened you, and that was a good thing. But Zehr said, "Trauma untransformed is trauma transferred," and that resonated with Sterling and Arnoldo. They knew this. They were living it.

Karuna Thompson, one of the prison's three chaplains, saw the two of them talking together after Zehr's presentation—they were deep in conversation, intent and intense—and she knew, in that moment, something was happening. That something *could* happen. Both men were thinkers. They were both leaders. They had struggled with and lived through the issues the men in that institution faced every day, issues that often led to conflict. Suppose instead of—or in addition to—bringing in experts like Zehr or offering a university class or having community volunteers facilitate programs, these two men became the planners and facilitators themselves? Together they might be able to do something outsiders could not do. They could identify men at the edge of shifting their behavior. They could reach out to them. The combination of Sterling and Arnoldo together could be a powerhouse. Arnoldo's stature in a gang and Sterling's cred as a lifer would resonate inside. The hard time they had both served in the hole was a badge of honor. They would be seen not as men co-opted by the system, not as cons trying to con anyone, but as legitimate players. Karuna thought they could work together to create a trauma transformation program, a chapel-sponsored series of events and talks organized by the prisoners themselves. It could be a way to make a difference not just in their two lives and not just in the individual lives of the men they could persuade to participate but in the culture of the prison itself.

They could also take the lead, or at least be involved in important ways, with how the prison might incorporate RJ within its walls. Out in the yard or in chow hall or on the tiers, they—and the men they would reach in workshops—might help resolve conflict before it erupted. These two were wise to the culture. They could smell a conflict coming. But more than that, Karuna thought that their extended time in isolation had helped them understand who they truly were. They knew their own minds. They had achieved a kind of equanimity born of self-reflection and a resolve born of the psychological and emotional rigors of years in the hole, of not just withstanding but growing from that experience. She believed they could be capable of stepping into confusing, potentially explosive situations without getting shaken. And that they would be respected for doing so. The chaplain believed in change. Change was always possible. Change came from the hard, gritty work of soul-searching and the quieter work of self-awareness. The path forward was through the practice and development of morality, through the slow gaining of wisdom. She was a Buddhist. She was also a plain talker, a nurturer who could be both tough and stubborn. And she was funny in that dark way people who work in dark places can be funny. Sterling and Arnoldo liked and respected her. And she liked and respected them.

Encouraged and supported by Karuna, fueled by their growing friendship, Sterling and Arnoldo began to work together on programs and events. The bonds between them, both personal and professional, grew stronger. They were comrades and brothers. But they knew their time together would not last. Arnoldo's release date was fast approaching. He would soon walk out a free man. Sterling's legal case was stalled. He would be left behind—perhaps forever.

One day, up in the chapel library in the southeast corner of the prison, Sterling pointed out the yellow hydrant to Arnoldo. Sterling had written a little essay about the hydrant. He was a talented writer, a poet who harnessed the power of both words and performance, a creative force. Had he not been in prison since his teens, he might have had a thriving literary career. He stood in front of that barred window often, maybe every day. He looked over the massive wall and saw birds landing near the creek. He saw joggers trotting down the sidewalk, cars pulling in and out of the prison driveway. He imagined himself feeding the birds. He imagined himself walking down that sidewalk. Sometimes he allowed himself to imagine sleeping in a comfortable bed in a quiet room. Sometimes he allowed himself to dream of the life he could craft outside the walls, a life defined by more than his worst failures. He stared at the spot of yellow in the distance. The hydrant became a symbol of a life of freedom, of the life Sterling might never have a chance to live, and the lives his released friends would struggle to recapture.

"When you get out, go touch that hydrant. Touch it for me," he said to his friend. They were standing together looking out the smudged window. He said this not with longing, not with envy, not even with sadness for the loss of the friendship. It came from a place of hope. He wanted Arnoldo to succeed. He wanted him to remember to cherish every moment of liberty.

That July morning of his release after nineteen years,

Arnoldo hugged his mother, his brother, his nieces, and then walked out the front entrance of the prison, down the driveway, and over to the hydrant. He had left his family in the visiting room, but he wasn't alone. Sterling's wife, Cheryl, walked with him. Sterling had introduced the two of them at some event in the past, but Cheryl didn't know Arnoldo very well. Sterling, like so many people behind bars, compartmentalized his life. He very purposefully kept his two worlds separate. There was a saying in prison, "Don't let your family do your time," which translated as *keep your incarcerated life to yourself. Or what happens in here stays in here.* But although Cheryl didn't really know Arnoldo, she did know about the hydrant. She knew what it meant to Sterling. And Sterling had asked her to come to the prison this morning to take a picture of Arnoldo touching the hydrant. She could print it out and show it to him at the next visit.

Out on the grassy strip that bordered State Street, Arnoldo crouched next to the yellow hydrant, balancing himself with a forearm on the weather cap, smiling, squinting into the sun, striking a pose for Cheryl as she tapped her smartphone to take pictures. Then the two of them stood side by side and looked back up at the prison. In the distance, over the wall, they could see a row of four heavily barred windows on the top floor. The second one from the left was the window Sterling had gazed through when he first noticed the hydrant, the window the two friends stood in front of when they talked about the future. Arnoldo's future was beginning today, right now. Could he make a successful life for himself after two decades of incarceration? What would that path look like? Sterling's future was persistently, agonizingly uncertain. Would his byzantine legal case—bolstered by U.S. Supreme Court decisions and various state rulings—move forward? Would he have the same chance Arnoldo now had?

From their vantage point on the street, Arnoldo and Cheryl looked up. The windows were dark; whatever was on the other side was obscured. They were about to turn and walk away when they saw something, a square of white near the bottom of the second window. Sterling was holding up a sheet of paper, signaling that he was there.

CHAPTER 2

When Arnoldo walked out the gates that July, he left behind his friend and comrade, Sterling, and the more than two thousand other men who would continue to live their lives inside that maximum security prison. And he left behind the almost 2.3 million men and women enmeshed in the American criminal justice system, a system that has grown to include 110 federal penitentiaries, 1,833 state prisons, 1,772 juvenile correctional facilities, 3,134 local jails, 218 immigrant detention centers, and 80 Indian Country jails, as well as military prisons, state psychiatric hospitals, and civil commitment centers. With just 5 percent of the world's population, the United States accounts for close to 25 percent of the world's prison population. One out of every six Latino boys, like Arnoldo, can expect to go to prison in his lifetime. One out of every three Black kids, like Sterling, will spend time behind bars. (For white kids, the figure is one out of seventeen.)

Another statistical insight into what has long been called our national epidemic of mass incarceration is the per capita numbers. The United Nations estimates the median rate, world-wide, at 145 people behind bars per 100,000 population. Western Europe and Scandinavia's rates fall far below this—76 in Germany, 60 in Norway and Sweden. The U.S. incarceration rate is 655, according to the same U.N. database. This is greater than the rate in Russia, China, or North Korea, countries known for their repressive governments and blindness to individual and civil liberties.

It was not always like this.

The U.S. incarceration rate used to be similar to those of other high-income countries and western democracies. But in the early 1970s, after fifty years of stability, the nation's prison population began a dramatic period of growth when politicians from both sides started to push for and legislate increasingly punitive policies. Richard Nixon opened the door—literally *opening the door* to the country's jails and prisons—by declaring a "war on drugs" that translated not into funds for community-based programs and treatment centers but rather into lengthy prison sentences, even for minor drug offenses. This approach, branded then and now as "tough on crime," was part of a broader cultural, political, and institutional shift toward the use of punishment to solve social problems.

Then, during the Reagan years, the prison population exploded when changes in federal and state legislation led to longer sentences, mandatory sentences (no judicial discretion), determinate sentencing (no early parole or time off for good behavior), and Three Strikes laws. These Three Strikes state statutes significantly increased the sentences of those who had been convicted of prior crimes, often leading to life sentences for felonies that would never have incurred such harsh punishment. Add to this the default use of prisons as mental institutions, an unforeseen consequence of the reform-based deinstitutional-ization movement that had hoped to improve the lives of the mentally ill. Instead, they landed in jail. When Ronald Reagan entered the White House, the total prison population was 329,000. Eight years later, it had almost doubled to 627,000. A National Research Council report that tracked incarceration rates from 1980 to 2010 found a 222 percent increase—and attributed it to changes in policy not crime rates. In 1969, the U.S. crime rate (reported crimes) was 3,680 per 100,000, and the incarceration rate was 97 per 100,000. In 2018, the crime rate was slightly lower (3,667), and the incarceration rate was seven times *higher* (692 per 100,000).

This half-century prison boom has had a disproportionate and disastrous impact on people of color and on poor urban communities, deepening divides and exacerbating existing racial and socioeconomic inequities. It has meant that on any given day one-third of adult Americans are either incarcerated, on proba-tion, or on parole. It has meant that one-quarter of all Americans have an arrest record of some kind. And all this carries an $81 billion a year price tag.

Those are a lot of numbers. And none of them are good. What we have, as *The New Yorker* writer Adam Gopnik put it, is "the caging of America." He calls it "the moral scandal of American life."

But why should we care that there are so many people behind bars? If they broke laws and did harm, don't they deserve to be punished, to be caged?

We should care because some of the punishments are unnecessarily harsh, because all people are not treated equally under the law, because sometimes innocent people get caught in the system, because a large body of research suggests that our approach to punishment doesn't actually work. But there is another reason, a compelling and immediate reason that has nothing to do with whether wrongdoers deserve the punishment they get, a reason that is unrelated to politics, social reform, economics, ethics, or morality.

The reason is this: selfishness.

Ninety-five percent of those we put behind bars get out. That's about 600,000 people each year. They may get out in four days. They may get out in forty years. But they eventually get out. They leave their cages and reenter our communities. They walk the streets we walk. Wait for the bus at the same bus stop. Shop at the local grocery store. Their kids sit in classrooms next to our kids. They are our neighbors. Living inside cages behind walls can have profound effects on personality and behavior, on health and attitude, on what kind of a person rejoins our community. That, in itself, is a reason to care.

Here's why I care: I spent more than three years going into a maximum security prison twice a month to meet with—and teach writing to—men who had spent most of their adult lives behind bars. One of these men was Sterling. What I saw, what Sterling and the nine other men revealed to me in their writing and our many hours of unguarded (literally) conversations, was that the constrained, routinized, rule-bound, hierarchical lives they were living took away more than physical freedom and privacy. Incarcerated life took away their personal agency, their power to make decisions, even the smallest ones like when to eat breakfast, how often to take a shower, what color pen to use when writing a letter. Over time, the inability to make decisions, the persistent, entrenched, institutionalized barriers to exercising personal agency over almost anything had led to what psychologist Martin Seligman called "learned helplessness."

The men in the group had never heard of that term. But they were living it. Or fighting hard against it. Sterling was perhaps the fiercest warrior, holding on to his sense of self as he—and Arnoldo—helped others inside try to do the same. But it was a mighty struggle.

Prison life, I also learned from these men, teaches the masking of feelings and emotions. It's not just men; Belinda was good at this, too. Just as athletes have an impenetrable game face, inmates have an unreadable "prison face." It is at best impassive; at worst menacing. There is only one allowable emotion in prison, Sterling once told me, and it is anger. Showing any other emotion is showing vulnerability. Showing vulnerability is dangerous. In the writing group, slowly, over time, the masks came off. It helped that they were there in the group by choice—perhaps the only freely made choice they had that day or that week. It helped that they wrote, sitting quietly with their thoughts. It helped that there wasn't a guard in the room. It helped, I know, that I was a woman and an outsider, which made me less of a threat. In prison, when they were faced with threats, dominance became a form of self-protection. That meant, for both men and women, adopting strategies like establishing a personal reputation for toughness, joining a protective and insular group (a gang), or self-isolating. These strategies work well in prison. Because they work, because they are practiced for decades, they become deeply ingrained—tactics that become attitudes, then behaviors, finally personality traits. The tension that underlies every encounter, the fear that anything could happen at any time for any reason, the often barely suppressed (or not suppressed at all) threat of violence, the violence itself, the noise, the absence of the healing touch. This is incarcerated life. A medical researcher from Brown University put it this way:

"It is unrealistic for us to imagine that people can emerge from prison psychologically intact."

Yet they emerge, hundreds of thousands of them a year, simultaneously joyful and overwhelmed at the prospect of freedom. They are anxious, confused, sometimes terrified, and often ill prepared to face the challenges of life in the free world. To reenter.

Reentry has a clear goal—to reintegrate offenders back into their communities. But the path to achieving that goal is anything but clear. In fact, "path" is not the right metaphor. That image is of a peaceful, pastoral lane, manicured, cultivated—a garden path, a bridle path. Reentry is not that. It is a rocky, winding, switchbacked trail, overgrown in some places, terrifyingly steep in others. Sometimes the trail disappears. Other times it is so crowded with fellow travelers that it is impossible to go forward. Occasionally the trail crosses with another, and that other one looks better, easier, but (discovered too late) is neither. Sometimes the trail winds back on itself, and the journey has to begin again. There might be a map of the trail, and it might be available, or not. It might be accurate, or not. It might be too dark to read the map. Those holding the map might not have map-reading skills.

Maybe it's not about maps and trails. Maybe reentry is best imagined as a story with complex characters, flawed as we all are, alternately motivated and discouraged, progressing, plateauing, backsliding, recovering, or not. Reentry is a story that moves in fits and starts, with plot twists and flashbacks, with endings that can be trite or completely unexpected. It is not a perfect narrative arc. It is not a neat three-act play.

Decades of research—often studies that end up tracking failures—have detailed the specifics of what successful reentry can look like. Ann Jacobs, executive director of the John Jay College Institute for Justice and Opportunity, one of the country's leading champions of reentry, lists six basic life needs: livelihood, residence, family, health, criminal justice compliance, and social connections. Each one is a story—or a winding, rocky path—of its own. Nick Crapser, former deputy director of a wraparound services reentry organization, an ex-con who used to be a client of that organization, likes to talk about the "Three Es": environment, employment, and education.

Jacobs's six needs and Crapser's "Three Es" represent checkpoints along the journey, dots on the map, chapters in the story. But as important as they are, they highlight only the obvious part of the journey, the externals: jobs and housing, training and treatment, relationships, parole restrictions. These are challenging goals, but they are, at least, definable and quantifiable. The barriers to achievement of these goals, the rocks on the trail, are also definable and quantifiable: poverty, mental illness, addiction, poor health, lack of education. Some of these barriers are so formidable that they are almost impossible to overcome, not rocks to stumble over or kick aside but boulders that stop all progress. But reentry is also a hidden-from-view process with no quantifiable goals, no visible stumbling blocks, a mapless journey that involves cognitive, psychological, and emotional transformation. It is the internal journey from caged to free.

More than twenty years ago, the U.S. Department of Justice issued a report stating that successful reentry depended on developing a plan that began at the moment a judge sentenced a criminal and continued through to release and beyond, a plan that mobilized a network of both formal and informal support. Two decades later, there is no such plan. Two decades later, the effects of the tough-on-crime legislation of the 1980s and 1990s are even more deeply felt. "Tough on crime" translated into longer prison sentences for more people. The longer someone is inside, the more prison life is accepted as the norm; the more deeply ingrained the habits, behaviors and mindset; the harder the transition is to the outside. And tough-on-crime sentiment has, in many states, translated into lack of resources for rehabilitation efforts—central to any plan for successful reentry—including educational programs, meaningful vocational skills training, therapeutic groups. These are the opportunities that can prime inmates for success when they reenter. But these programs are often seen as "extras," benefits that the guilty do not deserve, ways in which their time inside is softened, made more palatable. And why should prison be palatable? But a punishing environment, from beginning to end, is not an environment that promotes, teaches, nourishes—makes possible—the transformative change that may just be at the core of successful reentry.

When Arnoldo, in his spotless white T-shirt and fresh-off-the-Target-shelves baggy black shorts, stepped out the gate on that summer morning, he left behind not just his six-by-eight-foot, two-man cell and not just the walled-in world that had been his home for almost twenty years. He left behind—he wanted to leave behind, he vowed to leave behind—the prison-industrial complex that had formed who he was from his teenage years. He wanted a job, of course, and, as soon as he could manage it, a place of his own. But he wanted more. He wanted a *life*. Like the more than ten thousand other men and women released from custody that week in July, he now faced the obstacle course that was reentry.

CHAPTER 3

They line up outside Bethel Lutheran, a big, prosperous church just down the street from the capitol building in downtown Madison, Wisconsin. It's a few minutes before six in the evening. There's a woman with her young son in tow, a nurse, a man who owns an apartment rental agency in town, a group of grad students from the university, a psychologist, a trio of older women who belong to the church, a store owner, two colleagues who work in social services, a retired cop. It's a long line, more than fifty people tonight. As they enter, each is handed a folder with a name written on it. It is not their name. It is the name of a fictitious person whose identity they will assume this evening. These fictitious people are just-released prisoners: men, women; Black, white, brown; short-timers who've been in and out of county jail, lifers who spent three decades behind bars. Some have children in foster care; a few are sex offenders. Several have parents who will welcome them home. Many more have no one waiting for them. The biographies may be contrived for the purpose of tonight's exercise, but they represent the realities of those being

released from prison. This evening's event, a simulation originally created twenty years ago by JustDane, a Wisconsin-based
nonprofit, and since presented in church basements and university classrooms and corporate conference rooms throughout the
Midwest, will challenge the participants to complete the set of
reentry tasks that routinely face those just released. It's a "walk
a mile in my shoes" exercise that is both harrowing and instruc-
tive, an hour-long immersion designed to both foster empathy
and spur community action.

This evening's participants make their way down to the
church basement. They eat a buffet dinner, chat with each other,
watch a documentary about a released prisoner, listen to a short
speech, and then sift through the papers and documents in their
folders. They find birth certificates and Social Security cards,
travel vouchers, gate money (a sum given upon release) that var-
ies from $40 to $2,000 depending on circumstance. Some find
driver's licenses in their packets. A few lucky ones have notices
of jobs waiting for them; a few unlucky ones discover that they
will be on restrictive electronic monitoring (ankle bracelets).
Some packets contain court decrees that obligate the person to
pay child support or letters instructing them to make victim restitution payments. In all of the folders are documents detailing
the conditions of the individual's parole, from required check-ins
to drug tests to mandatory treatments. And all contain a list of
tasks to be completed. The participant-parolees will have one
hour to complete these tasks. That hour represents one month—
the first month—following release. The simulation is divided into
four timed fifteen-minute (one-week) segments. A large, audibly
ticking clock in the middle of the room counts down the minutes.

Around the perimeter of the large room are rectangular conference tables, each with a sign representing a different service,

from a community health clinic to the Division of Motor Vehicles, from a resale clothing store to a credit union. There's a rental agency, a parole office, a job center, a church, a paycheck cashing establishment. United Way has a table. Alcoholics Anonymous has another. A diverse group of volunteers staff these tables, from people who work in social services to people who have spent time in prison, from college students to members of the church's congregation. Unlike the participant-parolees, they have all been trained in what to do. Many are veterans of other simulations. In the hallway outside the large room are tables labeled "County Jail" and "Police Station."

A whistle blows to begin week one. Clutching their folders, the parolees rush—or try to rush—from table to table. Should they get their SNAP (Supplemental Nutrition Assistance Program) food benefits first? But, wait, they need to cash that gate check. A few go to the credit union desk but find the minutes ticking away as they are asked to fill out lengthy forms. Others make their way to the paycheck cashing desk, where they will be charged a premium for the service. When asked to present their ID to cash the check, several discover that the driver's license they were given in the folder has expired. They have to go to the DMV table. But there is a long line there. And as they are waiting to get to the front of the line, the clock runs out.

The whistle blows, ending the first segment. During that first "week" hardly anyone managed to check in with their parole officer, no one looked for a job, no one had time to go to the clinic to fill prescriptions for necessary medication. No one was able to find time to go to an AA meeting or attend mandatory treatment.

The whistle begins segment two. Anyone on electronic monitoring must stay in their seats for the first two of the ten minutes, a disadvantage that mirrors the difficulties of ankle monitors in real life. These monitors track the wearer's movements by sending GPS coordinates to their parole officer. If the wearer leaves a specific geographic area, an alert goes out, which could trigger a parole violation or the imposition of even more restrictive geographic boundaries. This can complicate navigating an unfamiliar place, taking buses that might stray outside boundaries, following up leads on jobs.

The others rush out, hoping to accomplish more than they did the first week. At the rental agency table, one person is turned away because he has no rental history. Another is turned away because she doesn't have the necessary funds for the common upfront payments of first month's rent, last month's rent, and damage deposit. Both have been waiting in line for precious minutes.

Meanwhile "police" roam the room, arresting some people for parole violations (not checking in with their parole officer, not attending treatment, not looking for a job). A few participants are arrested "mistakenly." All have to spend valuable minutes in the hallway police station, unable to accomplish anything. Their folders are taken away so they cannot use the time to plan or strategize. When the whistle blows again and week two is over, few have accessed any of the mental health and social services that might be able to help them. The lines are so long. The "distance" between one office and another eats up the minutes. They have run out of travel vouchers.

When week three begins, a "choice" character roams the room, arbitrarily stopping participants, demanding that each pick a card. The cards represent random good and bad luck, mostly bad: Your belongings were stolen from the halfway house. You injured yourself. Your brother kicked you out of his apartment. A lucky person gets a $100 bill. A few feet away, a "cop" arrests someone waiting in line for a housing voucher for nonpayment of child support. The room is noisy. No one is smiling. Everyone is either waiting on a too-long line or rushing from one desk to another. At the end of week three, almost all of the participants are still wearing their prison-release clothes. There has been no time to go to the resale shop.

It's a game, but several participant-parolees are now in tears. The organization running the simulation actually has real counselors in the room to help with such not uncommon meltdowns. *I'm doing everything, and it's just not working. This isn't fair. This is a rigged system. I don't have time. There are too many rules. The enforcement is too tough. The service providers are so busy they can't help.*

The final whistle blows, signaling the end of the fourth week. During that hour a handful of people were able to complete all the tasks on their lists. Of the many who did not, a sizable percentage just gave up trying.

A week after debriefing with Jackie Austin, a veteran prison reform activist and mover-and-shaker at the nonprofit that runs the simulations, I am texting with Leah. Leah was just released from prison after serving two years. I have signed on to be her community mentor, part of a program run by a local nonprofit. What was a simulation game is now playing out in real time in front of me.

Leah is a thirty-nine-year-old white woman from what used to be called "the wrong side of the tracks," but in this case would be the wrong side of the freeway. Her mother didn't teach her much, but she did teach her about addiction. As in how to be an addict. Meth was the mother-daughter drug of choice. It landed the daughter in prison after a chaotic, dysfunctional marriage during which her two children were taken from the home and placed in foster care. And it landed the mother in the morgue. The mother didn't die of an overdose. She died of a lifestyle. She was crossing a busy four-lane highway on a winter night, not in the crosswalk, to go to a liquor store. In an incident that sounds like the plot of a bad movie, she was struck not once but twice, both hit-and-runs. One car, driven by an eighty-six-year-old woman, was soon apprehended; the other by a seventy-six-year-old man who, a week later, committed suicide. Leah had written to me about her mother's death. It happened six months before the release. She thought she might have a meltdown after she got out, but she also confessed that she was "relieved" about her mother's death because it would make staying clean easier.

And now she is out. And the messiness and tumult that was her life—and her mother's—has followed her out the gate. I hear about it in a phone call so intimate and revealing that you'd think we were close friends instead of two strangers who've exchanged a few letters. As she tells me about the obstacles she encountered immediately—within hours of her release—I think about the community members in the basement of that Wisconsin church, clutching their assumed identity file folders, rushing from table to table trying to check all the reentry boxes, access the services that are out there, keep themselves on track. Leah thought she'd have a week to get herself settled in the temporary women's housing provided by a local reentry agency. Instead, minutes after she arrived, her ex-husband dropped off her two children, six and nine, along with a garbage bag full of their dirty clothes, which, she tells me, didn't fit them anyway. She had no clothes either, other than the ones she wore out the gate. They were several sizes too big. She had lost almost fifty pounds in prison.

Another woman at the housing unit told her the city buses were no longer in service because of the pandemic, which was not true (in fact, the buses were now operating free of charge), so she started walking with the kids to Walmart, a three-mile trek by the side of a busy highway. The kids lasted about ten minutes before she had to turn back. That was only a part of the tale of her first afternoon, which also included an aborted attempt to get SNAP food benefits and misleading advice about applying to the TANF program (Temporary Assistance for Needy Families). The world of social services is replete with acronyms. The acronym agencies each have their own application processes and forms, their own requirements and deadlines. Leah, without a computer, was trying to navigate all this on the tiny screen of her new phone. She had the cheapest plan, the only one she could afford, and data downloading was an issue.

This was a woman who went into reentry with advantages. She had been behind bars for only two years. Although the COVID-19 world she entered was alien to her, the way the world *generally* worked was not. Unlike Belinda, the woman paroled after two decades who I had hoped to be able to help more than five years earlier, Leah knew how to text and Google. She knew that cards and swipes had long ago replaced cash and checks. And thanks to the local nonprofit, Leah had, at least temporarily, a roof over her head, a room in a house especially established for women with young children. She could feed herself and her kids. She would have to donate her SNAP benefits, whenever she could arrange to start receiving them, to the house's food budget, but for now the nonprofit would cover the cost. Amid the tension and confusion and uncertainty of this day, the nerves, the fear, the excitement, Leah was in a better place than many who set off on the reentry path.

———————

Reentry is—and this cannot be repeated too often—both a per-
ilous and an exhilarating journey. The release date, the promise
of freedom, and the anticipation of a new life, all fuel the exhil-
aration. Most people leave prison with high hopes. The level of
optimism is actually quite astonishing given the inmates' lack of
resources and connections and what they know, because they've
seen it firsthand, about recidivism. All those prison friends who
left and then returned. Yet, in the Urban Institute's *Returning Home*
study, three-quarters of those asked said they thought reentering
was going to be "very easy" or "pretty easy." And what researchers considered a "staggering" 42.3 percent "strongly agreed" (and
another 37 percent "agreed") that a former prisoner could make
it if he or she wanted to. The American Dream, the Horatio Alger
rags-to-riches myth, is alive and well behind iron bars.

But reentry is neither "very easy" nor "pretty easy." Once
released, most people encounter obstacles big and small, fore-
seen and unforeseen, obstacles that can fast-track them back
to prison. That's what the simulation is all about. But there is
another side to this. In facing these same obstacles, in dealing
with and overcoming them, a person can learn persistence, resilience, and self-confidence. To understand this complicated reentry journey is to understand what it takes to remake a ruined
life, to live what University of Michigan historian Charles Bright
called "the corrected life." Most of those who succeed do so without the resources the rest of us take for granted, the economic
and social "capital" that we have acquired over time. And many
do so when who they are—poor, uneducated, often unskilled,
sometimes in poor health, and disproportionately a member of
an already marginalized minority group —is the biggest obstacle

of all. Or when their own traumatic backstories of abuse, addiction, homelessness, or gang affiliation conspire against successful reentry.

What success looks like from the outside is stable housing, a living-wage job, and healthy relationships. What it looks like from the inside may be just the ability to fall into a restful sleep, to get up every morning and not reach for the pipe or the needle, to navigate the aisles of a grocery store without suffering a panic attack. Whatever success is, it begins with the simplest of things, right out the gate: transportation from prison to the community; clothing that fits and does not look like you just got out of jail; a little money so that your first act of freedom will not be asking your family for a handout or spare-changing on the street.

Most states have some policy about handing released prisoners gate money, from Alabama's $10 to Colorado's $100 to California's $200. The average is $40 to $50, according to a report from The Marshall Project. California's seemingly generous amount has not increased since the 1970s. In many cases, prisoners are receiving their own money back, funds taken from prison wages and put into a separate account or money family had deposited in their commissary accounts. If no transportation is provided and there is no family support, the first cost will be paying for a way to get off the prison grounds. Family support has its own costs. One inmate, inside for ten years, spent his entire gate check in his first hour out when he took his wife for dinner at Applebee's. She had picked him up at the gate. She had stuck with him all these years. She had sent money to his account. It was a gesture he needed to make. And then he was broke.

Some states have programs to help with reentry; others have nothing. In some cities and counties nonprofit agencies offer resources like temporary housing, food banks, job boards.

Getting out of prison only to land on the streets, homeless and hungry, is the quickest way to go right back in. But just as there are food deserts with limited access to affordable and nutritious food, there are reentry resources deserts, especially in smaller towns and rural areas, with few or no support services.

And simply providing services—although this is anything but simple—is sometimes not the answer or not the definitive one. In 2008, the Second Chance Act awarded federal grants to government agencies and nonprofits to provide employment assistance, substance abuse treatment, temporary housing, family programs, and mentoring services. It seemed like a recipe for success, a way to take the wind out of the sails of recidivism. Ten years later, in a report to the National Institute of Justice based on interviews with almost a thousand ex-prisoners at eight different sites that had gotten the grants, researchers found that those receiving the enhanced services were more likely to have a reentry plan and a case manager they trusted. They reported more stable employment and higher earnings. But surprisingly—or perhaps not—they were no less likely to be rearrested than those who did not receive these services. Reentry is not about checking the boxes. It is far more complex.

One reason (among many) that the Second Chance Act grants failed to make the hoped-for difference is that meaningful help with reentry needs to begin far in advance of release. That's what the research indicates. But prisons in some states have no such programs. Others have programs that are not well advertised or promoted within the institution or have particular restrictions on eligibility. In some institutions, like the one Arnoldo emerged from, the programs are oversimplified, superficial—and optional. "I had no idea how unprepared I was for freedom," wrote ACLU strategist and ex-con Lewis Conway.

"I thought it was going to be as simple as the woman that taught the prerelease class said it would be."

The Vera Institute of Justice reports that today most prisons run limited programs on anger management and drug addiction, often a vital piece of the reentry puzzle, but that only a minority of prisons run college programs. This is in the face of Department of Justice findings that every dollar spent on education in prison translates into four dollars saved on incarceration. Education can lead to better job opportunities, more stable employment, and higher wages, not to mention helping to write a new narrative for the "corrected life." The Vera Institute also reports that only 9 percent of inmates earn either a trade school certificate or a college degree while in prison.

Employment, as steady as possible, as soon as possible, paves the way to successful reentry. But getting a job can depend on having an address and, of course, a phone number. How likely is this if a person is released to the streets with no money and no support? Getting anything other than a pick-me-up-on-the-corner day laborer job depends, these days, on internet access and the skills to search and apply online. Again, an obstacle. Those online applications often ask for résumés that include job histories. My children learned how to write résumés in middle school. The forty-something-year-old men I work with as a volunteer at a reentry resource center—the one that matched me with Leah—didn't have a clue. This was on top of their inexperience—and confusion—around connectivity and the online world.

Housing is an obvious—and formidable—obstacle upon reentry. Some prisoners have family that can take them in, which can be a mixed blessing. Some are fortunate enough to be released to cities or counties that have agencies offering temporary, transitional, and halfway housing. Others, as a condition of parole, are sent to in-treatment drug programs, where room and board is provided. Those who have some funds, some prospects, and some of the technical and social skills necessary for the task, can look for housing they can afford. "Afford" does not just mean the monthly rent. It most often means being able to pay first month's rent, last month's rent, and a damage deposit upon signing a rental agreement. Even for the most affordable, low-income apartment imaginable in most cities and towns that means upwards of $1,000. Those with no funds, no family, and no support live on the streets or in homeless shelters. With no funds, no housing, and no employment, they are unable to meet the demands of parole: paying for (and participating in) mandated treatment and programming, paying victims' restitution costs, charges for weekly drug tests. The deck is stacked against them. As ACLU's Conway put it, "I thought serving my time in prison was my punishment; I didn't know I was facing a life sentence after leaving prison...for many people that's what reentry is—a life sentence."

This "life sentence" can be a result of the stigma we attach to those who've been incarcerated and, just as important, their internalization and acceptance of that stigma. That perception and self-perception is, write the sociologists who studied prisoner reentry and detailed it in *On the Outside,* "arguably harsher punishment than the sentence itself."

The life sentence plays out in more definable, quantifiable ways, too, the result of what have been called "collateral consequences," the invisible punishments that follow previously incarcerated people after their release and, sometimes, for the rest of their lives. There are, according to the American Bar Association, some 45,000 federal and state statutes and regulations that affect a convicted person's ability to get—and stay—on their feet and to live a fully engaged life. These include everything from not always being able to qualify for SNAP benefits to not being eligible for federally funded public housing, from not qualifying for financial aid for college to not being eligible to hold public office.

The largest category of such restrictions pertains to employment. State governments require licenses for hundreds of occupations, from real estate agents to manicurists. The Bureau of Labor estimates that about one-quarter of all full-time jobs in the United States require professional licenses or government approval to practice. The opportunities for jobs or careers in law, banking, medicine, education, counseling, physical therapy, security, home healthcare, child care, and other fields can be affected. In the words of law professor and criminal justice reformer Michael Pinard: "The United States has a uniquely extensive and debilitating web of collateral consequences that continue to punish...long after the completion of sentences."

The list of consequences continues. Legislation passed in the late 1990s intended to prevent foster kids from languishing too long in the system before being eligible for adoption has resulted in accelerating the termination of parental rights for women whose children were put into foster care when their mothers went to prison. Ex-con status also results in what is called "felony disenfranchisement." Although casting a ballot may not be on the top of the list for those reentering society, losing the constitutional right to vote is a kind of civil death that confers second-class citizenship. Each state enacts its own felon voting laws. In nine states former prisoners may lose their right to vote permanently. In nineteen states their rights are restored after serving parole and probation. The average time on probation is five years, but some serious offenders are on lifetime parole.

This exile—from participating in democracy, from parenthood, from jobs, from the everydayness of life—keeps those who are reentered from fully reentering. They are *in* but not *of* the larger society. "We keep them at a distance," says University of Wisconsin–Milwaukee criminologist Thomas LeBel, "and avoid them entirely when we can." He likens them to lepers.

Nick Crapser, the ex-con now working in reentry services, puts it simply: "Imagine the worst thing you've ever done and just print in on a T-shirt you have to wear every day of your life."

———————

The final—and the most difficult—part of reentry is the cognitive transformation, the hard work of developing, reinforcing, and maintaining this new role of a "free" person, a role some ex-prisoners have not played for decades. It is about creating and embracing a new identity. This is what Belinda was in the process of doing when she sat across from me at that steak house, texting madly in the grip of a hasty, high school–style romance.

Maybe two years after that dinner, I was giving a talk to a university audience about mass incarceration. In the lecture hall was the usual assemblage of students with a sprinkling of faculty. Six rows up, to the left, sat a woman, fortyish, but with that embattled look of someone for whom a number of those forty years had been tough going. Her hair was that particular orangey-straw color that dark hair becomes when it is mercilessly peroxided. She was wearing an oversized sweatshirt. I noticed her not only because she didn't look like the other women in the room, but also because she alternately stared at me, hard, and then bent her head to furiously scribble notes. During the Q&A session, she stood up to introduce herself, saying that she had served twelve years in prison and had been out for two. She was now a university student, living an entirely different life. She said she had recently been at a support group for formerly incarcerated women. They sat in a circle and introduced themselves by stating their name, years out of prison, and inmate ID number—the number that is a key part of your prison identity, that gets you your mail, your pass to go to work, access to your commissary account. It *is* you. When it was her turn, she rattled off her name, years, number. Then caught herself. She had given her university ID number not her inmate number. "That's when I knew," she said, pausing, looking down. "That's when I knew I wasn't who I was anymore." She paused again. "I was who I was gonna be." The room erupted in applause. It was more applause than I had gotten at the end of my talk. And rightly so.

This new identity must be constructed, piece by piece, over time. The process involves shedding those behaviors and attitudes that worked in prison, that kept a person safe and sane, perhaps powerful and, within that setting, privileged, but that are inappropriate, counterproductive, self-defeating, and sometimes downright harmful in the community. Imagine the self-awareness that takes. The insight. The initiative. The courage. Sociologist Peggy Giordano outlined the steps toward cognitive change in groundbreaking research published back in 2002. Based on a long-term follow-up of female and male "delinquents" and their paths to what criminologists call "desistance" (cessation of offending or other antisocial behavior), she and fellow researchers identified four steps to cognitive transformation: openness to change; exposure to and receptivity to "hooks for change" (defined as environmental stimuli that are perceived as incompatible with continued criminal behavior); contemplation of alternative, noncriminal identities; redefining of criminal behavior as negative and undesirable. In other words: a complete paradigm shift, a rethinking of not only behaviors but of underlying self-image.

For some this can and does begin in prison. It happened for Sterling. It happened for Arnoldo. Maybe it's a class or workshop they were able to take, a therapeutic group they joined, a book they read. Beginning this internal change, stepping on this path before release, can be one of the keys to successful reentry. But for too many, incarceration means the opposite: the daily reinforcement of the criminal self. There are few hooks for change inside. In a closed enclave populated by hundreds or thousands of fellow criminals, there are few alternative, noncriminal identities in evidence. There may be an openness to change, a yearning for change, an optimism about the possibility of change, but many leave prison without the tools to make that happen.

What they leave with, instead, is what mental health professionals have begun calling "post-incarceration syndrome." Of course it has an acronym—PICS—although it is not yet officially recognized by inclusion in the bible of the field, the *Diagnostic and Statistical Manual of Mental Disorders (DSM-5)*. PICS is a discrete subtype of PTSD that results from long-term imprisonment. It is a recognizable cluster of symptoms that behavioral therapists who work with released prisoners (and researchers who study this population) say includes depression, anxiety, panic disorder, agoraphobia, alienation, and sensory disorientation. In an in-depth study of men and women released from state institutions after an average of nineteen years, the former prisoners reported nightmares, insomnia, fear of crowds, paranoia, emotional numbness, and confusion and helplessness when faced with decisions. They talked about persistent roadblocks to forming relationships because of an inability to trust and difficulties in judging the intentions of others. They talked about profound alienation, of feeling as if they did not belong in any social setting, that the only place they belonged was back behind bars. There was also the strong sense that whatever good was happening in their post-incarceration lives was temporary, that freedom itself was temporary. The researchers suggested that the longer the period of incarceration and the more trauma experienced, the worse the symptoms.

There are, in some communities, mental health and counseling services that work specifically with released prisoners and recognize PICS. There are, in some communities, therapeutic programs and support groups. But they are siloed, each doing what it can but not in a coordinated manner, not in conjunction with one another, not as part of a carefully thought-out and managed plan. When people need help, when they are panicked or depressed, when they are unable to function, they need help right then. But the wait times for such services can be (or at least seem to be) endless. And then there is maybe the bigger hurdle to getting help, even where it exists, even where it can be timely. Prisoners have learned to be quiet, stay in line, wait in line, be compliant. That is how you get by inside. But in the free world, especially in the bureaucratic, oversubscribed world of social services, it is often—as they saying goes—the squeaky wheel that gets the grease. Waiting your turn can mean not getting a turn at all. And to be in line, even quietly, patiently waiting in line, means you have to reach out. Men, who make up more than 90 percent of those released, are, in general, far less likely than women to seek mental health counseling and support. To ask for help is to be vulnerable. Vulnerability is not a trait that works in prison.

And yet, despite all of this—the obstacles and roadblocks, societal stigmas and damning self-perceptions, the sometimes overwhelming psychological challenges, the grinding bureaucracies, the lack of resources—former felons do, in fact, reclaim their lives, *live* their lives. Yes, recidivism rates are distressingly high, with 68 percent of those released rearrested within three years. But that also means that reentry works for more than 30 percent of released prisoners. The glass may be two-thirds empty—those are the stories we hear the most, the ones about the ex-con who robs the neighborhood 7-Eleven within an hour of his release, the identity-thieving meth addict who picks up where she left off—but the glass is also one-third full. Thousands of men and women who have lived lives on the edge, who have done bad things, who have hurt others, are reentry successes. The few stories we hear about these people focus on those with spectacular accomplishments: the drug dealer who transforms himself into the executive chef at Caesars Palace; the forger who becomes a renowned psychotherapist; the bank robber who becomes an activist dynamo. But just as the persistent stories of recidivism feed our fear of those coming out of prison, the cherry-picked stories of the wildly successful obscure the realities of reentry. The truth—the *many* truths—about life after lockup is more interesting, more nuanced, and both more troubling and more deeply triumphant than these alpha and omega tales.

Meet six people whose stories help tell this nuanced tale.

CHAPTER 4

VICKI

The young woman with purple hair behind the bulletproof glassed-in booth makes a call, and a few minutes later, Vicki comes through the locked door. She's a big, strapping white woman, five-foot-eleven, dressed in black jeans that span wide hips. She's wearing tattered black vinyl knee-high boots. Her hair, a faded orangey-red with a half inch of gray roots showing, is pulled back into a too-tight ponytail. Her face is scrubbed and shiny, her skin radiant, like she has lived a healthy, outdoorsy life. She hasn't. Vicki has spent more than twenty of her fifty years behind bars for a litany of "paper crimes"—identity theft, credit card fraud, check kiting, forgery—the crimes drug addicts turn to when struggling to support their habits.

I am at the women's drug rehab facility that Vicki, newly released from her most recent stint behind bars, will call home for a while. I've come to pick her up for our weekly outing, part of my commitment as her community mentor. I am volunteering at a local reentry services nonprofit, hoping to help Vicki navigate the transition from prison to home as I learn from her what that takes, what that really means. Sponsors is the name of the nonprofit that has matched us and trained me. It is a pioneering agency that offers a wide range of services for those recently released from prison, including this mentorship program. Vicki reached out to Sponsors. She needs and wants to connect with someone outside her toxic bubble of prison and drugs. She is addicted to both heroin and meth, although she's tried just about everything. Heroin has been a part of her life since she was sixteen, a soon-to-be high school dropout growing up in a small town that went bust just as she was coming of age, the kind of high-unemployment, low-education burg that checks all the boxes in those reports of "Substance Abuse in Rural America." The meth, she says, is not really a drug of choice. It's a drug that keeps her sane, a form of self-medication. She believes she suffers from attention-deficit/hyperactivity disorder (ADHD). Meth normalizes her, she says.

She served this latest stretch behind bars, five years, in federal prison for bank fraud and identity theft. Before that she spent four and a half years in a state prison, convicted of ninety-eight counts of identity theft, and before that, another four years for similar crimes. And then there were all those shorter stints in county jails, in and out, in and out. She doesn't remember how many times. She does remember that someone at the jail once told her she had the second thickest folder on file. She learned how to do small stretches of time. She thought it was no big deal. She didn't think she was hurting anyone. She figured they could all get their money back. Meanwhile, there was a benefit to jail time. It kept her off drugs.

Her story comes in fits and starts, loops and spirals. It's hard for anyone to tell a coherent story about their lives. It is even harder for a drug addict. There are whole stretches of time she doesn't remember, months, even years. Time folds in on itself, overlaps, disappears. The ADHD doesn't help either.

But her childhood comes back with clarity, maybe too much. She was seven, she remembers, when her father kept sending her outside to bring in more kindling. He used the sticks to beat her, and the sticks kept breaking. He was a biker—"patched," which is slang for a charter member of an original chapter of a motorcycle club. Her mother, she says, was a raging alcoholic. When Vicki went to her grandmother for help, the woman told her she couldn't get involved. Vicki ran away from home eleven times. By sixteen she was on the streets, part of a new family, a family she felt she could trust, a family that looked out for each other: her street family.

Her first drug was hash, smoked in the alleys with her new family, but her first addiction was prescription pain pills. She had dental surgery and was prescribed Vicodin. She loved the way it made her feel, carefree and floaty. She says she had two teeth extracted just to get more prescriptions.

On her seventeenth birthday, another memory comes into sharp focus. She was crashing at the house of one of her father's biker friends and his girlfriend. They were shooting cocaine. They wanted her to join in. They were, she thought at the time, creepily insistent that she join in. She left, got drunk, got wasted, came back, and let the guy, her father's biker buddy, shoot her up. And she thought: *Oh, this is what life is like. Why didn't someone tell me how wonderful this was?* She says the drug "filled her up." And that's what really started it all.

What follows is a tangled, hard-to-follow story about her adventures with the friend she moved in with after the biker. The girl's mother had been murdered (Vicki reports this as if everyone knows someone whose mother has been murdered), and there was insurance money, and the girl all of a sudden had $20,000, and she and Vicki went on a two-month bender. The $20,000 went in their arms. Heroin, she discovered, was even more euphoric than cocaine. The warmth was palpable; pleasure was intense. With her street family, high on heroin, she felt cocooned, loved, safe.

And then she got pregnant. And left the baby, her son, with her parents. A few months later, standing on a street corner, high on acid, she flagged down a guy riding a motorcycle. His name was Steve. They have been together, on and off—the off being the years she has spent incarcerated—for more than thirty years. How she hid her drug addictions from him is difficult to comprehend, but she says she did. She says she lived a split life: one existence on the streets shooting up; the other in an apartment with Steve pretending to be someone else. She was, she says, whoever he wanted her to be. When he found out she wasn't who he wanted her to be, who he thought she was, he would get verbally abusive. She would escape to the streets, come back loaded. He would hit her. She would steal from him. Then he'd call the cops, and she'd be hauled off to county jail. When she got out, ten days or four weeks later, the cycle would begin again. The crimes escalated. The sentences lengthened. She was now doing serious time in serious prisons, gone for years from Steve, from her son, from the daughter she and Steve had together, and from her beloved street family.

When she got out, she went to drug rehab. Four times. And then she was back inside again. She was a tough woman, but the drugs were tougher. When I picked her up at what was her fifth residential rehab center that December afternoon, she said, matter-of-factly, "No matter how strong you think you are, the

addiction is stronger." And life inside was, in an odd but significant way, comfortable. She had an incarcerated self who knew
the ropes, had connections and relationships, could fit right back
in. Between prison terms, when she was out, she told prison stories. Then, during her last time out between prison terms, she
realized just how many of the stories she told *were* prison stories.
She really listened to herself. And she says she consciously made
the decision to stop telling those stories. She did not want to be
that person anymore. Telling those stories reinforced that part of
her life. She *was* that story. This last stretch behind bars was different, she says, because she decided not to fit right back in, not
to take up where she left off, not to live these stories anymore.

She would give drug treatment another try. Although her
parole plan mandated only a four-week stay at the locked, residential facility, she added another month. She thought this treatment center might be different. She said she was learning things
this time that were new to her, not the "same old cognitive stuff."
She was hoping the doctor she would soon see would give her a
"double diagnosis," one focused on the heroin addiction, the other
an ADHD finding. Maybe she could get a legal drug to replace
meth for the ADHD. Meth was much harder to beat than heroin.

Vicki walks toward me, smiling. She is happy to have a two-
hour reprieve from the insular rehab world where she sleeps in
a small, sparsely furnished room hardly bigger than the cell she
lived in for five years, shared with a fellow addict, where her days
are micromanaged, a tight schedule of classes and therapies and
group sessions, check-ins and screenings. No phone, no internet.
The purple-haired young woman behind the bulletproof glass
pushes a clipboard through a slot, and both of us sign our names
and note the time we're leaving and when we are required to
return. I hand Vicki her drink of choice, a twenty-four-ounce

salted caramel breve with whip. The extravagance of it reminds me of the banquet-sized meal Belinda ordered at that steakhouse more than five years ago, back before I started going into a maximum security penitentiary to teach writing, back before I knew much about the world of incarceration and the effects of a caged life. Vicki takes a sip. Her pleasure is palpable—and audible.

We drive to a women's halfway house that's run by Sponsors in another part of town. Today the house is hosting a holiday craft event, a break from the lengthy, often dispiriting to-do lists all these women face as they start down the reentry road. There are eight of us around the table. We settle into our work of gluing and glittering, making holiday cards, garlands, ornaments. We are not an artistically gifted group, but we are having fun.

A companionable silence descends as we listen to the Christmas music that one of the women has on shuffle on her phone. It's all the old stuff: Nat King Cole, Bing Crosby, Frank Sinatra. The next song starts. It's sung by a woman, an unfamiliar voice, and begins: "Old Mr. Kringle is soon gonna jingle / The bells that'll tinkle all your troubles away." It's a catchy tune. Then she sings the next line: "Everybody's waitin' for the man with the bag." And everyone at the table looks up at the same time. And we all, and I mean all of us, start laughing. The song continues: "He's got a sleighful, it's not gonna stay full / He's got stuff to drop at every stop of the way / Everybody's waitin' for the man with the bag." We can't stop laughing.

"I guess there are several ways of interpreting that line," one of the staffers from the nonprofit says, but without much conviction.

"Oh yeah?" says Vicki, stifling a smile. "I think we all had the same interpretation."

CHAPTER 5

STERLING

It's been years since I spoke to a group of a dozen inmates, educators, and prison staff about the possibility of starting a writers' group for long-incarcerated men, but I remember that afternoon clearly. We are sitting in a small room somewhere deep inside Oregon State Penitentiary, a big maximum security prison. I'm nervous, but not because I fear for my safety. There is so much security and scanning and wanding and shoe removing and ID checking to get into this prison and up to this room that there is zero chance of some Hollywood-style shiv-wielding/hostage-taking event unfolding. I am nervous because I want to make a good impression. I am nervous because I want to make a compelling case for starting the writers' group. I think the men hidden behind these walls, voiceless, have important stories to tell, stories we on the outside should hear. I teach writing. Maybe I can help them develop their storytelling skills, encourage their efforts. I also believe—I know—that writing can be powerful, self-administered therapy, a way to unpack a life, examine it, understand it. I need the endorsement of the people in this room to make this happen. I make my pitch. No one is asking questions. This is either a good sign or a bad sign. After the meeting wraps up, we all head for the door. One of the men in prison blues comes up to me.

We're standing by the door, maybe three feet apart. He is tall, six-three, and angular, dressed in a pair of baggy prison jeans and a dark blue prison-issue T-shirt that hangs on his frame. I have to crane my neck to look him in the eye. His eyes are such a dark brown that it is almost impossible to distinguish between iris and pupil. And impossible not to look into their darkness. They are the eyes, I think then, of an old, old man. Not tired eyes but eyes that have seen it all, taken the measure of the world and been saddened by it, or maybe made wise by it; at any rate somehow came to terms with it. But he is not old. He looks to be in his late thirties. He introduces himself. His name is Sterling. He asks a few questions about the writers' group. I answer. Then he says something. I don't remember anymore exactly what he says—something about "truth to power"—that is both weighty and unpretentious, a rare combination. It is delivered in a melodic voice, almost sing-song, which, oddly, adds to its power. I leave with the impression that I have met someone with a kind of gravitas not often encountered, a warmth and intelligence that, being prisoner to my own stereotypes about prisoners, I would never have expected to find in a maximum security penitentiary.

Then I learn why he is behind bars and has been since he was sixteen. Stories about crimes and violence, stories about murder, are always deeply unsettling and always make you question what humans are capable of and why. The story of Sterling's crime is even more unsettling because it feels like the person I met, the man whose eyes I looked into, could not possibly have done this thing. And yet he did.

In January 1994, Sterling and a friend approached a young couple outside their apartment building and forced them at gunpoint into their car. It was to be a simple carjacking, but it spiraled out of control. Sterling drove the car. They ended up on a gravel road at a park by the river where he and his buddy ordered the couple out of the car. Sterling shot the guy in the head. His friend shot the girl three times. They left the bodies on the road, drove back in the couple's car, and bragged to their friends about what they had done. Sterling was sixteen. The murdered couple, the eighteen-year-old girl and her twenty-one-year-old boyfriend, were engaged to be married.

———————

There's something lawyers call a "mitigating narrative," a backstory that contextualizes violent behavior and makes the "poor choices" of the accused more understandable. "Poor choices" is the euphemism for decisions so damaging, so cruel, so amorally thoughtless—the "poor decisions" that led to or underlie the crime—that they are almost impossible to fathom from the outside. A mitigating narrative is not about innocence. It is about circumstance, about the life events, the influences that brought this person to the moment of the crime. Without context, what Sterling did was the act of a person without a conscience. A reckless, cold, heartless person. With context, with both backstory and what we now understand about the teenage brain, Sterling becomes more knowable, more human—not less guilty, but less frightening.

What is understood now, but was not widely discussed back

in 1994, is the nature of the teenage brain, how the "executive function" lobe, that part of the brain that weighs actions against consequences, is not yet fully developed—and won't be until the mid-twenties. A teenager's prefrontal cortex, the seat of moral reasoning, rational decision making, and emotional regulation, is a messy construction site in the process of being wired and rewired, not fully operational. Because it does not work very well, sometimes other parts of the brain are enlisted to "help." That means that sometimes the most primitive part of the brain, the amygdala—aptly nicknamed the "lizard brain"—takes over to respond. The response is quick, powerful, impulsive, without a thought of consequences, with no moral compass.

That said, very few prefrontal cortex–challenged teenagers kidnap, carjack, and commit murder. Sterling, at sixteen, had years of "training" to get to that moment. Maybe it began at his birth to a teenage mother, serving time, shackled to a hospital bed. At school—he was good at school, a smart kid—his mixed-race status, his kinky, light-brown hair with a touch of orange, his café au lait complexion with a dusting of freckles—made him the target of bullies. Everyone around him was white. He was not. But, at least for the first twelve years of his life, a loving grandmother created a bubble of security. When she died, everything changed. Shuffled off to the home of an abusive grandfather and an alcoholic step-grandmother who were enmeshed in their own dysfunctional lives, he became accustomed to a new normal: flaring tempers, rages, beatings. He was shunted off to an uncle thousands of miles away, a man only barely out of his teens who supported a drug habit through petty crimes. The uncle moved every few months, to different cities, to different neighborhoods. Sterling followed, stopped going to school, took to the streets. In this world he now inhabited, violence was how you proved you were a man. Not expressing emotion, not seeming to care—and ultimately not caring—was how you showed you were a man. Bragging about your exploits, the riskier and more horrific the better, was how you got street cred. Street cred got you respect. Respect made you a man.

The mitigating narrative continues with a journey through the juvenile justice system and foster care where Sterling establishes a routine for himself that he, much later, identifies as a "behavioral pattern" of running away, stealing cars, partying, getting caught, spending time in juvie, being sent to yet another group home where the boys spend their time proving to the other boys how tough they were and the girls, he remembers, swap sex for compliments. When he was fifteen he started carrying a gun, proof to others (and to himself) that he was truly hardcore.

On that day in January 1994, the day of the crime, Sterling and a friend from his last group home were crashing at a party house, telling (as Sterling later recounted it) "outlandish lies about gun battles, mafia connections, and sexual conquests." They were spinning a tale, inspired by some movie they had watched, about a carjacking they'd done in Chicago—a town neither had ever set foot in. One of the men in the house, older, a player, confronted them, calling their bluff, challenging them right then to repeat this crime they had bragged they'd committed.

And so they did. They found a young couple outside their apartment building and embarked on a chain of events that would, within hours, ruin four lives. How did a carjacking turn into a double murder? Was there posturing and verbal aggression and threats, the classic escalation cycle? Was there a triggering incident? Were Sterling and his friend one-upping each other, emboldened by their own "bravery," wanting to ratchet it up so they could tell a truly bad-ass story to those men back at the party house? Events take on their own life. Sterling was to understand this many years later when he learned, from trauma experts and restorative justice teachers, how to de-escalate violence between inmates and between warring factions in prison. At sixteen, he had none of those skills. At sixteen, he had no moral compass.

Now, twenty-six years later, Sterling has the possibility of getting out, of reentering society as a middle-aged man who might, if given the chance, do good in the world. He doesn't imagine that what he does with the rest of his life, should he be able to have one, will make up for the devastation he caused. But he has grown into someone who wants to be of use.

Sterling and I have now known each other for more than six years. I've helped him with many writing projects. Before the pandemic closed the prison to all outsiders, we saw each other twice a month in the writers' group. Now we exchange letters. One afternoon, a half a year into the COVID-19 restrictions, we're talking on the phone. He is telling me about the latest setback in his long-running attempt to get his case before the parole board, to get a release date. What he tells me is 90 percent awful. Barrier after barrier, disappointment after disappointment. Delays, defeats. He mentions one small bright spot, one inch forward, the whiff of hope. We're both silent for a moment. Then I hear that singsong voice through the phone. "I celebrate that which does not crush me," he says. It's just the kind of sentence—beautifully parsed, insightful, erudite but not showy—that he uttered that first day I met him.

CHAPTER 6

TREVOR

Trevor is sitting in a banquette by a window at the back of a Denny's. He has chosen the very last table. His back is to the wall. He has short brown hair, newly buzz-cut, and neat facial hair that is more than "designer stubble" but less than a serious beard. His smile, when it comes, is tentative, like his face is just learning how to do this. His hands are resting on the table, motionless. There is a stillness about him, a mixture of purposeful self-containment, quiet alertness, and studied composure. He is in his early thirties, a millennial, but absent all the stereotypes of his generation. Coming of age in prison, behind bars since he was fourteen, he is not a product of a culture that is said to have forged the defining characteristic of his demographic: entitlement. For close to eighteen years of his life, his entitlement looked like this: He was entitled to a six-by-eight-foot cell and three chow hall meals a day—the proverbial "three hots and a cot." He was entitled to a few hours of yard time. He was entitled to stand in line to make timed, monitored phone calls to family. He was entitled to see his mother during week-end visiting hours.

His generation is accused of being lazy. But Trevor, behind bars, became a paragon of self-motivation. Industrious, con-scientious, tireless, he grew into a man who was both modest enough to learn from those who were wiser and self-confident enough to assume power when he earned it. I first met him when I came into the penitentiary to run the writing group. He didn't join, but he was then-president of the inmate club that took on sponsorship of the group. He was interested, but not involved. We didn't speak much until he was out. Trevor had, quite liter-ally, worked his way out, embracing every opportunity to learn organizational and management skills, to learn how to plan and problem-solve and troubleshoot, to learn how to navigate hierarchies and mediate between groups with conflicting goals. His generation is accused of lacking aspirations. For almost two decades, most of them spent in an adult maximum security prison, Trevor lived a life that was all about aspiration.

But even before his crime, he lived a different life. It was in some ways bucolic, idyllic, even. He and his older brother grew up on fifty-two acres deep in the mountains of southern Oregon in a home built from the ground up by his mother and her sec-ond husband. They lived a peaceful backwoods life, off the grid with no television, no internet, a life that was equal parts sur-vivalist, hippie, and good ol' boy country. The boys were home-schooled. They helped with their parents' antique business, traveling to swap meets and fairs. They did odd jobs for neigh-bors. They rode dirt bikes. In their tiny, isolated community they were known as good kids.

But there was a dark side to that life. Like many rural households, there were firearms in the house: rifles, shotguns, pistols. And there were drugs: the marijuana that the parents knew about—in fact, Trevor's father had been convicted and had served time for a marijuana charge—the methamphetamines that they probably did not. There was also an undercurrent of criminality and the glorification of violence that Karen, Trevor's mother, recognized only many years later. At the time, she thought their purposefully insular life was protecting the boys from the worst of popular culture. They were, as an Associated Press story about the crime put it, "seemingly sheltered against evil." But in 1990s America, this was not possible. Investigating the crime, not really believing that these good kids could have done something so bad, local detectives searched the cabin on the property that the brothers shared and found these handwritten lyrics from a Marilyn Manson song: "Dealing with insanity, smoking pot, hating this fucking world, murder is the answer, I only kill to know I'm alive."

After the crime, after years trying to make sense of the crime, Karen thought about the movies they took the boys to see when they all went into town for groceries, movies—like so many—that were plotted around violence in which the most popular and admired men were the ones doing the killing. And she remembered that her husband used to regale the boys with stories about his own criminal behavior, mysteriously leaving it up to them to imagine what he did.

But there was no making sense of this crime, no making sense of that day, July 26, 1998, when Trevor carjacked a sixty-five-year-old man at gunpoint, drove his Chevy Suburban down a remote logging road, and shot him in the head, "execution style," as the media later reported. The victim was a beloved local businessman with deep roots in the community. The killer was a fourteen-year-old kid. He was tried as an adult and sentenced to life in prison with the possibility of parole after thirty years. His brother, eighteen at the time, who knew what happened but was not directly involved, was tried as an adult and sentenced to twenty-five years.

Now, at thirty-one, Trevor is newly free, the second juvenile lifer released under a "second look" state statute, legislation passed in 2015 that allowed people convicted as minors to have the chance to get out of jail after serving half their sentence. For Trevor that amounted to fifteen years.

He was, his lawyer and many others thought, a great candidate. He had spent his years in prison amassing an extraordinary record of education, rehabilitation, and accomplishment. He had worked his way into a top position at the prison's biggest employer, a vast commercial laundry operation. He was the youngest elected president of the prison's biggest and oldest inmate organization, the Lifers' Unlimited Club. He was instrumental in the development and ongoing operation of the prison's Inside-Out Program, part of a national education network that brought together college students and inmates in classes taught behind bars. His record in prison, his actions and interactions, his behavior, his affect—everything pointed to a man who had become sincere and trustworthy, measured and thoughtful, dependable and responsible. At his hearing, character witnesses lined up to testify on his behalf, including three university professors, two psychiatrists, and a correctional officer from the prison. One of the judges involved in the case called Trevor "a poster child for criminal rehabilitation." Still his "second chance" release was contentious. The state had appealed an earlier release ruling and was planning to appeal this one too. His victim had been a fixture of that small community, and the people in the community were not about to forgive his murderer. They were not ready to believe that Trevor had transformed himself into a moral, ethical, law-abiding citizen, or that such a transformation should earn him a second chance. The long list of Trevor's accomplishments in prison, all the testimonies on his behalf, could (and probably did) have the opposite effect on the people in the community. Here was a young man who was learning and growing and doing, who was—unlike his victim—alive. That, in itself, was unacceptable to many people in the community.

The story of his release carried on a community news site was headlined: "Walraven, cold-blooded killer, a free man." When the local television station posted its story online, eighty-eight people took the time to respond, all but two of them harshly. "His victim didn't get a second chance," someone wrote. Others were more blunt: "He should be put to death"; "An eye for an eye."

Forgiving is sometimes thought of as forgetting. Moving on is sometimes considered disrespectful to those who were harmed. And, in any case, rehabilitation is a hard sell. But the judge prevailed at that second hearing, and after spending not just half of his sentence but more than half of his life behind bars, Trevor was granted parole.

Sitting at the banquette in Denny's, where we arranged to meet a month after his release, Trevor looks both embattled and hopeful. There is still the possibility of an appeal by the state, so he is being careful not to let freedom be too exhilarating. Yet it *is* exhilarating. Next to him, almost but not quite touching shoulders, is Loraine, a sweet-faced young woman several years his junior. She is a community college student studying psychology and criminology. For years she had been corresponding with imprisoned adults who were youths at the time of their offense. One of her correspondents was Trevor. The correspondence grew into a friendship. The friendship grew into something else. And now, as Tom Petty put it in a song released when Trevor was a seven-year-old, carefree, dirt bike–riding kid: "The future is wide open."

CHAPTER 7

CATHERINE

"My name is Catherine Jones," she says, holding the mic with one hand, gesturing with the other. She's usually nervous when speaking before a large group, she tells them—there are maybe two hundred people in the audience this afternoon—but not this time. "You're like family," she says, her voice both amplified and intimate. And they are, in a way. In this room, at this national conference for the Campaign for the Fair Sentencing of Youth, are people just like her: survivors of violence, adults given extreme sentences as youth, advocates of prison reform, activists. She calls them "my distant cousins that I've never met," smiling a wide smile. It's not the smile you'd expect from a woman who has lived through what Catherine has.

She was thirteen years old, and her brother Curtis was twelve, when they shot and killed their father's live-in girlfriend four times with a semiautomatic 9mm handgun. They were charged as adults with first-degree murder, the youngest kids ever to be treated and processed this way in the United States.

It was the year of Columbine, the year two Colorado teenagers went on a shooting spree and killed thirteen people, the year of kids with guns, the year kids as killers seared the American psyche. Catherine and her brother were two kids with guns, the first national case. The jury never heard about the violence and sexual abuse in their home. The jury never heard that Catherine's mother had fled for her life after years of battering, leaving her children behind in the care of their father, a man once charged with second-degree murder. Catherine was four; her brother a year younger. The jury never heard about a family member living in the home who forced Catherine to perform oral sex and slept in the same bed as her brother, a man who had once spent six years in prison for armed robbery. There was no opportunity for the social service agency that had investigated the abuses to submit documentation. Catherine and Curtis did not testify and tell their story. That's because there was no trial. The two kids pleaded guilty to second-degree murder and accepted their sentences.

"That was the day," she tells me later, "that I ceased to be a girl, a daughter, a middle schooler. That was the day I was branded." I had met Catherine the year before at an all-day employee orientation session at Sponsors, the reentry nonprofit. She was about to start a job as a night manager at the agency's women's shelter. I was there to learn about the agency from the ground up. I knew nothing about Catherine's history until months later when I invited her out for coffee. What I did know, even in the context of that slog-through-the-employee-handbook day, was that her energy filled the room. It's that same energy, not explosive but like a banked fire, she is showing here in front of the crowd. No one cared about the circumstances of her case, Catherine tells the audience. She is not asking for pity or even sympathy. She is telling a story, her story, to make a point about the way the law treats kids and what that means to the kids. But it's not a story of the crime or even the sentencing but rather of her years of incarceration and the struggles she faced when she was released.

She spent the first three years of her imprisonment in solitary confinement, she says, letting that fact sink in. "They didn't know what to do with me." She makes it into kind of a joke. But the audience knows it is no joke. She paints a picture of her life behind bars, a traumatized kid in a prison with adults, overseen by guards that, she says with careful understatement, "probably should not have been guards in the first place." One of them raped her, in solitary, when she was fifteen.

And here she is, thirty-four, a survivor, a self-described "motivational speaker, mommy extraordinaire, and fierce advocate," delivering this plenary address in Montgomery, Alabama. To make this appearance, to travel here, she had to obtain special permission from her parole officer. Catherine is on lifetime parole. She is free—released from a Florida prison when she was thirty—but she will never be entirely free of the system. It has shaped her. Now she wants to help shape it, especially the treatment and sentencing of youth.

She continues with her story, relating how, once inside, she shut down completely. Probably, although she doesn't say this, the emotional detachment began much earlier, an attempt to insulate herself from growing up in what she later told me was "a household ruled by force and fear." Inside an adult prison, facing an eighteen-year sentence, a stretch of time that to a thirteen-year-old seemed interminable, she didn't want to think about what she did. She didn't know *how* to think about what she did, how to recognize, let alone process, emotions so deeply buried. And so she walled herself off. She also quickly learned that, as a kid surrounded by adults, she needed to protect herself. The institution taught her that the way to stay safe was to fight. She became a fighter. Her aggressive behavior was controlled with psychotropic drugs. A decade into her sentence, she described herself as "tough and hardened."

And now this audience wants to know—*needs* to know—how that damaged, numbed, tough, and hardened twenty-three year-old became this woman they see in front of them, this woman who speaks from the heart, who *has* a heart. This woman who took a human life and has, against tremendous odds, managed to reclaim her own. There is a softness to her: the sweet girlish face with upturned eyes under arched brows; the soft, comfortable body; a lilt to her voice; a hint of a southern drawl. But underneath it, there is a steely resolve, a resolve without bitterness or anger. How is that possible, those in the audience wonder, those who have been in prison themselves, those whose children are in prison, those who come to their activism by way of fury?

"I could have been a statistic," she tells them. A guy in the back of the room, a big man, an African American, like many in this audience, like Catherine, has been standing, sentry-like, staring ahead, expressionless during Catherine's talk. Now he crosses his arms, looks down, then nods slowly and keeps nodding.

What happened to Catherine at twenty-three was either luck or fate, depending on how you look at life. But what she did with that opportunity was all her, all will and effort and hard work. And grace, Catherine would be quick to add. Five years before she was to be released, she was transferred to a different prison where a husband and wife were teaching a class called Fresh Start. The name alone spoke to her. She knew she didn't want to be the person that she had become.

"I just wanted to feel," she tells the audience, "I wanted to have emotions." A fresh start was exactly what she needed, and so she signed up for the class. The question at the core of the class: "Who are you?" At first, she says, she answered superficially. She was smart. That's who she was. School was just something she was good at. It was also an activity that kept her head above water during those years in prison. It was her escape. She'd earned her high school diploma and went on to get an associate of arts degree and paralegal and computer support certifications. She was the sum of her accomplishments. But after the fourth or fifth time of speaking about her life as if she were reading a résumé, she realized she had to go deeper. The answer, she tells them—and why her voice does not catch when she says this is a mystery—was this: "I'm hurt. I'm angry. I'm wounded. I'm broken."

That was the truth of it. Once she admitted that, once she said it out loud, she could see the pieces. She could, in the vernacular of the self-help world, "own her story." This couple, this Fresh Start class, helped her put those pieces together, to heal. When the class ended, she worked with the couple to create a curriculum around self-worth and self-identity that focused on working with people like her, "broken women."

When she came out the gate of the Lowell Correctional Institution in Ocala, she emerged with a passion to help others and with big plans and big dreams. She thought she was, she tells the audience, shaking her head at her own naiveté, "completely prepared." She smiles that wide smile again. "I figured society was going to embrace me because..." she pauses, waiting to deliver the line, "because I was so awesome." She laughs and the audience laughs along with her. "But the reality of my release was so different than my fantasy," she says. From the audience comes a murmur of assent, a few "uh-huhs." They've been through, or know others who have been through, what Catherine is talking about. A few weeks out in the real world, Catherine realized that this new life she was so ready to live was not going to be easy to build. Society was not as forgiving as she thought. She cried a lot. She made mistakes—not the kind that got you sent back to prison, but the kind that ate away at your hard-won self-confidence.

———————

Her time is almost up, although the audience is not at all restless. She is a gifted speaker, both authoritative and intimate. She brings a light touch to a heavy subject. Her life is a lesson that she is willing, more than willing, to share. But she doesn't have time to take them through all that she experienced. What's important to her—and to these people in this conference room who work to reshape the lives of youth who've spent years in prison—is what she is doing with that experience. She tells them that the difficult time she had after her release "burned in me a desire to help those who were going to come home behind me." She wants them to have the resources they need to support them, so they don't have to go through what she went through.

"I want to pay it forward," she says. "I want to be that person they can depend on." She smiles again. The applause is loud. After the session has ended, as she makes her way through the room, people approach her. Many were in prison as juveniles like her. They need to tell her a bit of their story. They need to tell her that her story is their story. Like her, they survived something horrific. Like her they are working hard to beat the odds. She listens.

CHAPTER 8

DAVE

If I don't arrive at least ten minutes early, Dave will already be there, comfortably seated at an outdoor table at the bakery, and he will have bought my Americano, and despite multiple entreaties not to do so, he will already have ordered a slab of chocolate cake that he insists we will share. We never do. This afternoon, as usual during these twice-monthly meetups, I watch him dig into the cake, forking in huge icing-slathered hunks with the gusto and lack of self-consciousness of an eight-year-old. The chocolate coats his teeth. The teeth are his tell. If you didn't see the teeth, what you would see is a trim, fashionably bald, shiny-faced, clean-shaven, nattily dressed white man. But his teeth are gray and discolored. Missing bicuspids leave dark holes on the sides of his mouth. They are the teeth of a man who has not had the privilege of good (or any) dental care, a poor man, maybe, certainly not a man wearing slim-fitting black jeans and a tailored black sweater, stylish glasses, a thin gold necklace encircling his neck. In Dave's case, they are the teeth of a man who has lived thirty-four of his sixty years in prison.

Dave had been a mystery to me through our years together in the writers' group I ran at the penitentiary that had been his "home" for most of his adult life. He was one of the first three men to join the group. He came to just about every session for close to four years. He joined in the conversations. He did the homework. He responded to all the writing prompts. But, unlike the other men—the group eventually expanded to ten of them—he rarely wrote anything that revealed his inner thoughts. He was steadfastly outgoing without being in any way forthcoming, a combination that both confused and fascinated me. I plumbed his work for hints about his character, his persona, his past. Mostly, he chronicled and reported: his job, what he ate, the college classes he had taken. He once wrote a multipage account of the blueprint he had created for himself early into his long period of incarceration, a series of five-year plans, each segment devoted to another endeavor that would inch him closer to living a life outside the prison walls. But the overarching goal, really, was to stay sane by segmenting his time into imaginable chunks. Five years he could do. Thirty or thirty-five? That was inconceivable.

During his first five years, he wrote that he focused on education, earning a community college degree and then a bachelor's. It was easier to accomplish this back when Dave first went inside than it is now. Back then there were Pell Grants available to help fund education for those behind bars, and there were more than three hundred post-secondary education programs established in American prisons, including the one that housed Dave. After 1994, when Congress banned incarcerated people from accessing these grants, these full-on, degree-granting programs dwindled to about a dozen. At some institutions individual classes might be offered, but to actually earn a degree could take fifteen or more years, assuming—a very big assumption—that the right classes happened to be offered in the right sequence, and that the institution was making it financially possible for inmates to afford tuition. Dave, starting his sentence in 1985, had better choices.

During the second five years, he wrote that he turned his attention to his mental health, taking advantage of what was offered in counseling and therapy (which wasn't much), joining groups, and as he put it, "turning myself inside out." He does not write about what he found "inside," what he learned about himself that might have helped him untangle his past and understand and come to terms with his crime. In fact, he never mentions his crime. Or his family. His one and only reference to his past comes in response to a prompt I gave the group about describing a place they'd like to "transport" themselves to. Dave wrote about a restaurant in the town he grew up in.

Dave's third chunk of time was devoted to gaining new work skills in the prison industries and saving money. What those skills were, he does not say. He spent years working in the prison's commercial laundry and then in a call center. Saving money was an ongoing challenge given that prison jobs earn, at best, a dollar a day. Next came a period during which he paid attention to his legal case and, with the help of counsel, mounted a series of challenges and appeals and drafted letters and applications to the parole board.

The next stretch of time, which lasted until his release, was focused on personal finances, securing a credit card, exploring programs for first-time homeowners, making contacts with local banks and bankers, doing what he could from inside to set himself up for financial security once released. He read and reread Sheryl Sandberg's *Lean In* for inspiration and often ended his homework assignments with "Leaning in!" His optimism about his future, his discipline and focus, astonished me when I read this chronicle of self-motivation. This plan that had spanned more than three decades was extraordinary in its detail and rigor. His report was almost equally as unusual because, unlike the writing I was seeing from the other men in the group, it was reserved and impersonal. There was no emotional or psychological context for all he had done. Reading his work was like looking at a piece of cloth imprinted with an interesting design but no texture, no warp and weft to the fabric. Dave continued to be a mystery.

Then, in response to a prompt I gave the group about friendship, he wrote about a neighbor on his cell block that began with a deeply observant description of the man, his hazel eyes with flecks of green and blue that changed depending on the light. He commented on the man's "star power" and his graceful physicality, which reminded Dave of the Olympic diver Greg Louganis. Given the norms of Dave's caged world, the hypermasculine posturing, this description was unusual. I wondered if it meant something or if I was just reading into it. I wondered too about his handwriting. It was a severely back-slanted, left-leaning scrawl. I'd never seen handwriting like that before. Searching for clues about what made him tick, I explored what the "science" of graphology would say about such penmanship. Supposedly, a graphologist, analyzing the characteristics and patterns of a person's handwriting, could offer insights into the writer's persona and psychological state. I knew this was probably nonsense, but I sought out explanations from various websites. This one struck me: "The writer represses impulses and needs for affection and contact." Was this what Dave was doing? Did this explain why, despite so many opportunities to do so in writing, he never revealed much about his inner life?

And yet he apparently wanted me to know. One day, after maybe a year and a half into the writers' group, he handed me a very thick folder, his personnel file, with various commendations and certificates, letters of support, legal documents, and several psych reports. The folder also included a letter from his original lawyer detailing the story that underlay Dave's crime, the context in which it took place. It was a story, the lawyer explained in this letter, that he did not introduce in court. Reading this letter from the original lawyer is how and when I found out about Dave's crime: he murdered his father and his brother and then set the house on fire. The story presented at his trial was that Dave had met a girl visiting from Japan and wanted to marry her. He needed money to bring her over to the United States. His father refused, and Dave murdered him for the life insurance money. Maybe the brother witnessed this and had to be dispatched as well. The fire was to cover up the murders.

The very different story Dave's original trial lawyer wrote about in the letter in his file went like this: Dave, a "homosexual," a distinctly "feminine" man, a hairdresser, grew up in a small, conservative town. His father and brother were ex-military. They bullied him relentlessly. They made his life miserable. They made him ashamed. So he killed them. The lawyer wrote that he felt he couldn't use this in the trial because the attitude of the judge and jury would be so virulently antigay that this would hurt his case. This was 1985. AIDS had become a full-blown epidemic, igniting intense fear and ramping up entrenched homophobia. Dave was convicted of aggravated murder and arson and sentenced to life, so it's hard to see how much worse the sentence could have been had antigay bias entered into the verdict. The lawyer's explanation of Dave's state of mind is not an excuse. Murder is murder. But the story that led to his conviction, killing for insurance money, is calculated and cold-hearted and more chilling than the backstory sketched in by the lawyer.

I don't know the details of the real story—only Dave knows that, and he's not telling. But it is not difficult to imagine the pain of growing up effeminate in that household, in a sleepy, rural town of 17,000, in the 1970s. It is not difficult to imagine the bullying, the name-calling, the shaming. It might have begun early in his life. The research on bullying suggests that it is as psychologically damaging as physical abuse, that the effects persist into adulthood, that it is linked to depression, anxiety, anger, and hostility (also suicide). What drove Dave to the desperate act of murder? Was there a tipping point, a straw-that-broke-the-camel's-back moment? Had he examined this, with or without the help of any therapy or counseling he was able to get in prison? Did he, sitting across from me now, a free man, almost swooning over his chocolate cake, know himself? Nothing in his writing or in our scores of conversations over coffee and baked goods revealed answers. These were secrets long kept, still kept.

Inside and now outside of prison, Dave was mild mannered and polite. His affect was friendly, a little overly eager to please, but in no way creepy. I detected no banked anger, in fact no deep passion or fire. Today he looked as elegant as a bald, sixty-year-old man could look, all in fashionable black. A few weeks earlier he had come attired in snowy white, from sweater to slacks to shoes. Often he wore pastels, a sort of *Miami Vice* look accented by the gold choker necklace. The freedom to not wear prison blues must be intoxicating. The thrill of choice, of purposeful self-presentation, of, essentially, outing yourself through fashion. It was, I thought, a kind of bravery for someone who had spent thirty-four years being as cautious as he could be to not attract the wrong kind of attention. He was learning to be who he was. He was leaning in.

CHAPTER 9

ARNOLDO

At first Arnoldo doesn't trust me, and I don't blame him. He has been burned by stories that focus on his crime, on his gang activity, on his prison persona. He doesn't want to be written about that way, boxed into who he was, forever defined by what he did. He wants to be seen the way he sees himself these days, the way he is: a man who has reclaimed his life and is in the process of reinventing himself. It has been two years since his release.

The only reason he's agreed to talk with me by phone this winter morning is because Sterling has vouched for me, and Sterling's word is golden. The two of them share a long history inside and, before that, the experience of having grown up on the margins, products of childhoods branded by violence. Their friendship continues, and the respect that Arnoldo has for Sterling means that he is at least willing to talk to me, a stranger. Still, that first conversation is halting and somewhat strained. I know more about him, via Sterling, than he knows about me. Trust must always be earned, but the cost is higher and the earning harder when the gulf between the two people is as wide as it is between me and Arnoldo. Sterling is the bridge over that gulf.

An hour into the call, he haltingly sketches in some of his past for me, facts not feelings. It is too early for feelings. He was born and spent the first eight years of his life in McAllen, Texas, a small city—more like a town in the 1980s when he was a kid— just across the Rio Grande from Reynosa, Mexico. Hispanics or Latinos (as the U.S. census identifies them) comprise about 85 percent of the population, and Spanish is the lingua franca. Arnoldo's mother was from Mexico. Arnoldo fit into this cultur-ally homogeneous community, and for many years after he left, after his mother spirited her children two thousand miles away to escape her abusive alcoholic husband, he considered Texas his home.

Where he lived from age eight until his first arrest at fif-teen—a remote, overwhelmingly Anglo agricultural outpost in eastern Oregon—was in every way an alien place. The other Spanish-speaking kids in the small community were, like Arnoldo, the sons and daughters of field laborers, but most were transplants from Los Angeles, street-savvy city kids from dense urban neighborhoods where gangs were just as essential to life as family. Here, strangers in a strange land, the gangs they formed were safe havens from the prejudice. They offered a sense of identity to brown-skinned kids isolated in a white-skinned com-munity. To Arnoldo, a quiet kid, an introvert, a boy scarred by living with an unpredictable and violent father, gang member-ship offered instant friendship and camaraderie. He joined.

What he felt, he later tells me when we know each other better, when he can talk about feelings, was love and acceptance, brotherhood, the warmth of inclusion, the comfort of knowing you could depend on others to watch out for you. He knows that gangs are also about drugs, crime, and violence. He knows that's what people think when they think "gang." But from inside, he says, it doesn't feel like that. Nevertheless, when he joined, that was the life he signed up for. At fifteen he was remanded to a juvenile detention center for a gang-related shooting. He spent the next two and a half years there, more than two hundred miles from his family. Paroled to a halfway house in a nearby city, he connected with a fellow gang member, and he says, his voice low and quiet, "the cycle started all over again." Seven months and a hectic street life marked by random shootings later, he was back in custody, an adult facility this time, a maximum security penitentiary. His original sentence was for fifteen years. An assault charge for a fight inside earned him another two.

That fight, and others, were part of his gang activity inside. Inside it was even more important to have people you trusted looking after you, to know who your friends were. In the prison that housed Arnoldo, more than 70 percent of those who identified as Hispanic were gang-affiliated. Arnoldo was a leader. Over the years, his involvement in or proximity to gang-related assaults and fights, riots, and yard altercations landed him in the hole six different times. He spent a total of twelve years housed in isolation. Life for the men in the single-bed cells in that prison-within-a-prison unit followed a numbing, quarantined routine: twenty-three and a half hours in the cell with meals delivered on trays; thirty minutes out for recreation (access to a small outdoor space); a shower either two or three times a week. Depending on the severity of the already severe conditions, there might be reading material allowed in the cell or an occasional phone call. It was there, in isolation, that Arnoldo—and Sterling too—began to understand themselves.

When he was not in the hole, Arnoldo was learning about

restorative justice, taking a class, listening to speakers, participating in group discussions, talking with Sterling, thinking hard about what he valued. He continued to value the brotherhood of the gang, but he no longer valued or wanted to be part of the violence. Gang aggression and the hypermasculinity it both triggered and reinforced was part of the toxic environment he was just learning to recognize. This environment was so much the norm behind bars, so much the norm on the streets, that he hadn't seen it for what it really was: damaging, dangerous, *ab*normal.

He began to practice what he was learning about conflict resolution. He was seen as a leader and could use that status to place himself in the middle of situations and try to defuse them. His intent, the intent of conflict resolution practiced in the yard, in the thick of it, was to stop the immediate response, which was all too often, as he put it, "the big-ass reaction." The intent was to give people a moment to consider, to give them a way to step back without losing face. Even if the result still was violence—as it sometimes was—Arnoldo felt he was "doing the work."

When the situation could not be defused, when it got out of control, there continued to be a place for what he was learning, a way to continue as a mediator. Arnoldo told me about a yard fight between Mexican and Black gangs. I had read about it back when it happened, a brief news story based on one of those perfunctory reports prison officials release to the press. It was a riot that resulted in some inmates being transferred to other facilities and some being put in the hole. Arnoldo was one who went to the hole. He was not part of the violence, he said, but he was in the middle of "the situation." He told me about how, in the hole, the Black and brown men did not continue bad-mouthing each other. He helped guide the talk around de-escalating conflict.

Discussions continued in that way discussions happen in the hole, parlayed cell to cell down the line or scribbled on slips of paper sent skidding across the floor to a neighboring cell. "We brought our tools in there," he said. He was proud of that.

He tells me this story several visits into our ongoing attempts to get to know one another. He is talking about the way he has changed, his thoughts, his attitude, his demeanor, his body language. In prison, before his mediation and conflict resolution work on himself and with others, he would walk into an environment and his mindset would be: How do I come in and get you to put your guard down so I can take advantage of the situation and of you and have the upper hand? "I would puff myself up, like birds do," he said. "I would make myself bigger so I would be more threatening. I wanted my message to be: If you mess with me, I'll hurt you."

Now he thinks: How do I come into this environment and make people feel safe? What can I do to create a welcoming and healthy environment? Arnoldo is soft-spoken and articulate. He has an educated vocabulary, which he uses without affectation, and a street vocabulary, which he uses without posturing. He seems unflappable, self-contained. Maybe this comes from spending so much time alone.

Our meeting today, in the midst of COVID-19 shutdowns and precautions, is on Zoom. He is sitting in his living room, wearing what he always seems to be wearing when we meet: a knit wool cap pulled down so it almost meets his glasses and a dark, slogan-free hoodie. He seems both calm and alert—I've seen this in Sterling too—an attitude and affect that I think must come from long years of living a prison life. He excuses himself for a moment, leaving me to stare at the bookshelves in the room. I can't quite make out the titles, but there are a lot of them.

A few minutes later he returns with Sol, his sleepy-eyed eighteen-month-old son. The boy has his father's coppery skin, only a bit lighter, and long, dark eyelashes. He is a beautiful child. Arnoldo sits down, cradling the boy in his arms. Sol doesn't even glance at the computer screen. He looks up at his father.

CHAPTER 10

DAVE

It was cold that morning and still dark at seven. The sun wouldn't rise for another half an hour, and even then it wouldn't lighten the sky beyond a steely gray. It had rained on and off the night before, and the pavement was slick and puddled. Dave wasn't dressed for the raw weather. He wore khakis, tennis shoes, and a light windbreaker, clothes he selected from the "dress out" shelf in the prison. He hadn't worn anything other than prison blues—baggy jeans and a navy T-shirt—in thirty-four years. Today, February 4, 2019, was the first time he'd been on the other side of the penitentiary walls since he had been transported to a local medical clinic for hernia repair surgery more than fifteen years before. He remembered a lot about that long-ago day: how the prison transport van parked next to a brand-new Cadillac CTS in the clinic's lot—Dave loved cars; how the attending nurse had brought him a warmed blanket—it brought tears to his eyes; how one of the guards in the van let him look at his smartphone—the first mobile device he'd ever seen; how, on the way back that afternoon, the guard did him the kindness of not shackling and manacling him. He thought of it as a kindness, but really, what threat did he pose a few hours post-op, in pain, with stitches in his groin? He wasn't allowed to recover at the clinic. He had to go back inside and walk up three flights of concrete stairs to the infirmary.

He remembered all of this, but he couldn't remember the date of this excursion, or even the exact year. "Time is different in prison," he told me. What he meant is that you keep track of it, obsessively, but then you lose track of it too, sometimes quite purposefully. He wrote about the surgery, but once he was out, in those weeks after February 4, he threw out his journals. They were too painful for him to reread, he said. But on this February day, there was no pain, only excitement. And confusion. And fear. Dave's first parole hearing had been back in 2004. Now, a decade and a half later, he had gained release. He had big plans—graduate school, a late-life career in counseling for ex-offenders, home ownership, a loving relationship with Kevin, who had been his cellmate and had been released eight years before.

That was who was waiting for him at the entrance to the prison, Kevin. They had corresponded regularly since the man had left prison. He had visited Dave. They had talked about the future, their future. They had saved money to start a life together. In preparation for Dave's release, Kevin had gotten him a cell phone and added him to his plan. There were three others waiting by the door to welcome Dave that morning, two friends from inside with a bit of free-world time under their belts and a man named Roger Martin, an eighty-five-year-old, six-term state legislator who had been volunteering in the prison for years. It was still dark outside when they walked together to the parking lot outside the prison and drove west three blocks, past the Hall of Strains cannabis dispensary and the Plaid Pantry and the Graveyard Bar to Sybil's Omelettes, a breakfast joint that was the traditional first stop for the newly released. The guys inside talked about Sybil's all the time. At the table waiting for Dave were two more people, an octogenarian friend of Martin's and another long-time prison volunteer, a retired mental health professional who had known Dave for years.

Dave worked hard to maintain outward equanimity. Three decades behind bars had taught him how to feel one thing and show another. Plus he was a man long accustomed to keeping secrets. There was noise from the kitchen, doors swinging open and closed, plates and silverware clicking, people sitting down, getting up, busboys moving from table to table. So much activity, so much movement. People were talking around the table, asking him questions, laughing. He tried to study the menu. It offered so many choices that his brain shut down. The waitress leaned over to ask him what he wanted. It was so much. It was too much. Like an amusement park funhouse, he thought later, when he could think again. But at least he was not alone trying to negotiate everything by himself, like those participants in the reentry simulation.

The trip to the city that would be his new home was harrowing. His former cellie and, he hoped, his future partner, drove fast, or so it seemed to Dave. They were on the freeway, the scenery zipping by so quickly that Dave got carsick. He had that same disoriented feeling he had had in the restaurant, that he was on some kind of carnival ride—thrilling, wild, terrifying. His friend delivered him to the main campus of Sponsors, the reentry nonprofit that was offering Dave transitional housing for ninety days. He would be provided shelter and food, be case-managed, and have access to resources and support as he navigated his new reality. Sponsors was part of the burgeoning "reentry industry," a reaction to the flood of those released from incarceration without the benefit of meaningful and sustained rehabilitation programs that would prepare them for their new lives. In the absence of these programs, the responsibility had shifted to small local agencies and nonprofits. The good news — if good news can be extracted from this situation—is that from 1995 to 2010, the number of reentry services organizations and criminal justice agencies increased 300 percent. The bad news is that they compete for meager state and federal funds. They compete for donor dollars and community volunteers. They are often underfunded and understaffed.

Sponsors had agreed to take Dave in, even though he did not commit his crime in that county, which was usually one of the prerequisites for getting the services. The agency's director, a dynamo named Paul Solomon, who'd served a stint behind bars himself, sometimes made exceptions for lifers like Dave, men who had been in so long that the transition to uncaged life was particularly challenging. Dave's room would be larger than his cell, with a comfortable bed and an unbarred window that opened and closed. There was a communal kitchen, where he could prepare his meals, and a living room that was shared with a dozen or so other recently released men housed in the unit. He could choose when and what to eat. He could leave the campus, take a bus to appointments or just to explore. He could have coffee at Starbucks. But there was also a curfew and bed checks, random urine analyses for drugs, a daily schedule of programming, and the enforced expectation that he would, within ninety days, find a job and be ready to move on. It was, in many ways, an institutional setting. But for someone so new to the free world, it was a necessary first—and big—step on the reentry path.

Within his first twenty-four hours out, Dave had met the

Sponsors staff, conferred with his case manager, checked in with his parole officer, and taken a bus to the Department of Motor Vehicles to get an official photo ID. The only one he had was from prison. The next morning, with the help of Sponsors staff in the computer-equipped Reentry Resource Center, he went online for the very first time. Nothing was intuitive; nothing came easily. But with assistance, he managed to apply for SNAP benefits and health insurance. When the insurance came through he could get his eyes tested for the first time in years. He needed new glasses. He could go to the dentist. He knew how bad his teeth were. That afternoon he took a bus to Goodwill where he bought a new wardrobe. Nothing blue. With support and guidance right from the start, he was able to get more accomplished in those three days after release than most of the reentry simulation participants managed in their constructed month.

Dave knew he was fortunate to land at Sponsors, but he didn't realize how fortunate. Back in the early 2000s, Urban Institute's *From Prison to Home* report had called for an approach to reentry that focused on a holistic coordinated continuum of services located within the community. This was echoed by Jeremy Travis, former director of the National Institute of Justice and an expert on reentry challenges, who called for "a seamless set of systems that span boundaries of prison and community." But most who transition from caged to free do so without thoughtful and informed guidance. Many exit prison with no support and nowhere to go. They've got a trash bag full of belongings, a bus ticket, and maybe some gate money. They are understandably jittery, anxious, fearful—and also exhilarated, an overwhelming rush of feelings known as "gate fever." The experience is at once thrilling and debilitating. And often lonely.

The Boston Reentry Study, part of Harvard sociology professor Bruce Western's important and ongoing work on the experiences of those released from prison, found that in the first week after release, about 40 percent of the more than one hundred respondents the research team was tracking described feelings of anxiety or panic. (Consider that the designers of the reentry simulation found it necessary to provide on-site counseling for their sometimes distressed participants, who were merely playing a part and not actually living the experience.) Those in the Boston study reported anxiety when using public transport and in crowded places like stores. They avoided people. Western used the words "despair" and "isolation" to describe their state of mind. In a similar study of those released from a Michigan prison, a man named DeAngelo, interviewed by the Berkeley and Michigan researchers studying reentry and reintegration, said this about his experience out the gate: "My first day was the worst ever. The hardest, and the most intense challenge for me... was the anxiety... It's not just a jittery nervousness. It's like... you're just scared shitless...overwhelmed with just life." He and twenty-one others were part of the ambitious sociological analysis presented in the 2019 book *On the Outside*. DeAngelo had a lot going for him. He was picked up outside the prison by a supportive girlfriend. He was only twenty-seven at the time. He had been behind bars for less than five years. And still, the shock was visceral. Startlingly, or perhaps not, other researchers studying inmates released from Washington state institutions found that the former prisoners' mortality rate during their first two weeks out was thirteen times greater than a matched cohort who had never been imprisoned.

In interview after interview chronicled in *On the Outside*, the released prisoners talk about their overwhelmingly positive hopes and expectations for their future. This turns out to be both a good and a bad thing. Optimism can fuel change. It can spur what psychologists call "self-efficacy," confidence in one's ability to take control, to make things happen, to change and grow. But these prerelease hopes can also set the bar so impossibly high that moderate success can feel like stagnation, and a slipup can feel like abject failure. Maybe that accounts for some of those post-incarceration deaths noted in the Washington state study or the quick reversion to alcohol and drug use that can scuttle any chances at making a new life. Vicki was well acquainted with that path.

VICKI

It was a Friday in April 2017. She doesn't remember the exact day. This would seem odd. A release date is long anticipated and planned for, circled on a calendar, starred in a journal. But Vicki had been in and out so many times that she had lost track of the particulars. She remembers it was cold and dark. She was wearing ill-fitting clothing from the free box. She waited outside the gate for a Department of Corrections shuttle van to the Greyhound station. She didn't want Steve, the man who had stuck by her for decades, to have to drive four hours up the freeway to pick her up. She and another woman waited together, jittery, shivering, silent. They waited for the shuttle for what seemed like a long time. The ride into town to the bus station took forever. And then there was a long wait for the bus. And the six hours, with stops along the way, to get home. She read a book. She wrote in her journal. Everything was slow, but everything was also fast. She was on edge the whole time, barely holding it together. Steve met her at the bus station, another reunion, another chance. Vicki felt this time was going to be different.

She had a home to come home to—Steve owned a somewhat-worse-for-wear 1970s ranch in a safe neighborhood—but she had no plan, no services lined up to help with her transition. And most important, no help with her addiction. Or rather, addictions. Like three-quarters of those in prison, she had a long history of substance abuse. Fewer than one-third receive treatment while behind bars. Vicki had long admitted to the meth addiction. Meth was, with her street family and in prison, an "acceptable" addiction. But heroin, her twin addiction, was another thing. In her world, heroin addicts were losers. She never told anyone, including Steve about the heroin. She'd been clean in prison. She thought she could stay clean on the outside.

A few months later, she was back in custody for drug theft: pain pills, opioids she may or may not have needed for back pain. She was out again in late fall 2019. This time she got herself released directly to the inpatient drug program where I first met her and became her mentor. It was a substance abuse and treatment center, a residential facility for women with a full range of therapeutic services, mental health counseling, support groups, and mandatory classes in relapse prevention. Here she could work with a counselor to develop a treatment plan and a list of specific goals. Meeting those goals might take two months, or three, or more. She vowed to stick with it. Being honest about her hidden addiction was key. So was getting an official ADHD diagnosis that would allow for therapeutic treatment and prescription medication instead of the meth she used to self-medicate.

The rehab facility was tucked into a quiet, modest residential neighborhood near a park. She would live in a small, two-person room in a locked dorm. She would live a controlled, tightly structured life not unlike the one she had been used to in prison, with twenty-four hour monitoring, bed checks, drug tests, and daily accountability. Wake-up was at seven, meals served at seven-thirty, noon, and five in the small cafeteria. From nine to four she would follow a set schedule that included cognitive behavioral therapy sessions, debriefings with her counselor, group therapy sessions, doctor appointments, trauma healing activities, art therapy workshops, classes, and required homework assignments. She could leave the facility to participate in drug court, a county-supervised program of monitoring, oversight, and coordinated treatment for drug offenders with long criminal histories. She could also sign out to spend time with an assigned community mentor (that was me) for what the prison system called "prosocial activities." For us that meant working out at my gym, going to a craft fair, hanging out drinking coffee, taking walks.

She stayed with it, going to every appointment, trying to learn something new from the relapse prevention classes, taking advantage of special opportunities like weekly acupuncture sessions. When she felt overwhelmed, she calmed herself by coloring in a kids' book she carried in her purse, a suggestion from her therapist. She quit tobacco and transitioned to vaping. Her confidence grew. If she could control the addictions, she told herself that she could permanently exit "the life," a life that not only included the drugs but also the crimes committed to support the drugs.

She could have "coined out"—graduated from the program by receiving a special coin—by Christmas, but she asked to stay another month. It was hard not to be home, especially for the holidays. But this time she was, she told herself, finally going to learn the lesson she had been failing to learn for decades. She realized now that she needed help. She needed to admit and own her mistakes. She needed to truly change. Being at home meant everyday exposure to her old life. Being at home meant facing the trauma and chaos her life had inflicted on her two now-adult children. And then there was Steve. He had stayed with her all these years. Had that support, that safety net, also enabled the life she had been leading? She refused to think about that.

TREVOR

Seventeen years, six months, and three days after he was imprisoned for murder, at age fourteen, Trevor emerged from the maximum security penitentiary that had been his home all of his adult life. He was wearing a state-issue T-shirt and a thin jacket he had gotten from the prison's supply of street clothing. He had been given twenty-four-hours notice about the release. His case was a complicated one, and his release this chilly February morning was both controversial and contentious. He had been sentenced to life in prison with the possibility of parole after thirty years. But at his Second Look hearing that allowed for juvenile offenders to be considered for early release once they had served half of their original sentence, a long list of character witnesses testified to his rehabilitation. A judge listened, agreed, and ordered his release. But the state appealed, and for more than a year had fought to keep Trevor behind bars while the appeal was pending. The state lost. Now, today, this morning, Trevor was free.

He might have had only a day's notice about the release, but he had been preparing for that day for most of his time in prison, worked his way into a top job in the prison, showing determination, leadership, and an ability to navigate both the system itself and the culture it created. He had a quick mind, ambition without ego, and—nurtured by his extraordinary mother and his half brother, who was his codefendant and cellmate—he had a belief in his own power to remake his life.

His mother, Karen, should have been there this morning to meet him at the gate. She had uprooted her life, ended her marriage, changed her career, and become a prison reform activist to support Trevor and his older brother. This was the moment she had worked for and dreamed about for years. Instead, because the release was so contentious with the state still jockeying for position, Trevor was released directly into the custody of his parole officer who drove him to the county's parole office where he was fitted with a GPS ankle monitor. His mother and his attorney were waiting for him there and were able to see him for a few minutes before they were told to leave. It would take all morning for Trevor to be processed. He had an hour-long psych evaluation at the office. There were questions to answer, forms to read and sign, restrictions and rules to learn about. It felt surreal. He was out. But was he? He was "in the world," but right now that world was still the controlled, rule-bound world he had known since he was fourteen. He spent more than three hours in that office, full of both uncertainty and wonder. There was a chance the court could reverse his release. There was a chance he could go back.

It was early afternoon when his parole officer drove him to his mother's house. That's when it began to sink in. There was another person in the house besides Karen. It was Loraine, the young woman he had met while in prison. Karen had connected with the girl and honored the relationship. In fact, she had taken Loraine in, giving her a place to stay while she attended a local community college. Trevor spent a long time walking through the house, slowly, room by room, in an odd state between hyperalertness and somnambulance. It surprised him how low the ceilings were, how small the spaces. His cell had been closet sized, but all the other spaces he had inhabited for more than a decade and a half were institutional—the cavernous laundry facility, the high school gym–sized activities floor, the echoing chow hall. Karen watched her son as he worked to make sense of his new surroundings. Then she asked if he wanted to go out for lunch. It had been a very long morning at the parole office. It would be good to get outside, to be part of the wider world. Trevor said no. A police car was parked in front of the house. Daily surveillance was part of the parole plan, at least for a while. Trevor did not want to be tailed by a cop car. Instead, Karen went by herself to pick up some sub sandwiches. For dinner that night she made one of Trevor's favorites: pot roast.

The next morning they drove to the Department of Motor Vehicles where Trevor took—and effortlessly passed—his permit test. Driving was a very big deal to him. He had a street-legal motorcycle when he was thirteen. He had, in fact, at thirteen, taken the bike for a spin on the interstate and gotten a ticket from an astonished highway patrol officer. When, permit in hand, he got behind the wheel of his mother's car, it all came back to him: the freedom, the speed, the open road. He couldn't wait to get on a motorcycle again, but he would have to. He needed to pass another test for that. Until that happened, there was no chance he would risk a violation. So he contented himself with the lesser thrill of being behind the wheel of a car. Together, he and his mother drove around town taking care of the business of rejoining the world. He bought a phone, opened a bank account, shopped for clothes. With his mother's help, and his mother's car, his own sense of urgency coupled with his self-nurtured motivation, he accomplished those first important tasks of reentry—the ones that stymied the simulation participants—in short order.

He wanted to truly start living his new life, but he couldn't. The supervision he was under was intense, the strictest possible. Beginning in the 1970s, the focus of the parole system had shifted from assistance to surveillance. Trevor had to report to his parole officer in person every weekday. On weekends, the local police came by his mother's house to check on him. This level of surveillance, in addition to the ankle monitor, was not just because of the early release but also, he was told, for his own protection. He was getting threats and hate mail. *You're a piece of garbage. You don't deserve to be free.* The police were concerned someone might track him down and try to harm him. Meanwhile Trevor was also concerned that the state was not finished with him. The district attorney was contemplating another challenge to the second-chance release. The rug might be pulled out from under him. His parole could be revoked. In fact, it was not until late 2018, almost two and a half years later, that all the litigation was finalized and Trevor could be sure of his future.

CATHERINE

Prisoners are usually released from Lowell Correctional Institution at nine in the morning, but Catherine was released at midnight. The authorities were concerned that her release would turn the parking lot into a media circus. Even after seventeen years, both her crime and her sentence remained notorious. In 1999, after she and her brother, thirteen and twelve at the time, had shot and killed their father's live-in girlfriend, they became the youngest murderers ever to be tried and sentenced as adults. They pleaded guilty to second-degree murder and were each sentenced to eighteen years. Now "under cover of darkness"—that's the way she thought of it—that girl was emerging as a thirty-year-old woman.

Catherine was in the dorm, her stomach in knots, waiting for her name to be called. At five minutes past midnight, the call came. She was scared, anxious, excited, and she suddenly realized, overwhelmingly sad. She would be leaving behind the women who had become her family, who had supported her, befriended her, mothered her. She cried as she was led down the hallways to a room where she would undergo her last strip search. As she removed her prison uniform for the last time, discarding the pale blue cotton shirt and pants that looked like nurse's scrubs, she felt enormous relief. She stripped faster than she ever had before. She actually smiled. Then she dressed in the clothes her family had brought in for her—girl clothes, summer clothes—shorts, a tank top, and sandals. As she was led through the last set of gates to the guardhouse, women from all the dorms called out to her from behind the barred windows, waving, screaming their goodbyes. Had she ever seen a prison movie, this scene would have been familiar, a cliché even. But it was real. It was happening. At the guardhouse, the processing continued. Her papers were checked. Her identity was confirmed. She received a bag with her personal items. They were called EOS items—End of Sentence. This was it.

Was it her imagination or was the air somehow different on the other side of the gates? It was a typical midsummer night in central Florida, seventy-five degrees, the air thick and sticky, yet she had the impression as she stood waiting for the machinery of the prison bureaucracy to grind along, that the air was fresh and cool. She saw her mother and father—long divorced but together for this moment—pull up in the parking lot. She wanted to run to meet them, but there were more forms, more documents. Finally, she was told she could go, and she ran, sandals flopping, to hug them both. But she broke it off quickly. She wanted to get far away from this place as fast as she could. It would be a two-hour drive home.

Twenty minutes later, they pulled over to stop at a McDonald's. Catherine had dreamed of this moment so often: free-world food, choices, whatever she wanted. But now, faced with all those choices, she didn't know what she wanted. Or even if she wanted anything. Finally, she chose a yogurt parfait because it had fresh fruit on top. She so desperately wanted fresh fruit. Inside there had been the occasional banana and, ironically given that Florida grew three-quarters of all the oranges in the country, hardly ever any citrus. Next to the McDonald's was a convenience store. She wandered the aisles, in awe of all the selections, frozen with indecision. She got nothing. Back in the car, she realized she had no appetite. She ate the parfait anyway, tasting nothing. The year before, in a letter to a local newspaper, she had written that she was fearful of being released into a "foreign society" where she would have to "learn how to function like a normal person." She was imagining, at the time, the challenges of learning to drive, to fill out job applications, to build her credit, to get insurance. She hadn't imagined that deciding what to eat at McDonald's or what candy bar to buy at a 7-Eleven would be on the list.

The rest of the trip back to her father's house went quickly. She talked nonstop to her parents. They made plans to go to the beach as soon as the sun was up, but she could barely concentrate on that. Soon, now within minutes, she would see her brother Curtis—she still thought of him as her "baby brother" although he was now twenty-nine—for the first time in seventeen years. He had been released just two weeks before. So many years ago Catherine had tried to protect him from abuse in their home, abuse she also suffered. They shared that pain, that history, the crime it pushed them to commit, and the years of imprisonment that followed. She bolted out of the car, into her father's house, and into her brother's arms. She remembers drinking in his scent, a man's scent now, not a boy's. She remembers staring into his eyes, burning this memory into her brain. Their time together was limited. The next day Catherine would be on a flight to Kansas with her mother. She had transferred her probation there, away from the trauma of her girlhood home. Her brother would stay in Florida with their father.

Embracing her grandmother was next. She had come from Alabama to welcome Catherine home and had busied herself in the kitchen for hours that night cooking all of Catherine's favorite foods, the special dishes she told her grandmother she missed most. And so, at 2:30 in the morning, the family sat down to Cornish hens, collard greens, candied yams, corn bread, and mac and cheese. This time, Catherine tasted it all. Then she, her brother, and her mother slept for a few hours in a spare room. In the morning they drove to the beach, the place she wanted to go more than anywhere else. She and Curtis splashed together in the surf, acting like kids. She still couldn't believe she was free, that they both were free. The next day, her new life would begin in Kansas. It would be so much harder than she thought it would be.

ARNOLDO

He headed for the yellow hydrant. Of course he hugged his mother first, and his brother, and his nieces, but the hydrant was on his mind. It was only after he got there, after he looked up and caught a glimpse of Sterling at the barred fourth-floor window, that he could focus on what this day meant to him.

It was a gloriously sunny mid-July morning, the sky cloudless and almost blindingly blue. His family came out to join him at the hydrant. They posed as Sterling's wife, Cheryl, took their picture to commemorate the moment: Arnoldo, squinting into the sun, kneeling next to his pretty, long-haired niece, his arm around her waist; his mother on the other side, leaning into him, her hand resting on his shoulder; his brother bookending the shot, his brother whom he hadn't seen in ten years. They looked a lot alike, both with sturdy athletic builds, both with clean-shaven heads. He wished his sister could be there too, part of this picture. But she had given birth just four days before.

His was, in many ways, a dream release. He had a support-ive family waiting for him and not just a physical place to go—his mother's house—but an emotional soft landing. And he was not nervous about the transition. He had prepared for it, not so much with services or workshops offered by the prison—meager at best—but rather with his own research over the years. When men who had been released came back, he talked to them about what problems they had, what they experienced, why they hadn't made it on the outside. He educated himself about the pitfalls.

The most important thing was being with his family. As they headed back from the hydrant to the prison's parking lot, his brother suggested going to a restaurant. But Arnoldo wanted to go home, to his mother's home, to eat his mother's cooking. They had a meal of tacos, nothing fancy, but Arnoldo savored it. Then they all headed off to his sister's house to meet his four-day-old niece.

He didn't do a lot those first few days, just chilled. It was all a little surreal. But it wasn't the shock of being free and being with his family. It was the shock of how completely at home he felt, how he seemed to just slip back into life as if he were never gone, as if those nineteen years had just evaporated. He had had an epiphany when he hugged his mother in the penitentiary's waiting room. As a kid in eastern Oregon, he had always felt he was living in a foreign land. Texas was home, that rich Hispanic culture of his early childhood was home. But when he hugged his mother in the waiting room, in that moment, he knew that home wasn't a place. Home was people. He was with his people now. He was home.

At his mother's house he had his own room with a brand-new queen bed. He hadn't stretched out in so long he had to teach his body how to fully occupy this vast, new sleeping space. All those years in prison in that single cot with the thin plastic mattress, he had learned to sleep on his side. The pillows were fluffy. The blanket was soft. He slept well that first night and every night thereafter. He defined it, remembered it, as sleeping "well," but really he slept only two hours a night. His sense of freedom awoke him. He lay in that comfortable bed thinking to himself *I can get out of bed and walk out the door any time I want to.* And the urge was just too great. So he got out of bed. He walked around the house. He walked to the front door and opened it. He didn't think of this as insomnia or anything negative. In fact, he enjoyed the wakefulness. He loved that there was a place to go from the bed. In segregation, where he had lived on and off for twelve years, he did everything in bed. It was where he slept, where he read, where he sat to eat.

When he was conducting his own research about post-release life, talking to guys who had not been successful, he learned that the biggest problem they faced was having too much free time. You revert to old behaviors, they told him. It's hard to find a job, and without a job there is no structure to the day. Sitting alone during those first days in his mother's house while she worked where she had worked for the past twenty years, an Alzheimer's facility, he created his own structure. He cleaned her house. Really cleaned it. He scoured everything. He scrubbed the floors. He went through her closets and gathered six bags of clothing and household items that he dropped off at Goodwill. He did yard work. He did this all to stay busy, to stay sane, and because it was the only contribution he could make at the moment. She was providing a home. She was providing food. And she was working full time at a physically demanding job. Although he also created a daily exercise regimen for himself that included a morning run through a nearby park, he worked on his mother's house because it felt safer to be indoors. This strategy of isolation to deal with—or avoid—the potential stress of social interaction is one remarked on by the released prisoners interviewed in the *On the Outside* study. Arnoldo lived at this mother's house for three months. He began, slowly, to make a life for himself. He thought of Sterling, inside, for who knew how much longer.

CHAPTER 11

In the big, featureless meeting room on the fourth floor of the prison that has housed Sterling for a quarter of a century, just down the hall from a smaller room with the window he stands in front of when he gazes out at the hydrant, people are filing in and finding their seats. Half of the more than sixty or so who will eventually make their way in are either prison volunteers like me or community members who were carefully selected and personally invited to attend this evening's event. They have been vetted by the Department of Corrections, supplying their driver's license number for criminal checks. When they arrived downstairs—following instructions to come at least a half hour early—they handed over their licenses, emptied their pockets, removed their shoes, walked through the metal detector, and proceeded through three gated checkpoints. The others in this room came from their cell blocks, scanning in with the IDs that hang from lanyards around their necks. They know the drill.

Sterling, who has orchestrated this event, directs people to the folding chairs that line the perimeter, alternating inmate with community member. Most of the inmates are Black or brown. Almost all of the community members are white. In the center of the room are three chairs set in a circle. On one sits a Latino prisoner, on the another, an African American. Both are big men. Both sit in that way men sit when they want to send *I am someone you do not want to mess with* signals: torsos leaning in, legs spread-eagled, jaws jutting forward, hard stares. Sterling stands behind the third chair, holding himself uncharacteristically rigid. He is usually a graceful man, fluid in his motions, a relaxed public speaker, a spoken word poet. But this evening he is not that person. Something else is going on.

He looks around the room, slowly, unsmiling, clearly on edge. "We've been planning tonight's event about restorative justice for a long time," he tells the crowd, silencing the cross talk. "We were going to explain about RJ, its principles. Be all theoretical about it." Sterling has been doing restorative justice and conflict mediation outreach in the prison for several years now. He's read, he's studied, he's spent countless hours talking with Karuna Thompson and Avrohom Perlstein, two of the prison's chaplains, about how to create and foster an atmosphere of calm, of conversation over confrontation, how to—as ambitious and impossible as it may seem—basically remake the prison culture. He and Arnoldo worked together on smaller projects until Arnoldo's release. The event tonight is the first of its kind, bringing inmates and interested community members together to learn from each other.

Sterling pauses, crossing his arms, looks around the room. "We were planning this presentation," he says, repeating himself. "But we're not gonna do that." Another pause. "That's because there was trouble in the yard last week. A fight broke out between Black and Latino gangs. So we decided to use this real situation to see how the process actually works." The two prisoners on the chairs in the center of the room, Black and brown, have not moved. They stare at each other as Sterling explains how the session will start.

He explains that it will begin the way all RJ sessions do, with each person stating the facts as they see them while the other person listens without interrupting. The Latino guy starts. A group of his friends out in the yard were minding their own business, he says. They were approached by a Black inmate. Then another Black inmate, then another, came over. "They were disrespecting our guys." The other man, the Black man, shakes his head, leans in. He starts telling what he saw happen in the yard. For maybe the first thirty seconds or so, the two talk back and forth. But soon their voices start to rise. And now they are yelling at each other, interrupting each other. Then they bolt out of their seats and stand facing each other, almost nose to nose. In an instant, the prisoners around the perimeter of the room jump up out of their chairs too, the Black and Latino men glaring at each other, bodies tensed, readying for a fight. They start yelling.

The community members, seated, sandwiched between inmates around the room, shrink back into their chairs. I cross my arms and legs, hunch my shoulders, tuck in my chin, instinctively trying to take up as little space as possible. I can actually feel the pulse throbbing in my neck. I've been coming into this prison for more than three years, walking unaccompanied across the control floor that sits at the center of the institution and up a long flight of stairs and across the activities floor, passing dozens of men along the way. I've spent hundreds of hours in a room without a guard in the company of ten convicted murderers. And I have never been afraid for my safety. Until now. I am in a room on the fourth floor of a maximum security prison with thirty-five very angry men. There is one exit.

"Freeze," Sterling calls out, his voice louder than the others. "Stand down." The two men in the middle move away from each other and sit back in their chairs. The prisoners around the perimeter retreat from their fight-ready stances and return to their chairs. The silence, the stillness, is sudden and complete.

I see Sterling's body relax. "This was all a setup," he says. I don't understand. I look across the room at a woman I know, a long-time volunteer. We make eye contact briefly, eyebrows raised, then focus on Sterling. His body language has changed from rigid to relaxed. He is now the person I recognize and know, the loose-limbed man who navigates this foreign world like the native he is. He explains this was all a rehearsed "play"— the escalation of the argument between the two men, the way the others jumped up from their seats. Yes, he says, there was a fight in the yard last week between two gangs. That is true. But this moment we have all been living through, this was staged. There is a palpable change in the room, almost a temperature drop or a change in atmospheric pressure.

The men laugh. The community members laugh, too, but nervously.

"Now you see what can happen," says Sterling. "Now you can see how easily a conversation can go off the rails, how violence can be so easily triggered." Sterling smiles for the first time. Each of the men around the room turns to the community member seated by his side, smiles, extends a hand. Another bit of orchestration, but the connection, in that moment, is intensely real. Before there is chance to talk, or even process what just happened, Sterling sets up an activity. A few of the men circle the room distributing note cards to everyone seated around the perimeter. We all get five cards and a pencil with instructions to use each card to list one thought or emotion we had during what just took place. Then we get up and tape these cards on the walls around the room, instantly transforming this bare, institutional space into a gallery. Sterling tells us to take our time walking around, to read and study each card. We don't know the author of any card, whether it was an inmate or a community member, what race, what gender, what age, what life events brought them to this space, this room.

Those seemingly vital details turn out to be inconsequential. The reactions scrawled on the cards transcend all of this. *Scared, panicked, vulnerable, helpless, confused, powerless, angry, frozen. Terrified, exposed, defenseless, intimidated, triggered. Hyperalert.* The same words appear and reappear. What is most astonishing about this is that the men who knew this was a setup and those of us who thought it was real reacted the same way, our limbic brains, our fight-or-flight responses kicking in automatically.

"Was there something written on one of those cards, not something you wrote, that you're going to remember long after you leave here tonight?" Sterling asks. A community member, an older man—by his appearance an octogenarian—is first to speak. He had walked into the room leaning on a cane and had lowered himself into his chair with great caution. "I am used to feeling vulnerable," he says. He has a strong, clear voice that belies his fragile body. "Seeing that so many of you, you who are young and strong, felt that way just now... I will be thinking about that for a while."

"And that *men* felt that way," says a young woman, a university student who has come into the prison to take a class with inmates. "That was a revelation." Two people note how many times the words "trauma" or "traumatic" appeared on the cards. A woman mentions that one of the cards mentioned family. "That was my first thought," she says. "What will happen to my family if I don't come home?" She says she didn't write it on the card because she thought it would appear melodramatic, an overreaction. The room is silent. The silence feels important.

Sterling, still standing in the middle of the room, takes a breath so deep, an exhale so purposeful, that everyone can hear it.

"This is what it feels like to be in conflict," he says. "This is how it feels *all the time* inside. This is what our life feels like. This is how *we* feel."

Restorative justice is understood as repairing or mitigating the harm an offender does to a victim, Sterling explains. But those inside who have caused this harm also harm each other, he says. And it is this way of dealing with—or *not* dealing with—differences and potential conflicts that is at the core of what brought the inmates here in the first place. This is why restorative justice inside can be so powerful.

There is more to the evening: a small-group exercise that gets the whole room buzzing, an inmate who shares his edgy art, a musician from the community who sings and plays guitar. It is an event so full of both content and emotion that I will think about it for months. What I come back to is that visceral fear response, that body jolt I felt when the men around the room—and most especially the big men on either side of me—jumped up from their seats. We pay moviemakers to make us feel this way, to vicariously experience the "thrill" of fear from the safety of our own lives. But to feel it in real life is another thing entirely. What stays with me much longer, though, is the knowledge that this fear, this panic and anxiety, is part of everyday life inside prisons. It is embedded in the culture. And, over time, it is not just embedded, but *embodied*. The body becomes attuned and accustomed to the hyperalert state, the react-now-REACT-NOW response. If you stay in prison long enough, this is who you become. And then, one day, you get out. You reenter society, but you carry what you learned, what the prison culture taught you, what your body absorbed, out into a culture that doesn't work this way.

When I think about that evening, I also think about the energy and creativity it took to bring it off, the genius of the theatrical approach, the tricky work of corralling thirty-plus inmates to participate, the negotiated trust between the Black and brown-skinned men, the dedication and time it took to rehearse. Many cooks, yes. But one chef—Sterling.

———

A few months later, I am back in the prison for another event, this time one I have orchestrated with considerable assistance from Karuna, the chaplain, and Steven Finster, a prison "recreation specialist" who has long supported my efforts to run writing workshops inside the walls. Tonight, for the first time, the men in that group will be sharing—reading aloud—excerpts from some of the longer pieces they've been working on. It's taken many months to secure the necessary permissions and clearances from up the chain of command. And it has taken just as many months to persuade the men in the group that, although reading aloud can be terrifying, sharing their stories with others can also be empowering, both for them and their listeners. The eight men currently in the group have invited friends from within the prison, and together we've brainstormed a list of community members and supporters to invite. As with the restorative justice event, this one is taking place in the big, windowless meeting room on the fourth floor of the penitentiary. And, as with the other event, the invited visitors have been vetted, screened, and scanned. One of the visitors is a man I've brought with me, a friend who cooks meals for the homeless and has used the nonprofit's professional kitchen to bake industrial-sized trays of brownies for this event. Getting permission to bring in food is an exercise in patience, persistence, and (given the chaplain's efforts) prayer. I expect that the brownies will be the hit of the evening and that my friend Jesse will be the most popular man in the room.

I introduce each man from the writers' group as he makes his way to the wobbly podium to read. We have discussed the order of appearance so there are no surprises, and the men have all rehearsed. Some are more nervous than others. One man is visibly sweating. Another, at the last minute, enlists a fellow writer in the group to read for him. He just can't do it. They read stories about work and family, about sleep and dreams, about friendship. One man, the oldest in the group, an early 1960s Vietnam vet, reads three scenes from encounters he's had with inmates in the throes of PTSD episodes. He is an on-call volunteer trauma counselor. His delivery is crisp, clinical, and chilling. Another man, the quietest and most self-composed member of the group, gets halfway through his story about helping a mentally challenged inmate train for a prison 5K when his voice cracks. He turns away to compose himself, tries again. Maybe he can feel that the audience is pulling for him. He manages to finish and quickly makes his way to the back of the room. The last man to read is Sterling.

We planned it this way both because Sterling is the strongest writer in the group and the other men didn't want to follow him and because he has chosen not to read one of the stories he's worked on in the group but rather to perform a poem. It feels like the perfect way to end the evening. Or at least the literary part of the evening. The brownies are the sweet coda.

BIRD POEM
Sterling Cunio

The whole world in an uproar
Prophesy say end times come with war
Such is the nature of man, they say
And therefore there will always be struggle
Yet I. Don't wanna struggle. No more.
And I. Know. We. Will. Win.
Light started life
Has been there from the beginning
It's inherent. Within.
It don't mean easy paths to victory.
It means daring greatly and choosing to pursue bliss
Don't fall for shit
But stand with love
And fly motherfucker, fly
Like birds.
Kaww
Watch me soar
Even in my chains
Watch me soar
Way above the shame
Watch me soar
Even through the pain
Watch me end the struggle and build forever
Destiny is legacy
It's one and the same
Fly motherfuckers, fly
Kaww
And pay no mind to those who allege

That war's the only way
'Cuz Bob Marley already say
Only love can conquer hate
And love like
Tap dancing on a cliff edge
And prisoners feeding the hungry
And love like
Floating on funnel clouds and retirement savings
And love like
Savoring life moments to nourish the soul's light
And love like
Listening to ancestral wisdom of enlightened insight
Shared with the world for future generations
So here I say
Never whisper in the presence of others
And be aware of whispering men
Because light cast shadows
And some sit in the dark speaking anger
While others illuminate the night speaking love
Who you gonna be?
Kaww
Every moment is a choice
We can always choose light
Be a torch
Olympian!
Because even in the deepest dark
Love sparks the heart
Beat. The heart
Beat. The heart
Beat that will be the beat that the soul sings its song to
The heart *beat*

That moves our feet with the rhythm we dance to
The heart *beat*
That society will advance to
The heart *beat*
That makes prisons a thing of the past
The heart *beat*
That humanity will evolve to
The heart *beat*
That makes rivers more important than pipelines
The heart *beat*
The most precious gift to the terminally ill
Even when they handcuffed to a bed still
The heart *beat*
That transforms the ability to kill
To helping people heal
The heart *beat*
Of revering mothers and respecting fathers
And honoring life as we ought to
The heart *beat*
Of I'm destined to go farther
Beat of never giving up on a dream
The heart *beat*
Of redemption achieved
Love sparked my heart
And now I dare fly
And I get so high
And where I land
I plant seeds
With heart *beat*
Every moment is a choice
We can always choose light

Be a torch

Fly motherfuckers, fly

Kaww

And most importantly

Love.

Everybody.

A month later I am sitting in a little back room at the Latino
Network's southeast Portland office talking with Arnoldo about
how well his life is going when his phone and my phone simultaneously chirp. We both reach for our devices, startled by the
oddity of this. The text message on both phones is the same.
Cheryl, Sterling's wife, is sharing the news that the U.S. District
Court for the District of Oregon has just handed down a decision
in Sterling's favor. Arnoldo and I beam at each other. Neither of
us understands the legal intricacies, but we know it's good news,
and that is, for the moment, all we need to know.

The next morning, I have a long conversation with Ryan
O'Connor, Sterling's attorney. The ruling is complicated. Most
legal rulings are, but this one is even more so. This is a civil
rights suit mounted in federal court. It involves, if I have managed to make sense of it, a federal statute, a twenty-five-year-old
state sentencing law, three (or maybe four) state statutes (one
of which has been thrice amended), a parole board decision, an
Oregon Court of Appeals reversal, a U.S. district court ruling,
and a landmark Supreme Court case. The gist of it is this: The
U.S. district court has ruled that the state of Oregon must provide Sterling with a release hearing, a so-called Miller hearing.
This decision orders the board to do so. The board had declared
that it didn't have the authority to do so (another complicated
decision mired in conflicting state statutes and federal rulings),

and Sterling and his attorney had sued the board over this. The federal magistrate agreed with Sterling. Now a hearing must take place. That is, O'Connor tells me, unless the Department of Corrections appeals this decision. If there is no appeal, and the board meets and hears convincing evidence of Sterling's rehabilitation, the board could order Sterling released from the entirety of the sentence he received for crimes he committed as a juvenile. As it now stands, Sterling's earliest possible release date is 2065.

There are a lot of ifs. There are strong personalities involved, from the DOC to the parole board, from the county district attorney's office and the victims' rights advocacy group to juvenile justice reformers and the victims' families. And there may be politics. There is always politics. Still O'Connor says he was "thrilled," that this was "the best-case scenario." I ask him how he celebrated this victory last night. He says he went home and wrote a press release. It was his wife's night to go out for drinks with her friends. He stayed home to put their two young children to bed. "It was a good night," he said.

———

The following day Sterling calls me from a phone in the chapel. "I'm excited, but I'm not jumping up and down," he says. "When I get out and get to the hydrant and get down on my knees and hug that hydrant, then I'll know I'm out. And then I can begin the rest of my life."

CHAPTER 12

Where will I be sleeping tonight?

When was the last time they had to think about that? Where they slept, where and what they ate, what they wore, when they showered, when they were able to go outdoors—all these decisions had been made for them. Now, emerging from the controlled, micromanaged world they had inhabited for years—for decades—they were faced with so very many decisions. But this decision, this question, demanded an immediate answer.

Some had no answer. They would end up on the street that first night. A 2018 Prison Policy Initiative report, the first national snapshot of homelessness and the previously incarcerated, found that people who had served a single prison sentence experienced homelessness at a rate nearly seven times higher than that of the general public. For those who had served repeat sentences, the rate was almost twice as high: thirteen times that of the general public. And then there were the men and women just out of the gate who were not technically homeless that first night because they found a place to sleep at a temporary shelter, environments too often just as or even more risky than pitching a tent under a bridge or sleeping over a sidewalk grate. Some of those released would be mandated by the conditions of their parole to report directly to community corrections centers, transitional facilities that housed offenders in monitored, structured settings, allowing them to leave only for approved activities.

But many of those released would spend at least their first few nights with family. That might mean crashing on a living room couch in their cousin's apartment. It might mean a spare room at their grandmother's place. This homecoming might be warm and welcoming; it might be tense and weird. It might be sustainable. It might be healthy. It might be dangerous. For many of the more than 600,000 men and women released every year, finding stable housing—finding *any* housing—is their first and biggest hurdle. And it is housing, say those who study the lives of those who leave prison, that is the foundation for successful entry.

———

Trevor, emerging from seventeen and a half years inside, was one of the lucky ones. He knew where he would sleep. And he was releasing not just to a physical space that was safe and comfortable—his mother's home—but to an emotional space that was loving, accepting, and fiercely loyal. Few people, ex-inmates or not, could count on the level of support that Karen, Trevor's mother, provided. It was unflagging, tireless, and in that way that only a mother's love can be, ferocious. Back when he was first arrested, Karen had steadfastly believed her boy, her fourteen-year-old, was innocent. It's not just what he had told her. It is what, as a mother, she *had* to believe. When she accepted that he was guilty as charged, that he had in fact committed murder, when she was forced to grapple with what that meant to his future, her belief in him never wavered. That belief propelled her out of her old life. She fashioned a new one from the ground up: a new town, a new job, a new career, and a new house, the house that was waiting for Trevor when his parole officer finally dropped him off that first afternoon.

The layout of the house offered privacy and separation of space. Trevor had his own room with his own private bathroom. He didn't feel wedged in. He didn't feel as if he were an addendum to someone else's life. And, although he was living in his mother's house and had never experienced independence, he did not feel like a kid the way a lot of us do when we come back home as adults. He was a man, thirty-something, who had grown into what it meant to be an adult while behind bars. It helped that his mother encouraged and supported this, that she saw him as the adult he had become. But it also helped, almost as much or perhaps more, that Loraine was waiting for him in the house. She was the young woman who had begun writing to him years earlier, who had visited him regularly, who had established a relationship with Karen, who saw her future with him. That private room in Karen's house was their room. Trevor was releasing not just to a house but to a new life that had at least the beginning of a structure to it, a foundation.

He was extraordinarily grateful for all this, and he understood how deeply indebted he was to his mother. He wanted to pay her back, and he knew exactly what that meant. The most important thing for her was seeing that he was on his way to a happy and fulfilled life. That meant taking care of himself, being productive, paying his own bills. Ingrained in him from his off-the-grid, backwoods childhood was his father's attitude that "when you turn eighteen, you're out of the house." He was more than a decade past that landmark, but his immediate situation, although seemingly about as ideal as a homecoming could be, was actually quite tenuous. His early release was contentious. He might be reincarcerated at any time. This was not paranoia. The threat was real, and it was with him every day. So, although he wanted to start an independent life, to leave his mother's house and find an apartment for him and Loraine, he held himself back. If they moved out and he was sent back to prison, he would be saddling Loraine, or his mother, or both of them, with the rent.

And so he did chores around the house. He made himself as useful as he could. But he also tried to enjoy his freedom. He and Loraine went for drives, often with no destination in mind, just to be out and about. Sometimes they'd go to a Walmart or Target and just walk the aisles, looking without buying. When he got clearance from his parole officer, they drove west an hour to the beach. He signed up for a motorcycle endorsement class, got his license, bought a bike. Then, six months later, a little more than eleven months after his release, he was rearrested, recharged with the original crime, and sent back to prison. This wasn't double jeopardy. Due to how his second look hearing had been adjudicated, his indictment was still alive. It would take another four months for the legal haze to lift and for Trevor to once again gain release, this time for good. Less than a month later, he and Loraine signed a lease on a duplex.

———

Stable housing is the doorway to what follows, what *has* to follow, for reentry to be successful. There is universal agreement about that and about how being housed matters immediately— from the first day out, the first week. It is not just the physical place—although safe indoor shelter is vital—it is that stable housing offers the consistency and control that helps to establish daily routines. It is a way of reducing exposure to what criminologists call "deviant peers." It is a base for seeking employment and, if needed, treatment. It is a statement of personal growth and independence. As Washington State University criminal justice researcher Faith Lutze put it: "Housing stability serves as a conduit to access and builds the social capital necessary to sustain long-term reintegration into the community."

Conversely, housing instability has been shown to undermine offenders' ability to take advantage of whatever support and treatment services might be available in their community or might be mandated by the conditions of their parole. Lack of safe and stable housing is related to poor health. Life on the streets or in temporary shelters is risky, and access to medical support is more challenging and more limited without a permanent address. Compliance, whether that means checking in with a parole officer, going to treatment, securing employment, or staying away from "known associates," is harder in the absence of stable housing. In fact, reentry studies highlight the link between homelessness and noncompliance. Not surprisingly, lack of stable housing is also linked to recidivism. Those without stable housing are far more likely to return to prison. Lutze's four-year study in Washington state highlighted this. Another study that focused on former inmates reentering communities in Georgia found that every time a parolee changed addresses the possibility of rearrest increased 25 percent. If stable housing is essential to reentry, if the benefits and the risks associated with stable housing have been extensively researched and are well known, if interrupting the revolving door of recidivism saves many millions of dollars and makes communities safer, then why is it such a challenge for so many of the men and women reentering society to secure a decent place to live?

One obvious, but incomplete, answer is that affordable housing is a problem for everyone in virtually all parts of the country. A Harvard Joint Center for Housing Studies report found that the availability of "low rent" (defined as $800 or less a month) apartments in most metro areas declined substantially—in some places sharply—between 2011 and 2017. In the Denver and Portland, Oregon, metro areas, affordable rentals declined more than 60 percent. In Miami, the decline was 40 percent; Chicago, 26; New York metro, 22. In Detroit, an impoverished community that already suffered a shortage of affordable housing, the decline was 15 percent. Lack of affordable housing leaves ex-offenders competing for the same limited inventory as those without criminal records. Even in areas where there might be what is deemed "affordable" rents, most inmates do not leave prison with enough money for the first month's rent, last month's rent, and cleaning/damage deposit required by landlords and rental agencies.

But even getting to the point of being asked for this money is a challenge. Many landlords and rental agencies require potential tenants to list past housing and employment references on their applications, thus immediately flagging (without directly asking about) incarceration history. It is true that the Fair Housing Act of 1968 protects a variety of potential tenants from being discriminated against, but "felon" is not a protected class. Even in states or communities that have attempted to ban discrimination against those with a felony record, there are many reasons a rental agency could easily reject a former felon without referencing a past conviction. For those without funds or in need of substantial support, public housing might be an option. Or not.

Federal law bans outright three categories of people from admission to public housing: sex offenders, those convicted on methamphetamine production (in a federal housing project), and people who are currently using illegal drugs. Public housing agencies, under the auspices of the U.S. Department of Housing and Urban Development, have the added discretion to deny applicants who have previously been evicted from public housing for drug-related criminal activities or who have a pattern of disruptive consumption, and a catchall category includes anyone who has engaged in any drug-related criminal activity, any violent criminal activity, or any other criminal activity, if the housing authority deems them a safety risk. Assuming a released inmate qualifies to apply for housing support—a Section 8 voucher to be used to offset rent—the processing of the application can take months. Once accepted, the person is placed on a waiting list. The wait list to get the voucher is one to two years. And then the hunt for a Section 8–approved rental begins.

The increasing challenges of the affordable housing market, the inadequate government funding to support subsidized housing, the released inmate's lack of funds to cover the initial costs of renting—all this stands in the way of a smooth transition (or sometimes any transition) to stable housing. But what also stands in the way, and cannot be budgeted or legislated out of existence, is the deeply ingrained learned helplessness of a person leaving prison after many years.

Patricia McKernan, a social worker and past president of the Reentry Coalition of New Jersey relates the story of Darryl, released from thirty years behind bars and instructed by prison social workers to head to a shelter. Prisoners know from other prisoners how dangerous these places can be. In *Beyond Bars: Rejoining Society After Prison*, Stephen Richards, a former drug offender who spent nine years in federal prisons and is now a professor of criminal justice, writes about the experience of spending time in a temporary shelter. It is not just that homeless shelters are often located in high-crime areas; and it is not just that many are seedy; and it is not just that a person's belongings are often not safe in such a place. It is, Richards writes, that an ex-con is often earmarked upon arrival, a target for, as he puts it, "folks slinging dope or women in miniskirts."

Darryl did not head to a temporary shelter. Maybe he had heard the cautionary tales from inmates who'd cycled in and out. He had released without a plan, without post-prison supervision, and without funds. Maybe he just didn't know where to go. He roamed the streets and slept in doorways. There was a snowstorm. He took refuge in a bus station. He had left the world that for half of his life had told him exactly what to do and when to do it. Released to a community he did not remember, where he had no one, where he had to take initiative to make something happen, he was at a loss.

———

Arnoldo's story could not be more different. During his almost two decades inside, and especially his long stints in the hole, he had thought hard about the kind of man he wanted to be on the outside, and he had methodically researched the challenges of reentry by questioning men who'd been released, hadn't made it, and were back again. He was prepared. And his smooth release to a welcoming household paved the way for successful reentry. But, as with anything that relates to family, there were issues. For some who leave prison to stay with family, the issue is the financial burden they place on their relatives.

For others, the household they are joining is already crowded and their added presence is a physical burden. If the family lives in public housing, the issue may be that the ex-offender's presence is a violation of the lease. It might be the family itself contributed to the life led and the choices made by the person now emerging from prison: alcoholism, drug abuse, domestic violence, abuse. The list goes on: Are there guns in the household? Is anyone living there also an ex-offender, perhaps on parole? The reasons a release to family can't or won't work are numerous.

For Arnoldo, the challenges were more subtle. Both his mother and his stepfather were employed. Money was not an issue, and neither was space. Like Trevor, Arnoldo had his own room in a safe, quiet, law-abiding home. He was, during those first few days and weeks, buoyant and energized, "all juiced up," as he put it. He was free. Everything was cool. Every day was great. He was on his best behavior, and so was his family. The last time he had lived with family was when he was fifteen, and the tendency now might be to treat him as the kid he was then and not the adult he had become. But that's not what happened. He was not confronted with rules, with curfew, with a list of chores. It was not anything they said or did; it was just being there. It was their home, not his. On the one hand, his days were gloriously his own. On the other hand, he felt pressured—from himself, not his family—to contribute. They didn't need financial help. But his mother, who worked full time at an exhausting job and, it soon became clear to him, shouldered the burden of virtually all the domestic chores on top of that, could use his help. Because he needed to keep busy, because he needed to create structure to his days, and because he needed to actively contribute to the household, Arnoldo spent most of his first month out of prison doing chores, cleaning and caring for the house, and doing neglected upkeep on the property.

As he settled into that rhythm, as the days and weeks went by, he began to see his family more clearly. He had changed during the almost two decades he was gone, and so had they. His little sister, eight years old when he went to prison, had written him letters all the time, signing off with smiley faces. They had developed a strong relationship during his time behind bars. Now they were both adults. She had her own life, and it was a complicated one. They got into an argument. She said some hurtful things, this smiley-faced little girl. It was hard to reconcile, hard to move forward.

Living in a household with his stepfather also became increasingly difficult. This was the man his mother had married back when Arnoldo was nine. There had been issues then, more between the stepfather and Arnoldo's younger brother than between Arnoldo and his mother's new husband. But Arnoldo felt the tension. And there was residual trauma in that household reaching back to his early childhood, from the years spent with his biological father, an alcoholic, a mercurial, sometimes solicitous, sometimes violent man. As a child, as a teen in juvie, as a gangbanger in prison, Arnoldo had, at first, repressed those feelings, then given into rage, and then finally, after years of reflection and hard work, gotten to a place of forgiveness, for both his fathers. It was not because he thought what they had done was okay. It was because he needed to forgive to move forward. But now, sharing the home with his stepfather, in his presence every day, there were just too many memories. He would have to leave. The soft landing was not as soft as he thought it would be.

Catherine had created a fantasy around her release to her family, a Hallmark movie version of her homecoming. She had never had a relationship with her mother, a near stranger who had left her and her brother when she fled her marriage. Now, Catherine would have that opportunity. This is what she told herself. This is what she planned for. Instead of releasing to Florida and to her father's house, she petitioned to have her parole transferred to Kansas, where her mother lived. Releasing to her father's home would have been traumatic anyway. The crime she and her brother had committed had been against her father's girlfriend. A few months before the murder, child welfare officers had found signs that the two children were being sexually and physically abused by their uncle, their father's brother. How could she make a new life while immersed in the environment that led to her crime? And how could the state of Florida have sanctioned this arrangement anyway? The state apparently did. Catherine's younger brother, her codefendant, released to that home.

The other alternative had its own challenges. Her mother had exited Catherine's life when she was four. During those years before her arrest at age thirteen, and during those seventeen years in prison, the mother-daughter relationship had not flourished. Now, as an adult, a woman of thirty embarking on a new chapter in her life, Catherine felt compelled to reach out. Maybe it was because of her prison relationship with "Ma Betty" from Fresh Start Ministries. Betty and her husband, Pastor (Papa) Charles, had come into the prison to teach and preach, and after getting to know and love Catherine, they had declared her *their* child, the "product of a spiritual birth." Ma Betty was a substitute mother. Perhaps that connection fueled her desire to unite with her biological mother. Maybe reaching out to her estranged mother was a step on the path of forgiveness that Catherine was determined to travel. Maybe it was just that every daughter longs for a loving mother. Whatever the motivation, Catherine wanted to live with her mother.

A day after her release in Florida, she and her mother were on a plane to the Midwest. The dream of a rekindled relationship died less than a month later. They were mother and daughter, but in truth, they were strangers. Catherine felt like a guest in someone's home. Actually, she felt more like she was living in a motel. It didn't help that her mother related to her—and treated her—like an adolescent. She was too old to have a curfew. Too old to have decisions made for her. Maybe if they had been able to talk it through, things would have gotten better. But they had no foundation for that. A few weeks after moving in, Catherine moved out. It should have been hard for her to find an apartment, almost impossible, in fact. She was an ex-con, a violent offender with no rental history. Her employment "history" included the job she had just landed at a fast food chain. Had she gone through a rental agency, she never would have found a place to live.

But Catherine was both resourceful and lucky. She had found a job. It was a menial one, but she poured energy into it. She showed herself to be an enthusiastic and reliable worker. Her supervisor loved her, and her supervisor knew someone who had an apartment to rent. The rent was affordable. She put in a good word for Catherine. And that was that. She had her own space for the first time in her life. Her mother gave her a bed. She would acquire the rest when she could. In the meantime, she was both overjoyed and overwhelmed. She shopped at the Dollar Store. She almost settled in.

But Catherine also had much bigger dreams for herself than working a minimum-wage, burger-slinging job in a small town.

In prison she had earned an associate's degree, as well as paralegal and computer support certifications. Through her work with Fresh Start Ministries she had discovered a talent for teaching and public speaking. She wanted to be living that life or at least pursuing it. She had met a guy at the fast-food place, a fellow worker who had his own prison history and was in recovery from addiction. Together they imagined a new life together, a fresh start as far away as they could get. They saw "the West" as the promised land, like the pioneers of old. They decided to move to Oregon, and it was this move that exposed her to the real estate realities she had avoided in Kansas.

To change her parole again, this time from Kansas to Oregon, Catherine would have to show that she had a permanent address in the new state. She knew no one in Oregon, had no connections. She applied for a travel permit—her Kansas parole restrictions did not allow her to travel outside the county without permission—and flew to Oregon to look for an apartment. But she was in the system as a violent offender, the same database used to track sex offenders. When her name popped up, no one would rent to her. She returned to Kansas, put in more hours at work, saved up money for a second trip, got another travel permit, and flew out again to make the rounds looking for a place to rent. This time, owing to some combination of fierce determination, faith, luck, and her vibrant personality, she found an apartment. The paperwork involved in the permanent move, in getting all her files transferred, and in reestablishing relationships with another parole officer took close to three months. During that time, in order to obey the conditions of her parole and satisfy the requirements of two states, she had to scrounge the funds to pay rent on the apartments in both Kansas and Oregon. But it was worth it. Now, finally, she thought, my life can begin.

———————

Vicki returned to familiar surroundings: the town that was home to the "street family" that had been part of her life since she was a teen; the house Steve owned that she lived in every time she was released from prison, this being the fifth; her estranged children who coped or did not cope with her revolving-door-repeat-offender lifestyle. Familiarity blunted the jolt of reentry, but it created its own problems. There were triggers everywhere—in the house, in conversations with Steve, on the street—reminders of the life she was, this time, determined not to repeat. It had been about a year since the last time she had been released to this town, this house, her family. That stretch of freedom—from prison, from her own addictions—had lasted only a few months before she was rearrested on drug charges. Now she was back out, again. But this time she hadn't gone straight from prison to home. She had spent close to three months in a women's residential drug facility several hundred miles from home. It was there that we became mentor and mentee. Now, back home, surrounded by her old life, she was determined to learn how to live it, as she put in, "unloaded."

Steve's house was dirty. That's the first thing she noticed when she walked through the front door. She was angry. But she was also, simultaneously, ashamed of herself. Steve had been the constant in her wildly fluctuating life. He was steadily employed, kept up the mortgage payments, waited for her over the years, welcomed her home. It was, she told herself, ungrateful to feel anything other than grateful. But she looked around, and the carpet was littered with dog toys, there were dishes in the sink, and the kitchen table and countertops were buried under clutter. The bathroom was filthy. There were clothes all over the bedroom floor.

She spent her first few days cleaning. It was cathartic—the physical effort itself, the literal "wiping the slate clean," the reestablishing of her presence in the house. She played music as she worked, alternately hugging and sidestepping Ziggy, her little dog. He was a papillon, a toy spaniel with big, tufted ears. She had missed him terribly. He was, as dogs are, loyal and forgiving. Her two adult children were another story. She was careful not to try to jump back into their lives too quickly. She had done that before, promising that this time would be different, then disappearing behind bars again. They had learned not to believe her. She would try to change that, to repair and rebuild those relationships. But not now, not right away. Instead, she cleaned, she cooked, she spent hours on the phone negotiating the world of health insurance, arranging doctor's appointments and clinic sessions, getting the prescriptions she needed to stay clean. Like the reentry simulation participants who were faced with tasks like this, she was often frustrated and harried. She made her way through phone trees, told strangers the same story over and over again, waited for callbacks, tried to access forms on her phone. She calmed herself by playing with Ziggy. She spent long afternoons in the crammed second bedroom of the house going through her rock collection. There was almost no room to maneuver, no open floor space. She had thousands and thousands of unsorted rocks stored in buckets and cardboard boxes, on shelves, in piles on the floor. She might do something with them, but she didn't know what. They reminded her of days walking on the banks of rivers. She was high then. She was always high. Her memories were all filtered through drugs, through heroin, through meth. She would have to make new memories. It was going to be hard.

Dave, master planner, inveterate list maker, had begun thinking about where he would sleep that first night more than a year before his release. He knew he would, by law, be sent back to the county where he was convicted. He would get a bus ticket to that now bustling upscale little city—a sleepy working-class town when he left more than three decades before—and he would know almost no one. He had no family there, and even if he had, he would not have found a place with them. His crime was against his own family. If he were remembered in that town, he would be remembered for this. He began researching his housing options. There was a faith-based agency in his hometown that offered temporary housing, but reading between the lines in correspondence with them, he thought his sexual orientation might be a problem. He found out that the state had an agreement with a low-end motel on the north side of town. He could be housed there. But he would be released in February. The weather would be cold. There would be snow on the ground. He determined that there was no bus service on that side of town. How would he get to his parole appointments? How could he go job hunting? Dave was an overthinker, and this time it worked in his favor. Had he not thought this through, had he not researched his options, he would have had a rocky start.

He found out about Sponsors, the reentry services nonprofit, from fellow inmates. The agency provided three months of transitional housing, but this and all the other services were meant for men and women released to Lane County, not the county Dave would be released to. He wrote a long letter to the agency explaining his situation and managed to get an exception based on his years behind bars. With housing secured—at least for the first ninety days—he was allowed to change the location of his parole. And so he spent his first night and the next three months in room in a men's dorm on Sponsors' main campus. The facility was attractive, with two-story dorms, a resource center, an administration and meeting building, and other structures facing a landscaped courtyard. The dorms were clean and plain and institutional—eight motel-style rooms with a shared living-dining-kitchen space. It wasn't homey. But it wasn't prison. Dave was kept busy all day with the nitty-gritty of reentry: getting IDs, signing up for insurance and food benefits, attempting to learn basic computer and internet search skills, writing a résumé. He had help, and that made all the difference. He was required to meet with a case manager, submit to random urine tests, and attend a behavioral therapy class. But most important, he was required to look for work. To stay in Sponsors' transitional housing for ninety days, you had to prove you were looking for work or applying to school. Dave was doing both.

And being a planner, he was planning. Where would he sleep, where he would call home after the ninety days in the dorm? He wanted to be independent and self-sufficient as soon as possible. Sponsors offered a class that fast-tracked the process for receiving a Section 8 voucher. The rental assistance he might get from that program could make it possible for him to afford his own apartment. He did successfully apply. The fast-track class worked. He was quickly approved. But the voucher was for only $400. He had sporadic jobs—selling food at sporting events, cutting hair—but his focus was taking community college classes so that he could become a citizen of the digital world, a necessity for decent employment, he believed. His income was so low that, even with the $400 voucher, there was nothing he could remotely afford. He thought about sharing the rent with someone. But the only people he knew were ex-cons with their own issues.

Then he heard about an opening at The Quads, a satellite facility owned by Sponsors. This was not temporary housing. It was not a case-managed life. The Quads was a twenty-eight-unit apartment building in a middle-class residential neighborhood. The tenants were, supposedly, all employed, drug-free ex-offenders. It was not exactly like having your own place. The seven "quads" in the building included four bedrooms, each with its own half bath, as well as a shared kitchen and eating area and full bathroom. It was how a lot of college students lived. The rent was an extraordinarily affordable (highly subsidized) $350 a month, including utilities. Dave moved in the day after his ninety days were up in the dorm. It wasn't the answer to his housing needs. He didn't want to live like a college student or an ex-con. But this was a clean, safe, inexpensive place that would buy him some time. For now, he would work. He would save money. And he would plan for his next move.

—————

If housing-first, wraparound services agencies like Sponsors were common in cities and towns across the country, the reentry path would look a lot different—and be a lot smoother—for the tens of thousands of those released without a safe place to land. But what is common instead is a patchwork of programs that struggle for funding and often serve only a small percent of those who need help. What is common are stopgap measures like homeless shelters or well-meaning initiatives and pilot programs that focus solely on housing and do not offer any of the other support services that go along with successful reentry.

Sponsors, which began with a nun giving an ex-con a ride home from prison almost fifty years ago, has grown into a constellation of services and a far-flung support network including a warehouse stacked with free furniture, a clothing store where every item is free, an organic garden, a bike giveaway and repair shop, a computer lab, an employment resource center, the mentorship program I am a part of, monthly support groups, weekly classes, and housing facilities in seven different locations, from transitional dorms to a cluster of tiny homes to fully furnished two-bedroom garden apartments. The staff has grown from that single nun to forty men and women, almost two-thirds of whom have incarceration histories. Their stories of recovery, reentry, and successful reintegration fuel the organization and help make believers out of those struggling to make new lives.

At the head of Sponsors is a man whose own story could be the plot of a noir novel. A lean, wiry guy who looks at least a decade younger than his fifty-plus years, Paul Solomon grew up working class in a socially conscious family in a yet-to-be-gentrified urban neighborhood. He started shooting heroin, as he dates it, "shortly after my Bar Mitzvah." His first prison sentence, two and a half years, was for drug dealing, robbery, and forgery. Six months after his release, he was busted for bank robbery. This time the sentence was for five years. He heard the verdict standing in the Gus J. Solomon U.S. Courthouse in downtown Portland, a building named after his grandfather, a highly respected and celebrated federal judge. Gus J. Solomon, appointed by Harry Truman, served as the court's chief justice from the late 1950s until his death in 1971. Paul was just a toddler. In the late 1990s, Paul had one last foray into the system, another drug charge. There was no "aha" moment that transformed him, no flipping of the switch. It was, for him, a long series of lessons, a slow climb. Maybe this was why he was so good at his job.

Paul was the one who bent the rules to give Dave a home.

CHAPTER 13

"You're like a ray of sunshine," the interviewer told her. And she was. Just released, almost giddy with optimism and the promise of a new life, Catherine radiated energy and goodwill. She was focused, articulate, and charming. Her smile was infectious. She was confident but not arrogant, poised but not scripted, warm but entirely professional. Her buoyancy, which might have seemed almost adolescent, was tempered by her composure, a skill born of years navigating a life behind bars. She was thirty years old, but for her this was the start of the life she was determined to live. Her résumé included a two-year college degree and a paralegal certification. She had designed and taught workshops for abused women. She wanted to be a teacher or perhaps a nurse. But first she had to establish herself, find a job that tapped into some of her skills and paid her accordingly so she could establish a work history and save for the future she dreamed of.

After the questioning and the conversation, after the smiles and the compliments, Catherine told the interviewer about her homicide conviction. The woman would find out anyway. She thought that if she told the interviewer right then, in person, within the context of the interview that had just taken place, that person would see *her* in context. If instead her record was later uncovered during the background check almost all employers did these days, the interviewer would think she had tried to hide her past. Her crime, a violent crime, a crime with a gun, would stun them. They would, she figured, just toss her résumé in the trash. So she told the interviewer that day. "We'll call you," the woman said.

Catherine, that "ray of sunshine," waited for a call that never came. She went out on another interview. *I nailed it,* she thought to herself as she left the room. "This is one of the best interviews I've ever conducted," this second potential employer had told her. And as before, Catherine was forthcoming about her past. And as before, there was no callback. After the third interview, she sat in her car and cried. And then she forced herself to go out again. Surely someone would see the person she was now and give her a chance. She kept trying long after she realized that the only kind of job she was going to get was exactly the kind of job she didn't want: mindless, dead-end, underpaid.

She took that job anyway, minimum-wage shift work at a fast-food franchise, because she needed to be employed. Employment was not just a condition of parole; it was essential to her independence. And she took that job because they hired her and no one else would. It was, as were the jobs that followed, dead-end "McJobs." The pay was so low that she could barely afford her rent. She was served with eviction notices for three months in a row and temporarily lived in a shelter. For almost four years she worked fast-food and convenience store gigs, trying to keep her aspirations alive. She had two toddlers now. They were going to have the safe, secure childhood she never had. And she owed it

to the people who believed in her, especially the evangelical couple she called Ma and Papa who had embraced her in prison and
showed her a nurturing spiritual path. And she owed it to herself. Life in prison works daily to erode self-worth, assuming a
person has much to begin with, which many do not—especially
women like Catherine with histories of violence and abuse. But
the day-in-day-out, year-in-year-out challenges of incarcerated
life can also teach stamina, perseverance, and resilience. These
were lessons Catherine learned.

———

As Catherine—and just about everyone else released from
prison—soon discovered, there are "vastly diminished employment opportunities" for those with criminal records. This is
according to a report from the Center for Economic and Policy
Research, a Washington, DC–based economic think tank. The
stigma of having an arrest record hurts an applicant's job prospects more than virtually any other factor (and those factors
include education, race, and gender), according to the National
Institute of Justice, the research agency of the Justice Department.
Researchers tracking employment of ex-felons in cities throughout the country report uniformly dismal statistics. In a compre-
hensive report of employment outcomes for released prisoners
in Ohio, Illinois, and Texas, researchers found that only 45
percent of the men had jobs eight months out. Another report
from that same *Returning Home* study included one-year-later
data from men released to Baltimore, Chicago, Cleveland, and
Houston. Just half were employed. In a Boston reentry study that
included both male and female ex-felons, a scant 25 percent of
the women were working six months out. The men fared better,

with 57 percent finding jobs. A Prison Policy Initiative report, compiled the year before COVID-19 temporarily upended the employment scene, offered these national unemployment rates for those with criminal records: white men, 18.4 percent; white women, 23.2 percent; Black men, 35.2 percent; Black women, 43.6 percent. And in the first-ever estimate of unemployment among five million formerly incarcerated people living in the United States, another Prison Policy Initiative study found an unemployment rate of more than 27 percent. In that year, 2018, the U.S. unemployment rate was 3.9 percent.

Yet at the same time, the research is clear about the importance of employment to successful reentry. Stable employment can reduce recidivism, or at the very least, it can lengthen the time between release and the commission of another crime. It's easy to see why. Wages earned through work lessen the chance that the person will be motivated to commit a crime to get money (and the higher the wage, the less the chance). Earning a wage can lead to a better relationship with family, particularly if the just-released ex-offender is living with family or depending on family funds. Earning a wage is also the first step to being able to afford a place to live. Beyond the obvious monetary benefits, employment, even a menial, minimum-wage job, gives order and organization to the day. It sets expectations and demands a level of responsibility, self-monitoring, and self-control. Psychologists who study unemployment and depression agree that having a job to go to every day is closely tied to a person's sense of self-worth and self-esteem. And the opposite is true. Unemployed adults and those not working as much as they would like are, according to a Gallup health index poll, twice as likely to be depressed as Americans employed full time.

Some prisons provide help before release, offering résumé-writing workshops, role-playing interview preparation sessions, or events that bring in potential employers. The Federal Bureau of Prisons operates a Release Preparation Program that intensifies eighteen months prior to release. Organizations that run informational websites, like Jails to Jobs, Help for Felons, and Jobs for Felons Hub, are out there for those who know where—and how—to look. Reentry nonprofits, where they manage to exist and keep funded, reach out to so-called "second chance" employers who are "felon-friendly." And still, dozens of extensive surveys show high and persistent unemployment among those with criminal records.

———

For those who do find employment in the weeks and months after release, the result may not be *gainful* employment. A study by University of Wisconsin–Milwaukee criminologist Thomas LeBel found that two-thirds of those previously incarcerated suffered from continual financial hardship, vacillating between periods of stability and survival. Some of that hardship comes from not being able to find work at all, but some comes from the kind of work these men and women were able to find. Like Catherine, they found themselves in low-wage, low-skills jobs with variable hours, few if any benefits, high turnover, and almost no room for meaningful advancement.

There is another side to this coin: media attention on the few ex-felons who make it big, from a notorious jewel thief who transformed himself into a motivational speaker and YouTube sensation, to a check kiter who became a highly respected forensic psychologist. The list of exceptions also includes a drug dealer who became the executive chef at the Bellagio, a carjacker who teaches poetry at the University of Maryland, and a man convicted of manslaughter who teaches law at Michigan State. And then there is the poster boy himself, Danny Trejo, an East LA drug dealer and thief, now famous for playing tough guys in *Breaking Bad* and *Sons of Anarchy*. Do these celebrated exceptions serve to motivate the ex-offender hefting boxes in a warehouse or slinging burgers at a franchise—or those unable to find any work at all? Or do they set the bar so high, present a dream so unattainable, that they lead to disappointment, failure, and lack of self-esteem? Probably both. Countering the dire statistics that emerge from two decades' worth of research on ex-prisoner employment (and unemployment) with the exceptionalism of the few only serves to highlight the extraordinary challenges of finding work when you have a criminal record.

———————

Why is it so hard for ex-felons to find jobs? There are obvious challenges, collateral and systemic challenges, and underlying challenges. Together they create a steep hill to climb, especially when added to everything else going on during the transition from prison to home, from reestablishing relationships to finding stable housing, from meeting the conditions of parole to learning how to operate in a world that has moved forward without you. For many there is also the challenge, immediate and ongoing, of staying clean.

One obvious impediment to securing all but the most menial of jobs is lack of education. A quarter of all those who've served time never graduated from high school. More than half hold only a high school diploma or GED, according to data from the National Former Prisoner Survey. (Three-quarters of those with GEDs earned those certificates in prison.) And these very basic educational credentials have diminished in job-marketable value. The percentage of low-skill jobs in the U.S. labor force available to those with no more than a high school diploma has declined by close to 25 percent over the past generation. Less than 4 percent of ex-felons have college degrees.

They also lack a key factor employers look for: a history of relevant (and steady) employment, a job record that can easily be checked. Able-bodied prisoners are required to work inside. They *do* have jobs to list on an application, but those jobs may involve either minimal skill (washing dishes, picking up trash) or skills likely uncalled for in the outside labor market (a prison-specific industry with particular processes and highly specialized machinery). It is easy, too easy, to lose a job in prison—as punishment for a minor infraction, for example, that has no relevance in the outside world, like having an unauthorized book or magazine in the cell or hoarding food. Prisoners are subject to surprise transfers from facility to facility, sometimes due to overcrowding, sometimes as punishment (known, with dark prison humor, as "diesel therapy"), another reason job history may be spotty. Supervisors, the people future employers want to contact, might be fellow inmates, who cannot be contacted (and might not be considered credible references anyway), or correctional officers without easily accessible email or phone contacts. There are nuances well known to those who have been in prison but largely invisible to the rest of us.

Recent job history counts, but one of the most consistent predictors of post-prison employment is actually *pre*-prison employment, which again creates a barrier, either because the employment dates back decades or because the "employment" was criminal behavior. Other factors add to the obvious challenges of finding a job: lack of experience filling out applications or writing a résumé, lack of experience being interviewed, lack of technological know-how in searching for and applying for jobs online. Conventional job searching, like responding to newspaper ads or signs in windows or dropping off a résumé at a business, is not the way it's done anymore. Yet this is the only kind of job hunt that Dave, behind bars for thirty-plus years, and hundreds of thousands of others released after long imprisonment, know.

Add to this the old school, but still relevant, method of finding a job: networking, tapping into friends and contacts who know of jobs, knowing people who work for likely employers. These connections are part of the "social capital" that those in prison do not often accrue or have long ago lost. What connections to the world of work would someone like Catherine have, incarcerated since she was thirteen? Or Vicki, in and out of prison with dizzying regularity for the past two decades? Family, assuming relationships have been maintained and there is the wherewithal to offer support, can function as social capital. But what if the crime the now ex-offender was punished for was committed against family, as Dave's was? There is little hope of support in that case. What if "the street" was the family, as in Vicki's life?

And then there are the obstacles to finding sustainable employment that have nothing to do with the ex-offenders education, job history, or job-hunting savvy. These are the institutional, the so-called *collateral consequences* of imprisonment, the embedded, continuing effects of punishment long after the term of punishment has been served. Felons are banned from working in many government positions due to perceived lack of accountability. Jobs at the post office or in federal facilities are unlikely, and many states ban felons from applying to police and public safety departments. Most states ban those with criminal records from working in top-level positions in the healthcare industry, like doctors, nurses, and pharmacists. Although regulations vary widely from state to state, there are consistent crimes that, no matter what, will keep a felon out of the teaching profession. Catherine dreamed of becoming a teacher, but her homicide conviction closed that door forever. Those who have served time for other serious crimes, like arson, rape, sex crimes with a minor, kidnapping, and domestic violence, are also almost always excluded from obtaining teaching licenses. Joining the military is not a great option either. Although recruiters can grant waivers that allow an ex-offender to enlist, some crimes (sex crimes, assault with a deadly weapon, kidnapping) are immediate disqualifiers.

Some states will not grant ex-felons the licenses required to practice certain occupations or trades like accountant (money) or barber (sharp implements). There is no law prohibiting a felon from joining a union, but those with certain convictions are generally not eligible to work in specific occupations requiring a license and involving union membership, like electrician or plumber. Where there is discretion involved, a license-granting entity could consider the nature and seriousness of the crime, the relationship of the crime to the purposes for requiring a license, and the extent to which a license might offer an opportunity to engage in criminal activity. But sometimes there is simply an iron door policy. And sometimes the barriers to employment in potentially lucrative trades like welder, carpenter, HVAC technician, trucker—all listed as "highest paying jobs for ex-felons" on an overly optimistic site for those recently released—are not about laws or licenses but about attaining (and being able to afford) significant training, being eligible to be bonded and insured, and having access to reliable transportation. It is also worth noting that these high-paying trade jobs have historically been closed, or at the very least unwelcoming, to women with or without criminal records.

Employers from Walmart to Wall Street routinely conduct background checks of job applicants. An estimated 70 percent of all employers use these reports as early identifiers of viable candidates. The least expensive background search ($4.50) goes back seven years and checks for arrest records and convictions within the state. Employers can also pay for more extensive investigations that capture criminal records from seven, ten, twenty or more years past, that include convictions in all states, and that scrutinize credit. Companies are governed by various laws concerning what they can and can't consider for employment purposes, and some states bar basing employment decisions on arrest records. But this does little to nullify the potential effects of background checks on hiring. As Catherine quickly learned doors get slammed in your face once a criminal background check is done. Even among employers who claim not to discriminate against those with criminal records and actually express an interest in hiring them, research shows that having a record reduces employer callback rates by 50 percent. In other research, a national survey of employers in five major cities, two-thirds said they would not knowingly hire an ex-offender. Not surprisingly, employers report that a criminal past raises significant questions about the character, trustworthiness, and honesty of the applicant.

Well-meaning criminal justice reformers thought they had a handle on this and could put a dent in the widespread discrimination against hiring those with criminal pasts when they worked hard, state by state, to "ban the box." The box they were referring to was the square appearing at the bottom of most job applications. If the applicant had a conviction on their record, they checked the box. The idea behind the reform was that, without that telltale check mark, employers would consider an applicant's qualifications first before viewing that person through the lens of a criminal record. The reformers' efforts were, at first blush, extraordinarily successful. Nationwide, thirty-three states and more than one hundred cities adopted "ban the box" policies, with three-quarters of the U.S. population living in jurisdictions that banned its inclusion on job applications. Additionally, eleven states mandated the removal of conviction history questions from job applications for private employers. But, as the painstaking research of Rutgers economist Amanda Agan illustrated, removing this information from job applications did not prevent employers from *wanting* this information. In the absence of the box, they used another characteristic to discriminate: race.

In an audit study, Agan and a colleague sent fifteen thousand online job applications for entry-level jobs on behalf of young male applicants both before and after Ban the Box laws went into effect in New Jersey and New York City. On the applications, the researchers randomly varied whether the applicant had a felony conviction and whether the applicant's name was distinctly Black or white. The results were stunning: The gap in employer callbacks between Black and white applicants grew significantly *after* Ban the Box. With the box, the white advantage for callbacks was 7 percent; without it, that advantage leaped to 45 percent. Without the box evidence, employers "inferred" whether the applicant *might* have a criminal record. Their inference? Black men were most likely to have convictions. Thus Black men—or rather those with "distinctly Black" names—were disadvantaged. Of course, this would include many with no criminal records at all. Their "crime" was being Black. The employers themselves were not being any more racially biased than the criminal justice system itself, where racial inequality exists and is well documented at every level, from policing to prosecutorial decisions to sentencing. The employers were right. Because of the racial inequity in the criminal justice system, it was more likely for a young Black man to have encounters with the law than for a young white man. Playing it "safe," in the absence of documentation, they chose not to call back the Black applicants. And so Ban the Box, which had been designed to level the playing field, did the opposite.

What's interesting about the Ban the Box experience is not that best-intentioned efforts sometimes backfire. It is that problems don't get solved from the top down. What is deeply embedded does not get legislated out of existence. The unconscious—and sometimes completely conscious—racism that underlies the hiring process is what underlies the criminal justice system, and the criminal justice system, in turn, reflects the larger culture. The experience also reveals our collective unwillingness to believe that people who have done wrong and own up to their mistakes, people who have served their time, are worthy of a second chance.

The stigma of having an arrest record can remain for a lifetime. That stigma may be the most profound challenge facing the ex-offender seeking employment, looking to secure housing, nurture healthy relationships, or fully reintegrate into the free world. That stigma may be more of an obstacle than lack of education, employment history, tech savvy, or the barriers of policy-based collateral consequences. The power and persistence of the stigma is that it comes both from the outside and the inside. It is the mark of disgrace the employer, the rental agent, and the neighbor sees when they look at an ex-con. It is also how many ex-offenders see themselves. They have internalized the disgrace; they carry the shame. Many believe what others believe of them, that they are no good, that they are unworthy, that because they cannot erase the past it forever dooms them. And prison is not a place to learn self-confidence.

Those emerging from incarceration are also held back, or hold themselves back, for another reason. To search for a job that might lead to economic security or advancement means to believe in the American Dream, the possibility that success is open to anyone who works hard. Yet it is often a rejection of that dream, or the direct experience of seeing how out of reach (or historically inaccurate) that dream is, that can lead to criminal behavior. Suppose you live in a community where that dream is denied, and you grow up in a household where no one dreamed that dream, and then you spend years—perhaps decades—in a closed society where no one has the freedom or opportunity or vision to dream that dream? And then some prison program (if you are lucky) or some parole officer who has the time and takes the interest (if you are lucky) tries to light a fire under you. There is no kindling.

———————

Yet against these considerable odds, Catherine, Trevor, Arnoldo, Dave, and Vicki all found jobs within the first few weeks of release. How did they manage that? What were those jobs and what did these five, newly released, encounter in the workplace? Stitched together, these small stories create a realistic picture of the varied—but almost always rough—roads traveled by those struggling to reenter and remake their lives.

Catherine is a warm, vibrant human being. But she is also a statistic. She was one of about a quarter of a million juveniles who are tried, sentenced, and incarcerated as adults every year. During the 1990s, the era during which many of our most punitive criminal justice policies were developed, forty-nine states changed their laws to increase the number of minors being tried as adults. Catherine was then, and still is, as of this writing, the youngest person ever to be tried as an adult for murder. When she was released after sixteen years and out looking for her first job, she was also a statistic—a Black female ex-felon, the category that researchers found to have the highest rate of unemployment, more than 43 percent. And she was not just a felon but a violent offender. Any deck—*all decks*—was stacked against her.

The degrees and certificates she earned in prison didn't open any doors. Or rather, they cracked open a few doors which were quickly slammed when she disclosed her criminal conviction. There was no box to check on the applications—the box had been banned—so she did get the initial interviews. And they went well—the interviewers themselves said so. She did not have to disclose her criminal past right then, but she thought it was better to self-report. Each interview—were there five, six, seven? She lost count—ended the same way: *We'll be in touch.* And then they weren't. One company told her it had a national policy against hiring ex-felons. Another said her homicide conviction disqualified her. But mostly there was silence. The only place that would hire her was a fast-food franchise. That job was followed by a job at another fast-food franchise, which was followed by a job at a convenience store. There was no upward mobility, no American Dream. In fact, like many minimum-wage workers, and like most minimum-wage working women with young children to support, there was downward mobility, economic insecurity, busted budgets, mounting credit card debt she couldn't begin to repay, daily anxiety that she would not be able to afford to put food on the table. She kept going because she had to. She said later that she "had no choice" but to persevere. But of course she had a choice. Hundreds of thousands of men and women released from prison make their way back into the criminal justice system. One of all-too-many reasons they reoffend is the inability to find and hold a living-wage job.

Catherine broke out of the McJob world when she found an ad online for a position as night resident manager at a transitional housing facility for women just released from prison. Here it was a different world. Catherine's years in prison were seen as a plus, not a permanent stain on her character. It was, however, an entry-level job, which meant the pay was not much better than what she had been making. The hours were rough. And the job involved more supervision and oversight—bed checks, pantry inventories, enforcing house rules—than it did helping the women who lived there. She wanted to be a mentor, a teacher, someone who could work to make things better for those with dark pasts, especially, like her, juvenile offenders.

She and the man she met at her first job back in Kansas, a man like her with a troubled and criminal past, launched a nonprofit by themselves, over the kitchen table in the apartment they no longer shared. It was called Breaking Free MVMT and featured this reach-for-the-stars mission statement: "We aim to eradicate juvenile incarceration through public education and community empowerment." It was a testament to Catherine's prodigious energy, even more prodigious optimism—and naivete—that the two worked together on this. It turned out that she didn't have to reinvent this particular wheel. There was already an up-and-running national coalition and clearinghouse that led, coordinated, developed, and supported efforts to implement fair and age-appropriate sentences for youthful offenders. It was called The Campaign for the Fair Sentencing of Youth, and Catherine found a job there. She was, initially, a "first responder" and mentor to young people transitioning into lives outside the criminal justice system. Her public speaking talents were soon recognized, and she began delivering talks and participating in panels at national conferences. She had, four tough years after leaving prison, found a home.

Like Catherine, Trevor's immediate post-prison job future was not promising. He was male and white, which "helped," but like Catherine, he had a murder conviction on his record and, like Catherine, he had been inside since his early teens. He thought he'd start working at a local 7-Eleven. He knew someone there who said they would hire him. It was a minimum-wage job that made use of none of the considerable management and organizational skills he had learned behind bars, but it was a job. He stopped by his mother's place of work to tell her. She had started working for an employment agency called All-Star Labor and Staffing that specialized in finding jobs for, as the website so delicately put it, "individuals who may have barriers to employment." The jobs were mostly the kind of work recently released ex-offenders could hope to get: general labor, construction, landscaping, food service, janitorial. But the agency performed a valuable service by working with felon-friendly employers to make the job search easier and, with a combination of empathy and professionalism, by helping their clients navigate the application and interview processes. Karen, Trevor's mother, had secured a job as one of this branch office's first employees just the year before.

When he stopped by the office that day, he had a chance encounter with the chief of operations for the agency who was checking in with staff. The encounter turned into a lengthy conversation, which, although Trevor didn't know it at the time, was an impromptu job interview. He was offered a job in that office as a coordinator, interviewing released felons looking for work, working with local businesses, and making contacts. When Trevor talks about this moment, it sounds more random than it was. In fact, the chief of operations knew Karen well and respected all she accomplished in the office. He knew about Trevor. Karen was a proud and vocal promoter of her son's talents. And the agency wanted to practice what it preached. If the mission was to help previously incarcerated people find work, then the office staff should reflect that. Then there was Trevor himself: articulate, self-confident, focused. A man—an employee—who had every reason to prove himself. The job made use of his organizational skills, but more than that, it allowed him to be—and to be valued for—who he was, just as Catherine's position at the nonprofit did.

For a little more than a year he worked there alongside his mother in a modest office less than a half mile down the road from the penitentiary. Meanwhile he joined the Youth Justice Project, a program helping and advocating for kids sentenced to life imprisonment. Like Catherine, he became a frequent speaker and panelist. Like Catherine, he was able to begin coming to terms with and making sense of his long period of incarceration by mining that experience to help others. The job he found next was also tied to the criminal justice system, but in a different way. He now provides support services for defense attorneys by collating, organizing, and managing the files, reports, and documents they need to mount their court cases. His job is to make the defense team's job easier, to give them more time to represent their clients. He overseas five others, all of whom he has trained. The work is meaningful and important, but it is also psychologically and emotionally challenging. It pokes at his own wounds, reminds him daily that people inflict harm and cause what can be irreparable damage. Like he did.

Arnoldo's transition to the world of work was smooth, perhaps too smooth. His younger brother was in charge of hiring at a trucking parts company. A month and a half after release, Arnoldo got a job in the machine shop there. His brother completed the application for him. Arnoldo didn't even come in for an interview. The family connection is what did it, but it didn't hurt that the boss was interested in hiring ex-felons. He saw them as hard workers who had a lot to lose if they messed up. There were already several working there, and it seemed to Arnoldo on that first day in the shop that everyone knew someone who had done time. It was that kind of place. No one cared, or even gave much of a thought to the fact, that Arnoldo been inside for nineteen years. The irony of this accepting workplace was that it reminded Arnoldo of prison. It was hypermasculine. There was a lot of tough talk, a lot of posturing. It was misogynistic. He had worked hard to first recognize, then understand, and finally transcend this kind of environment. He left that toxic world behind when he left prison. But here it was in the workplace. As soon as he could, he switched to swing shift where there were fewer men and the atmosphere was more relaxed.

He was grateful for the paycheck, but he knew this wasn't what he wanted to do. The restorative justice and trauma transformation work he'd done in prison, the classes and workshops and events he and Sterling had worked on, had changed him. He wanted to mentor others. He wanted to do something to help the overlapping populations he identified with: at-risk youth, ex-felons returning to society, the Latinx community. He reached out to people he knew from RJ work inside. He became part of a small group that met to brainstorm ways to work on reentry. But it was his parole officer who connected him to the woman who would hire him for a position at Latino Network, a thriving twenty-year-old nonprofit that worked on social justice, education, and family and youth issues.

It took five months to get that job, five months between his initial interview and his first day of work. He was the first previously incarcerated person to be hired there. They wanted someone with "real life experience," but they didn't know what that meant exactly. They were anxious. How would Arnoldo handle himself in challenging situations, especially those that involved law enforcement? His experience with gangs as a kid and in prison could be a plus, helping him relate to the youth in the Latino Network programs. But it could also be a minus. Would his past be triggered by the situations he encountered? Arnoldo understood these concerns. But he had confidence in himself. And more important, he did not go into the job with the idea that he had to prove himself. This was the attitude embedded in gang life, the engine that powered it. I am who I am, he told himself. When they see how I interact, when they see what I do, they will see who I am.

And this is just what happened. Arnoldo "proved" himself through his quiet diligence, his ability to listen and connect, the combination of empathy and gravitas he brought to the moment. His first boss saw this, as did his subsequent boss. He was given more responsibility. He now manages four programs that focus on Latinx youth, from working with homeless kids to mentoring those at risk for gang involvement, from reaching out to kids in foster care to creating after-school recreational activities. "You can't just go to work, see all this stuff, and then cut it off," he told me. We were talking at the end of a particularly grueling week of work almost a year into the pandemic. "I have to be there, be present," Arnoldo said. He was talking about work, but he was also taking about his life.

Arnoldo, like Catherine and Trevor, found meaningful employment in a job that put his past to service and became part of the long, perhaps lifelong, process of redemption. This is not the path Dave chose. He had thought, fresh out of prison, that he would enroll in a graduate program in counseling psychology and specialize in work with reentering ex-felons. But he wasn't accepted into the one program he applied to, and the experience of that soured him. It was not just the rejection—which came from the university's legal department—it was the whole confusing, confounding, tedious process of applying online. The technological world was completely foreign to him, and not just foreign but unwelcoming, intimidating, deeply and disturbingly off-putting. Had he been accepted, his classes would have been delivered online, a thought that terrified him even as he was limping his way through the application and student aid processes. And so it came as something of a relief when he wasn't accepted. He did enroll in a few community college classes in attempt to learn basic computer skills, but he felt like such an outlier, even in those relatively diverse classrooms. And then there was the cost of continuing his education. The student aid funds that came through were not generous. He considered the near future: three or more years in school accompanied by mounting debt. He was very conscious that he did not have a full working life ahead of him. He was healthy, except for high blood pressure and a mouthful of neglected teeth, but he would be sixty on his next birthday. School leading to a new career, a dream that kept him motivated in prison, now seemed like a bad idea. He needed to find work. He needed a paycheck.

His first job was a series of part-time gigs setting up, delivering, and serving at catered events. He got calls to come in for two, occasionally three, of these a week. Meanwhile he began looking for a job cutting hair. He had kept his beautician's license current while in prison, but he had not worked in a salon or barber shop for three decades. After several unsuccessful walk-ins to local businesses, he found part-time work at a chain salon inside a Walmart. They ran a background check, which he was told he passed. (It would have flagged convictions only for the past seven years. His dated back to the 1980s.) But he could tell from almost the first day at work that the manager was uncomfortable with him. She began making comments about him "invading her personal space." He felt like she was inventing issues to make trouble. He feared that if she reported some incident that she thought had happened he would get in trouble with his parole officer, and who knows what the repercussions of that would be. He quit a month and a half later.

Meanwhile, an attendant at a local gas station told him about an opening at Safeway, where he himself had a part-time job. It was a good place to work, the guy said. You should go in and talk to them. The closest of the three Safeway stores in town was just three blocks from Dave's quad apartment. He got a job there in the deli section, moving inventory from the freezer to the case, stocking the trays, taking orders, making sandwiches, and serving salads and prepared foods. His schedule changed from week to week, but the work was almost full time, and the pay was a bit better than minimum wage. It was indoor work in a clean place. He liked his boss. He got to talk to customers. He knew he was underemployed, and he knew he was going nowhere. But it was what it was. It was a job he could do until, as he put it, "I fall over dead." That's how long he'd have to work there, he figured.

———————

Vicki could have been, maybe *should* have been, the success story here. When she got out she had a familiar home, a long-time partner waiting for her, food on the table. Although she had spent considerable time locked up, almost half of her life, none of her prison terms had taken her away from the free world for longer than five years at a time. She did not have that shock of entry that the others had. And she was not a violent offender, which meant that her record looked less threatening to a future employer. She may also have had less of a burden to bear. She had not pulled a gun on anyone. She had caused damage, but identity theft was not murder. Yet her post-incarceration history of employment was successful only in the narrowest sense. She did find work. But there was no path forward, no path at all, just a stumbling from job to job. When she got out, a cousin employed her for a few days a week organizing racks in a small, dark warehouse stuffed with secondhand clothing. The business really could not support an employee. The cousin was doing her a temporary favor. Then she found a part-time, minimum-wage job at a convenience store. Then a bakery, work she actually seemed to like, but a boss and a coworker with whom she had almost immediate "issues," followed by a job making sandwiches at a Subway, where there was "drama" in the workplace.

Vicki was not the easiest person to get along with. She was opinionated, which was not necessarily a bad thing unless you were a just-hired, easily replaceable minimum-wage worker. And she seemed to be on edge much of the time, quick to react, difficult to keep on track. It might have been the ADD she believed she suffered from, or the residual effects of the drugs she abused for so long, or her constant fear that she might relapse. It might have been that her many years in close quarters with hundreds of women had made her crisis-prone, hyperalert to what could go wrong, too ready to give deeper meaning to the insignificant, finding irreconcilable conflict where there might be merely transient disagreement. Vicki, out of prison, off illegal drugs, still seemed to be in limbo, not truly inhabiting her new life, moving from one crappy job to another, with no goal, no ambition. Maybe it was the only kind of life she knew how to live.

CHAPTER 14

It was a warm, bright afternoon in late July. They stood together on a small, indigo-dyed rug set on the front lawn of the house they rented on a quiet street in northeast Portland. They faced each other, holding hands. He was wearing baggy white Bermuda shorts and a bright blue shirt. She was wearing a lemon-yellow sundress. Her canvas deck shoes were the same blue as his shirt. She had dyed the crown of her dark hair a brilliant chartreuse. There were flowers everywhere. Friends, neighbors, and family, maybe sixty people, were amiably crowded together in the yard, some standing, some sitting on folding chairs, the kids on blankets. Her parents stood on one side of them; his mother, brother, and sister on the other. Today was their wedding day.

The guy in the white shorts was Arnoldo. He had, by then, been out of prison for one year and ten days. The woman in the sundress was Nicole, an academic turned activist. He grew up in a Texas border town, the son of a man currently serving a fifty-year sentence for murder and a woman who did what she could to hold the family together. She grew up the child of California hippies, followers of Gurdjieff, the philosopher-mystic who taught that most humans live their lives in a state of hypnotic "waking sleep." He had spent his high school years in juvie and his twenties and most of his thirties in prison. She had attended private schools and earned a PhD from Berkeley. A more unlikely couple would be hard to imagine. And yet there they were, connected in ways that transcended stereotypes and defied expectations. And there was Sol, eleven months old on this day, the child that had come both too soon and at exactly the right time. Just like their relationship.

Karuna, the prison chaplain, was officiating this afternoon. She had known Arnoldo for years but had only recently met Nicole. The day they met, Karuna had brought fresh peaches, and the three adults watched as Sol had a total body experience with the fruit, smearing it all over his face, his hands and arms up to the elbows covered in juice and pulp. It was a mess, which no one cared about. What Karuna thought, in that moment, was that the joy and intensity of the relationship she would soon be blessing was right there in front of her, expressed in, as she put it, "this sweet little person."

Now Karuna stood in front of the couple, lighting a bundle of sage, explaining how it was part of a spiritual ritual to cleanse a person or space, to promote healing and wisdom. She handed the sage to Arnoldo, who smudged Nicole. Then Nicole waved the bundle over him. The couple walked in a tight circle around their families, smudging that space, then a larger circle, acknowledging the community that had come together on the lawn that afternoon. The ceremony that followed had been built from the ground up, pieced together from many traditions, carefully scripted. It was both solemn and quirky, indigenous and bohemian, self-conscious but also completely genuine. There was a sense that something big and important was happening here, and it wasn't just a marriage.

Karuna, a Buddhist by training and temperament, had never before officiated at a wedding. But then no one had probably ever officiated at a wedding like this one. She called forth the ancestors to bless the union. Then the parents were asked to come forward to offer their blessings. Arnoldo's mother probably loved Nicole from the get-go in that immediate and visceral way a mother loves the woman who so obviously loves her son. Nicole's parents came to the union more cautiously. "You need to allow me to show them who I am," he told her. "Don't fight for me. Let them just see me." There was bravery in that, given Arnoldo's history, given the gulf, both deep and wide, between his experiences and hers. He had Nicole's love, but he felt strongly that her parents had to both know and accept him for who he was. He had a long and candid conversation with Andrea, Nicole's mother. She began to see what her daughter saw. That afternoon, her blessing was unconditional.

It was time now to hear from the couple. Arnoldo faced to address the gathering, but he was clearly speaking to Nicole. The moment was both public and private, simultaneously communal and intimate. He spoke slowly, his voice low and measured. This came not from hesitation or awkwardness but from someplace else, a place a man who spent years in solitary learned to inhabit, a literal "dark night of the soul" few of us have experienced.

"For me, the first hug allowed me to feel safe and nurtured," he said. "It was like everything just fit." He talked about the moment he realized he loved her. He talked about the day they found out she was pregnant. "You have given me space to evolve as a person," he said. They work hard at their relationship, he wanted everyone to know. They work hard at communicating with both honesty and kindness. "More than anything," he told her and the people gathered on the front lawn, "you have given me the room to heal and keep my personal demons at bay."

Then it was Nicole's turn. She told the community about the instant connection she felt, how—although she had to allow herself the time and emotional space to ease into it—she knew early on that she had found "my person." She also talked about the pregnancy, which came so early in their relationship. Sol, as if on cue, started fussing. Arnoldo's mother had been holding him. Now a friend took a turn. Nicole continued. Like Arnoldo, she spoke both intimately and openly. "You put my anxiety to rest," she said, "and showed me that I could lean on you. You have always been present and stable and responsible." It is hard to overstate what this must mean to a man who could never count on his own father. "I love you," Nicole said, "and I love our family."

This relationship was both improbable and meant to be— but not in a syrupy "it was fate" way. It was meant to be in a Venn diagram kind of way. Nicole's circle included fifteen years of teaching in prisons and running programs and developing policy. It included a PhD in jurisprudence and social policy. Arnoldo's circle included gangs, guns, and almost two decades behind bars. But those circles overlapped. The space they shared was defined by activism, a deep commitment to restorative justice and prison reform, and a spirituality that transcended any particular culture or religion.

Those circles had overlapped in time and place two years before when, on a hot August day, both Arnoldo and Nicole found themselves at KBOO, a ragtag community radio station that had been producing progressive programming since the late 1960s. Arnoldo, released just twenty days before, was in the throes of a cleaning frenzy at his mother's house. A buddy from inside, Carlos, asked him if he'd like to come to the station to listen to a prerecorded episode of *Prison Pipeline*, a weekly one-hour show dedicated to educating the public about the criminal justice system. After the recording ended, Carlos asked Arnoldo to hang around. The collective that created the programming was holding a planning meeting to brainstorm another project.

———————

Nicole had been invited to that meeting too. She had finished grad school a year before and had decided, doctorate in hand, that she didn't want to pursue an academic career. She wanted to be in the thick of it. She wanted to be involved in community organizing and restorative justice work. She had been interviewed for a segment on the program earlier in the summer, talking about a class she taught on mass incarceration and the war on drugs. The interviewer asked if she wanted to be involved in the collective. Her life was complicated. This August meeting was the first one she was able to attend.

There were seven people in the room. Arnoldo remembers looking around, taking careful note of Nicole, exchanging a look, and thinking, not with heart racing but with quiet curiosity, "This is an interesting person." Nicole remembers looking around and taking careful note of Arnoldo as he introduced himself. She was in this phase of wanting to learn about the Oregon state prison system. Her work, education, and career, had been in California. She was in search of someone who could school her from the inside out. And there he was. She thought he had the look of someone just out: his energy, his demeanor. He held himself rigid, his face without expression. His head was shaved. She noted his clothes and thought someone else bought them for him. He doesn't know his style. He doesn't know how to wear civilian clothes. During the course of her fifteen years working inside prisons she had come to know men who were able to use their time to educate themselves and use their experiences to develop unique perspectives about how the system worked. They developed a political analysis fueled by personal awareness. She thought Arnoldo might be a man like that. When the meeting broke up, Nicole turned to Arnoldo. "Let's talk," she said. "I want to pick your brain." A week later they met at a pizza joint in a mall, and that's when she heard his story.

Meanwhile the collective began holding weekly meetings to listen to people, like Arnoldo, who had been incarcerated and were now trying to make new lives for themselves. What could the collective do to identify these people and help them advocate for themselves? That was the task they took on. Nicole, with her history of reentry policy work, and Arnoldo, with his in-prison restorative justice and conflict resolution work, were important members of the group. They all met at a homey-but-hip coffeehouse, brainstorming, making plans, sharing the excitement and the frustration of trying to get a new project started.

Nicole remembered the spark. At a meeting toward the end of September, Arnoldo walked into the coffeehouse wearing a black Carhartt T-shirt that fit him perfectly. His style, she thought. He's beginning to get his shit together. And she felt a little jolt of electricity. She jumped up and dashed to the bathroom just to get hold of herself, to talk herself down. She was in the middle of a breakup. He had only recently gotten out of prison. This was the wrong time to be attracted, she told herself, and definitely the wrong time to do anything about it. She needed to put a halt to this. She needed to get out of town. She left for California a few days later to talk to friends about her soon-to-be-ex-husband and about this new guy, Arnoldo. I have this feeling I just can't shake, she told one of her oldest friends. Yes, it is the wrong time, her friend agreed. But sometimes, her friend told her, the wrong time is the right time.

Two weeks later Nicole was back, her head cleared, a new resolve beginning to take shape. The most immediate shape it took was that she found herself picking out an "outfit" to wear to the next meeting of the collective. This was not a woman who wore, or thought in terms of, "outfits." She marveled that she was doing this; she laughed at herself; she did it anyway. She and Arnoldo found seats next to each other at the meeting, and although it was absolutely not her style, she casually put her arm around him. She was dropping big hints. Arnoldo remembered not the outfit, or even the casual arm, but that Nicole somehow seemed different at that meeting. She was happy on the outside, but he thought there was something else going on inside. He was right. There was the breakup of her marriage, the painful logistics of splitting up a shared home, the emotional turmoil of feeling these feelings she was not yet sure she should let herself feel. He didn't know any of that then.

After the meeting, he texted her. "If you ever want to talk, I'm here," the message read. "Thank you, that's kind," she responded, figuring that was the end of the conversation. But he texted her back and later sent her a picture of the park he ran in every morning. And then there were a flurry of texts back and forth. Were they flirting? She didn't know. Maybe he was just excited by this new thing called texting. Texting was not part of the way Nicole interacted socially. She texted to set up meetings, to confirm schedules. But this was obviously something different. Then came the "date" text. They went to a restaurant for dinner, took a long walk, then went to a dance performance. The evening toggled between fun and awkward, spirited and somehow flat. Sitting in the car at the end of the evening Nicole was tired. And confused. Maybe this was it. Maybe they'd just say goodbye and move on. Or not. She had to know. He was talking about his childhood. She asked if she could put her head on his shoulder. Yes, he said. She was making all the moves. Later he told her that this was calculated on his part. He couldn't be the aggressor. He needed her to lean in. Literally.

"I want to kiss you right now," she said to him, as they sat shoulder to shoulder in the car. "But we have this professional relationship."

"It's too late for that," he said.

So they had what Nicole laughingly remembered as a "make-out session" in the car. Until five in the morning. It was like a scene from a movie, she thought, like the fantasy of the high school relationship she never had. It was all fresh and new for her, and for Arnoldo, too. It was exhilarating, a wild, emotional, youthful ride. But it was also deep and purposeful and mature. How could it be both? They never looked back. A few months later they moved in together. By the end of the year she was pregnant. Sol was born that next summer. Now, eleven months later to the day, they stood on the front lawn in the warm sun.

It was time for the rings. Karuna talked about the symbolism, the circle they form that connected not just this couple but this couple with the community. The rings are gold. Gold is malleable. Gold does not tarnish. Arnoldo slipped the ring on Nicole's finger, reciting, in Spanish translation, a Mayan poem. His voice quavered. Standing on the lawn a few feet away Cheryl Cunio, Sterling's wife, noticed that there were tears in his eyes. She and Sterling had been married for fifteen years by then. She had thought Sterling would be out by now, that they would be here together. She listened as Arnoldo recited:

> *Tu eres mi otro yo*
> *Si te hago dano a ti*
> *Me hago dano a mi mismo*
> *Si te amo y respeto*
> *Me amo y respeto yo*
> *Tu eres mi otro yo*

Then Nicole slipped a ring on Arnoldo's finger, reciting the English translation, her voice clear and measured:

> *You are my other me*
> *If I do harm to you,*
> *I do harm to myself*
> *If I love and respect you*
> *I love and respect myself*
> *You are my other me*

"Here is where you kiss," said Karuna.

———

Over the past generation, sociologists and criminologists have studied many variables that they suspect make for, or stand in the way of, successful reentry. They have focused on the impact of age, race, education, employment status, housing accessibility, neighborhood context, and criminal history on the ability of ex-offenders to remain *ex*-offenders. Marriage, however—the institution itself, the quality of the relationship, what the partners bring to it—has gotten much less attention. The research there is intriguingly ambiguous, much like the institution itself.

On the one hand, a subset of researchers who study the importance of transitions and turning points in pre- and post-incarceration lives (they are known as "life-course" criminology scholars) believe that marriage has the potential to "knife off" an offender's past, to create a clean break between a criminal past and a crime-free future. Marriage can forge new, healthier social bonds. It can lead to stability and accountability. It can contribute to a change in self-perception, an awakening to a new identity as a noncriminal person. At the very least, attachment to a marriage partner might mean less hanging out in unsavory places with unsavory people.

But, as anyone who is or has ever been married knows, a live-in, intimate relationship with another person can also be a source of significant stress. When one of those partners has a criminal background and a history of incarceration, when one of those partners is emerging from a world where hiding feelings is a way of life, where showing emotion makes one a target, where trust is hard won and easily lost, the chance for tension, anxiety, and stress is even greater. Finances, considered one of the top stressors in any marriage, can be magnified when one partner—the ex-offender—is unemployed or underemployed, when that partner does not bring a savings account or a credit rating to the marriage, when that person has not had to manage a budget or pay bills, perhaps for decades. There are other common marital stressors—going through a challenging time, experiencing family difficulties, struggling with communication styles, trust, sex—any or all of which can challenge (or tank) a marriage that does not have the heavy overlay of incarceration.

It's not surprising, then, that life-course criminology scholars, while seeing evidence of marriage as positive and protective, also have discovered that it can amplify the already significant stress of reentry. It is one more change—a very big one—and change is uncomfortable, particularly for those accustomed to the routine, monotony, and uniformity of incarcerated life. The research also suggests that reentry marriage partners can be ill chosen. This is a result of what researchers call the "assortative mating process," meaning that former inmates choose former inmates as partners. There is no "knife-off" benefit in those cases. The opposite is true. Marriage to an assortative mate more deeply embeds the ex-offender in criminal life and increases the risk of committing new crimes.

———

What made Arnoldo and Nicole's marriage different was...*every-thing*. But mostly it was who they were. He emerged from prison with both a strong sense of self and a strong sense of purpose. Despite all those years of incarceration, he had resisted becoming institutionalized. His years in solitary had taught him patience, endurance, resilience. His work with Sterling on conflict resolution and trauma-informed transformation helped him become an open and honest communicator. Nicole was resolutely her own person, a smart, funny, no-nonsense woman, a hopeful realist. More than just about anyone who had not served time—which she had not—she understood the world Arnoldo came from. She had worked in prisons for years. She was a student of the criminal justice system. Their union was different also because it was fast and furious. It took them by surprise. When something is that powerful, and when two deeply thoughtful otherwise cautious people feel it, the result transcends the research.

Sitting on a folding chair on the lawn watching the ceremony, Cheryl Cunio took pictures on her iPhone. She would share them with Sterling when she next saw him in the visiting room at the penitentiary. Theirs was a different kind of union altogether. They had gotten married fifteen years before. She was, in the parlance of a mostly hidden subculture of women who are married to incarcerated men, an "MWI." This stands for Marries While Incarcerated, a woman who meets her mate after he is already behind bars. This distinguishes her from an "MBI," Married Before Incarceration, a woman whose marriage predates the incarceration of her spouse.

Thanks to a headline-grabbing bestseller, *Women Who Love Men Who Kill*, there is an entrenched narrative about women who are attracted to, and marry, men who do bad things. A national sensation back when it was first published in 1991 (an updated edition was published in 2021), featured on CNN, the *Today* show, MSNBC, *Good Morning America*, 20/20, Fox News, and NPR, the book declared that women who were attracted to killers in prison were "universally damaged." The author, Sheila Isenberg, explained it this way to an interviewer: "They've been sexually abused, psychologically, emotionally abused. These are women who've been hurt. In their earlier lives they've been abused either by their parents, their fathers, their first husbands, their boyfriends. When you're in a relationship with a man in prison, he's in prison. He's not going to hurt you. He can't hurt you. So you're always in a state of control because you're the one who's on the outside." In other words, women who married men in prison were emotionally and psychologically scarred control freaks.

The noted New Zealand psychologist John Money had considered such women so psychologically damaged that, back in the 1950s, he had declared the attraction a mental illness for which he coined the term "hybristophilia." Sandra L. Brown, referred to as a pioneer in the field of pathological love relationships (and author of *Women Who Love Psychopaths*) focused on the role of the men and the methods they used to seduce and lure unsuspecting women. Her take on this was that the women who loved such men were either duped or self-deluded (believing their love could redeem the psychopath)—or both. The verdict seemed to be that MWIs were damaged and deranged or messiah-complex control freaks or pitiful victims. MBIs, on the other hand, were self-sacrificing, celibate saints who had given up a normal life to stand by their man.

In fact, the reasons women marry or stay married to men behind bars are as diverse, quirky, openhearted, misguided, optimistic, rational, irrational, well considered, and impulsive as the reasons women marry and stay married to men in the free world. Many women who marry incarcerated men simply—although there is nothing simple about it—fall in love with them. The sociologist Megan Comfort interviewed dozens of women married or involved with inmates and found little pathology or victimhood involved. The women she profiled in her clear-eyed but compassionate book, *Doing Time Together*, were not attracted to the "bad boy," not attracted to the thrill of risky choices, but rather quite the opposite. The women she interviewed were attracted to what we would consider these men's "feminine" qualities. The men were thoughtful and communicative. They were listeners. They were interested in establishing and nurturing a lasting emotional relationship (a sexual relationship not being possible, not now and maybe never). They were interested in finding a soul mate not a bedmate.

This was the story of Sterling and Cheryl.

———————

Cheryl never knew anyone who was in trouble. No one in her family had ever had a brush with the law. There was no swearing at home, no drinking, no drugs. She was in her mid-twenties living in Colorado, working at a T-Mobile collections call center at a job she despised but was good at. Her best friend told her she was corresponding with someone in prison. It was an assignment for a college class. Cheryl thought that would be a nice thing to do, to reach out to someone, to learn about a life so different than her own. She googled "prison pen pals," and scrolling through the profiles, she found one that was particularly well written. The guy seemed very respectful. He was looking for a friend, not a girlfriend. His name was Sterling Cunio. When she first wrote to him in November 2003 she was so cautious that she used a fake name. And she didn't use her own address. She rented a PO box.

They started corresponding. Men in prison often write long letters. And as Megan Comfort discovered when she explored these relationships, they often communicate in a reflective, emotionally resonant way that can be unexpected. Sterling and Cheryl wrote to each other about family and friendship, about books and music and poetry, about beliefs and principles. He was careful with his words. He never gave an easy answer. She thought he was smart, and not just book smart. He was only two years older than she was, but he seemed wise about the world, about people, about himself. She'd never met anyone like him. She knew why he was in prison—a quick internet search early on told the tale—but she compartmentalized that knowledge. She knew that she wouldn't be able to correspond with him, to get to know him, to admit that she was beginning to like him, if she thought about the crime. He didn't talk about it, not in those early days, and she didn't ask.

Four months into the correspondence, they spoke on the phone for the first time. That cracked open a door that opened wider and wider with each conversation. They talked weekly, then several times a week, then almost daily. At twenty-four, she had had a few serious relationships, but this one was different. She had to see where it might go. She needed to meet him in person. And so, eight months after that first exchange of letters, she got in her car—enlisting her mother to come along—and drove twelve hundred miles west. She had never set foot in a prison before. She was terrified. But she was even more terrified that their relationship wouldn't survive an in-person encounter. Maybe he would take one look at her and decide...no. Maybe she would realize how crazy this whole thing was. That's not what happened.

She drove or flew out to visit him six more times before deciding to leave her job, her family, and her home to be with him. "With him" meant weekend prison visits, but that was only for the short term. Back then they both thought he would be getting out within a year or two. He had had a positive ruling from the courts. It looked good. In fact, he was optimistic enough about his future to propose marriage. And she was optimistic enough to accept. They married in late April 2006, standing next to each other on the worn linoleum floor of the visitors' room at the penitentiary. She wore slacks and a white blazer. He wore prison blues. His hair was plaited in cornrows; hers was thick, black, waist length. There were no decorations, no flowers, no music, no friends to share the moment, no photographer to capture the event. Her mother and sister were there as witnesses. She had never dreamed of a big fancy wedding like some girls do. Whatever she had imagined, though, was not this.

The minister, a Christian counselor who had known Sterling as a youth, came in to officiate. When he intoned the word "God" in the vows, Cheryl and Sterling—neither of whom was a believer—looked at each other and whispered "Jah," the Rastafarian word for the higher being. It was a spontaneous moment, a magical moment. Cheryl thought how very lucky she was to be marrying this amazing man.

In all the years since, they have never seen each other outside the prison walls. In the visitors' room or, on a warm day, in a chain-link-fenced outdoor area, they can talk. They are permitted a hug and a kiss, as long as the guards watching over them do not deem the encounter "excessive." If so, Sterling can be written up. On one visit Cheryl had extended her wrist for Sterling to smell the brown sugar lotion she was wearing. The guard saw it and wrote up Sterling for an infraction.

Sterling says now that, had he known he'd still be behind bars seventeen years after their wedding day, he never would have proposed. Cheryl says that, had she known, she would have married him anyway.

CHAPTER 15

Catherine was twenty-eight when she and Navy Senior Chief Ramous Fleming exchanged vows in a small chapel in west central Florida. The chapel was inside the Hernando Correctional Institution, the women's prison that housed Catherine. Fleming was dressed in his officer's khakis, insignias and five rows of ribbons above the right pocket, a compact, well-built man with a shaved head and fashionable three-day stubble. Catherine, her smile radiant, her makeup perfect, wore shapeless pull-on blue pants with a white stripe down the leg and a short-sleeved blue shirt. Her prison blues matched her eyeshadow.

Catherine became, on that day, an MWI. But the research, the stories, the podcasts, the one-off documentaries that explored the motivations and psyches of those who Married While Incarcerated were not about people like Catherine. They were not about women behind bars and the men who chose to marry them. They were all about free-world women choosing convict husbands. Maybe we don't hear about women like Catherine because women make up only about 10 percent of the incarcerated population and thus are (legitimately) less of a focus. Maybe it's because, as the feminist school of criminology argued back in the late 1960s, criminology research—like so much other social science and science research—routinely focuses on men with the "add women and stir" approach.

But marriage is a deeply gendered institution, both in the free and incarcerated worlds. Love notwithstanding, men marry women for different reasons than women marry men, and in general men expect different things from a marriage than do women. It is also true that, as a group, incarcerated women are significantly different from their male counterparts, which could easily have an impact on MWI unions. The ACLU has estimated that as many as 60 percent of women in prison have histories of physical or sexual abuse, as Catherine did. Rates of drug addiction and suicide attempts are higher among incarcerated women than men. Also, according to figures compiled by the Bureau of Justice Statistics, an estimated 70 percent of incarcerated women are mothers. These gender-specific characteristics combine to make imprisoned women less desirable—and more risky—as marriage partners. And it may be that men do not go in search of mates who could not, and might never, share their bed.

Yet, one day in 2011, a career Navy officer sent a letter to a twenty-six-year-old woman who had been behind bars since she was thirteen. The way the story goes, as reported by *Florida Today*, is that Ray Fleming, serving aboard the aircraft carrier USS *Enterprise* in the Persian Gulf, was spending off-duty hours entertaining himself by scrolling through crime stories from his home state of Florida. A "self-professed crime news junkie," he came across the stories of the crime Catherine and her brother had committed more than a dozen years before. They were famous not as much for the murder as for being the youngest murderers ever to be tried and sentenced as adults. There was no dearth of coverage. Catherine's story touched him, he told a journalist many years later. He couldn't get it out of his head. But he didn't act on his—was it curiosity?—until a few years later when, searching for the story again, he chanced upon a video *Florida Today* had produced back in 2009. In between images of police documents and newspaper headlines and archival photos of a very young girl in handcuffs and a tract house cordoned off with yellow police tape, there was a video of Catherine, who was twenty-four at the time. She sat with shoulders squared her hands clasped on the bare table in front of her, dressed in prison blues—the same institutional uniform she would wear on her wedding day. She was wearing no makeup. Her hair was limp and appeared to be not recently washed. She looked directly at the camera. She was almost startlingly articulate and undeniably compelling. Not rehearsed, not glib. Not self-serving. She was a young woman looking straight at you telling a story. She lost control twice, but only briefly, her voice thickening, her hand sweeping away a tear, when she talked about not seeing her younger brother for more than a decade. Once, imagining what she might do when she got out—she mentioned how excited she would be to wear heels—she smiled. She had a dazzling smile. She was beautiful.

Whatever it was that Ray Fleming felt when he watched that video, the result was that he sat down and wrote a letter to Catherine. Later he told a reporter that her story had piqued his interest and that he "wanted to be pen pals." He was, he said, "fascinated." She responded to that letter, and he to hers, and a correspondence was born. They learned about each other via mail and, although he said "it never crossed my mind that it would happen," they began a courtship of words. What he saw in Catherine was a smart, determined, resilient woman with a clear understanding of what mattered and what didn't. Her home life, her crime, the first decade of her imprisonment had scarred and toughened her, had numbed her. But she had found a path through it, and the person she had become was someone with an open heart. What Catherine saw in Ray was, as she put it, "the complete opposite of every male figure I knew." She meant this as a compliment, but that bar was low, very low, set by the two other male figures who had played significant roles in her life: her father, a wife-batterer who had shot someone in a bar fight; and her uncle who lived in that tract house that was later cordoned off with police tape, the man who forced oral sex on her, the one who had masturbated in front of her when she was taking a shower. Ray was decidedly not that kind of man. He was solid and loyal, sweet and attentive, a "true Christian man." Since her spiritual awakening in prison, faith had been at the core of her life.

They wrote for close to two years, slowly getting to know each other the way that letters—long, honest letters—make possible. There was nothing whirlwind about this courtship. After many letters, there were phone calls and then, finally, when his duties in the Navy made it possible, in-person visits. By that time, they were in love. Their first meeting in the prison's visiting room, described by an imaginative newspaper reporter as a "display that rivaled Disney's nightly pyrotechnic extravaganza," was if not demonstrably explosive (given the venue, it could not be) then certainly momentous. Soon there were plans to marry. On their wedding day, November 27, 2013, she was twenty-eight and, although she didn't know it yet, one year and nine months away from release. He was forty. She had, in the words of that imaginative reporter, found her Prince Charming.

As it turned out, the reporter was not being overly fanciful. Fleming did consider himself a savior of a damsel in distress. "There's a lot she has to learn," he is quoted as saying in anticipation of Catherine's release. "There will certainly be a lot of adjusting to do, but I look forward to it," adding that his military training had prepared him for the challenge. Catherine fully understood the challenge of rejoining the world. "I am completely clueless," she admitted to a reporter. "I'll leave prison as clueless as I was at thirteen." She knew she would have to learn the basics of living adult life, from getting her first phone and jumping into a tech-dominated world to opening a bank account and getting insurance. She would have to learn to drive. She would need to find a job. She had never gone grocery shopping. "The idea of being completely dependent on others to teach me these basic things is not appealing," she went on to say.

But her Prince Charming wanted to be that teacher. In fact, in anticipation of her release, he set in motion his retirement from the Navy. If he remained on active duty, he would have to go on another deployment at sea. "I don't want to leave her alone," he said.

She was not alone the day she got out of prison. But she was not with her husband. By circumstance, they were separated from the beginning. Catherine was released in Florida but she was on a plane to Kansas the next day to reunite with her mother. Ray was stationed in Virginia waiting to be discharged. They could have figured out how to make it work. But Catherine almost immediately realized that she didn't want to make it work. Her decision to walk away from the marriage, to reject her husband before she even experienced married life, was in some ways the act of a child, the thirteen-year-old she was when she went to prison. It was almost like she was dumping her eighth-grade boyfriend: abrupt, almost heartless. But it was also the opposite. It was the act of a woman struggling to come into her own, a woman just awakening to the promise—the headiness—of independence. Her family had not been in favor of the marriage. They thought that her husband, thirteen years her senior, was not going to give her the opportunity to make her own choices. And that's how Catherine felt too once she left prison behind. Here she was, free. It came as a revelation: She did not want to be tied down. She did not want someone to take care of her. She wanted to learn how to take care of herself. But she was married to a man whose next duty assignment seemed to be attending to and overseeing her life. She had strong feelings for Ray and respected him. We should have dated, really dated, first, she thought. If we had met at a different phase, a different time, we might have made it. But stepping directly from prison into marriage was not what she wanted, or needed. She asked Ray for a divorce. He refused, perhaps believing that, with time, she would change her mind.

She didn't.

She met Damon in Kansas. A year and a half older than Catherine, he'd been in and out of jail much of his life, battling addiction and, as it is called in the psychotherapeutic world, "anger management issues." He had fathered four children. It didn't appear to be the healthiest of matches. In fact, it fit neatly in the category of "assortative mate." But their incarceration histories created a bond, and there was a special kind of energy they generated together. They both wanted fresh starts. They both wanted new lives. They both felt they had a mission, maybe even a calling. They were, at the moment, minimum-wage burger-slingers, but they started talking about how they could help people like themselves, or rather people younger than they were now—youth who had grown up "in the system," who were, as they both had been, at risk. The conversations were lively and empowering. And beyond that, there was no denying that he was a burly, good-looking guy with a big smile. And she was a young woman who wanted to have a boyfriend.

She soon had something more than that. She and Damon got pregnant within months. The exuberance of a new relationship—her first real romance—the ticking of her thirty-year-old female biological clock, her deep psychological need to create the sweet, innocent childhood she never had...the pregnancy was not surprising. What was surprising is that when she told her husband that she and Damon were expecting a child, Ray continued to refuse to grant her a divorce. Her son was born in August 2016. "You were the beginning of my redemption journey," she wrote when she posted a photo of them selfie-smooching. "You are my motivation, inspiration, my energetic ball of awesomeness." When she quickly got pregnant a second time, Ray finally agreed to the divorce. Almost exactly twelve months after the birth of her son, a daughter was born. She was Damon's child, but she looked exactly like Catherine. She called her "my mini-me" and "the better version of me" and lavished all the attention on her and her brother that she never had as a child. She dubbed herself "Mommy Extraordinaire," and that wasn't an exaggeration.

Catherine was not interested in marrying Damon, but they lived together, mostly amiably. They moved across the country together, started their nonprofit and parented the two babies, but the relationship began to fall apart. Catherine's yet-to-be-quenched desire to make it on her own; the complications of his previous life and four children; the heavy psychological baggage they both carried. It was complicated. They went through a stormy breakup, but they both knew enough about anger and broken families and children caught in the crossfire to mend what needed to be mended. As Catherine posted later, when the dust settled: "What the Devil meant for bad, God turned into our great. We decided that in spite of our personal pain and feelings, we would always put our children first." They would coparent. They would work to build a new kind of friendship. They would celebrate holidays together. They would go on vacations together. But she would take care of herself by herself. She would finally step into her own life.

———————

While Catherine was in prison missing out on her adolescence, her teens, and her twenties, other girls her age were out in the free world living those years. She emerged from behind bars "asynchronous," like Belinda had, out of step with her age cohort. That may have fueled her marriage inside to a man she never was able to date, her quick connection to Damon, her pregnancies. There was much catching up to do. She fast-tracked herself. Trevor also emerged from prison asynchronous. He was a year older than Catherine when he got out, a thirty-one-year-old man who had gone inside as an adolescent. Like Catherine, he spent his growing-up and coming-of-age years behind bars. And like Catherine, he had one day, well into his twenties, out of the blue, received a letter in prison from a stranger.

The stranger was a young woman named Loraine, barely out of her teens, in college and trying to decide what direction her studies should take. She was interested in psychology and thought she might like to work inside a prison. She was especially drawn to the idea of working with juvenile offenders, people like Trevor, like Catherine. In a book she was reading, *Inside the Mind of a Teen Killer*, she found interviews and lists of names. She wrote letters to fifteen of those people, adults who had gone to prison as kids. *I want to get to know who you are today after growing up in the system. And who were you when you went in? Who do you want to be now?* she asked them in that introductory letter. She told them, bluntly, that she was not interested in "a relationship" but rather in learning from their experiences. The last of the fifteen letters she wrote was to Trevor. She hesitated about that one. He was the only one on her list who lived in the same state as she did, a mere hour away. She thought that might be risky. She was not interested in actual contact, in even the possibility of visiting.

If she was hesitant, so was Trevor. At first he was concerned that she might have been a student in one of the Inside-Out classes he had taken. Those were university classes taught in the prison. Half of those enrolled were traditional undergrads who were escorted in once a week with the professor; half were prisoners. It was against the rules to communicate outside of the class experience, and Trevor played by the rules. When he found out she had not been an Inside-Out student, he was still hesitant. He had had a prison relationship that began with letters, and the experience had taught him about the extraordinary stress it puts on both people. But he was at a point in his incarceration—he was then about fifteen years into his thirty-year sentence—and in his own understanding of the prison system that he was open to opportunities to share perspectives. Through workshops and classes on restorative justice, he was gaining new awareness. If corresponding with Loraine would give him the chance to have such discussions with an outsider, and if that correspondence could help humanize the incarcerated population for this young woman, he would do it.

Their letters back and forth were about school, psychology,

the realities of incarceration, prison reform. He was educating her. In one letter he gently corrected her use of "inmate"—a term many incarcerated people equate with those committed to mental institutions. Refer to us as "prisoners," he counseled. Meanwhile, as they exchanged letters, much was happening in their own separate lives. Trevor had learned that he was eligible to apply for a Second Look hearing that might result in early release. There was much to think about, to talk about, to strategize with his attorneys. Loraine, too, was living a complicated life. She had been engaged when she first started writing to her many pen pals. Then she suffered a devastating breakup that fueled depression and anxiety so troubling that she checked herself into an inpatient facility for a week. While there, she encountered a seriously mentally ill man who later threatened her, stalked her, and, violating the court order she had taken out against him, came onto her father's property and shot through the windows of the house. She and her father barely escaped. Loraine referred to it as "my near-death experience." The man then shot himself, committing suicide in their backyard.

And so, for reasons that could not be more different, they began to meet in person during visiting hours at the prison. Trevor had some hope for release and could now allow himself to think about sustainable outside relationships. Loraine had just gone through the most challenging and disturbing experience in her life and now wanted to, as she put it, "take full advantage of being alive." Plus, she felt that because of his own history, Trevor would understand what she'd just lived through. Trevor really listened. He was caring, reliable, levelheaded, smart. People like this are hard to find anywhere, she thought to herself. It was weird, and she knew it, but she was finding solace—maybe more than solace—in this most unlikely place with this most unlikely man.

Meanwhile, Trevor was consciously tamping down any spark he might be feeling. He was a focused, analytical man with very little real-world experience. He was also a logical guy. What, he asked himself, is the likelihood that a person who writes you out of the blue will be the person you spend the rest of your life with? And, he asked himself, how can I think about a relationship when my life is in flux? A Second Look hearing was pending, but how long would it take for it to be scheduled, and would the hearing be successful? He had no idea how much longer he'd be in prison. It could be a roller-coaster ride through the criminal justice system. Did he want to burden her with this?

Some things, love being one of them, are not about logic, however.

For Loraine the moment came during one of their now-frequent visits when they stood next to each other posing for a prison photographer. It was common to have these photos taken and then given to the men as mementos. She remembered that they put their arms around each other to pose—there were very few opportunities for sanctioned physical contact in the visitors' room—and she felt electricity. She knew it was trite. She knew it was cheesy. But it was real. That electric jolt. She fell for him.

Not long afterward, Trevor invited her into the prison for one of the yearly banquets sponsored by prison clubs. It could have been the Lifers' Unlimited Club or it could have been the Athletic Club. Trevor was a member of both. These banquet events were opportunities for the men to invite a person from their approved and vetted visitors list to join them upstairs on the activities floor where long tables were set up to dispense whatever fast food—pizza was the favorite—the club had purchased from an outside vendor. To the men, any nonprison food was a banquet. When Loraine walked up to Trevor, they hugged briefly, which was now a usual greeting. But when she moved back, he kept holding her. "May I?" he asked. Before she answered, he kissed her. Throughout the banquet, they held hands. There was no talk about dating. What would dating mean in this context anyway? But they both knew, from that evening, that they were a couple.

Trevor did get his Second Look hearing, but it took almost two years. Based on the criteria for early release and his extraordinary record in prison, he walked out the gate after serving seventeen years. His parole restrictions were Draconian, but the couple made it work, slowly navigating their way toward a sustainable relationship. They had written and talked for years, but they had to learn how to interact outside the visiting room, how to be a couple. He found employment. She continued taking college classes. They tried to settle in, but their life together was tenuous. Hanging over their heads was the state's threat to appeal Trevor's release, a threat they made good on when, sixteen days shy of his first year of freedom, Trevor was rearrested. He spent the next twelve weeks locked up in county jail while the lawyers fought it out.

Released again, this time for good, he could now allow himself to make big plans for the future. He asked Loraine's father for "permission" to marry—a nod to traditionalism that he felt compelled to make. Her family had been slow to accept him. He fully understood why, and he knew, they both knew, that some members of her large Irish-Catholic family might never accept him. It was important, he thought, to take it slow, to build trust, to show his good intentions. He waited for just the right moment to propose: a day trip to the beach. He had the ring in his pocket. She knew he had the ring, and he knew she knew. She said yes.

Vicki also said yes. It was Christmas, about a year since she'd gotten out of prison for the fifth time. She had a just-inked tattoo on the inside of her left forearm. Underneath a stylized Hindu lotus design was the word *cuimhnich*, Gaelic for "to commemorate," "to not forget." Under that were three names: Jason, Steve, Jessica. Jason was the child she had given birth to a few months before she met Steve, before she flagged him down on the street, he astride a motorcycle, she high on acid. Jessica was the child she and Steve had eight years later. Vicki had wanted to get that tattoo for a long time. She waited until she was sure she could stay clean and sober. She had gotten clean and sober in prison, five times, and four times, within months, she was back on drugs again. This time was different. She was positive. If life was not perfect—employment was touch and go; she was estranged from her daughter who was not clean and sober—then at least it was livable. She was taking legal drugs prescribed by a clinic doctor who monitored her: an Adderall variant for the ADHD she had attempted to self-medicate with meth; an opioid agonist that relieved her heroin cravings without producing a high. The combination was working. She could do this. She *was* doing it.

This was one of the few Christmases she and Steve had spent in each other's company. They had been "together" for thirty-three years, but for twenty-one of those Vicki had been behind bars—weeks and months cycling in and out of county jails, hard time in state prison, even harder time in a federal penitentiary. Each time she came back to Steve. Each time he was there. The homecomings might begin well enough. All the right words were said—at least by Vicki; Steve didn't talk much—but soon she was lying to him about where she was, which was in some apartment shooting up. And then she was stealing to support the habit, sometimes from him, sometimes from mailboxes, later more sophisticated schemes. And so it went.

All relationships are, on some level, mysterious. But this one was close to unfathomable. Why did she return, time and again, to a disengaged and distant man who didn't really know who she was? Why did he support a woman who could not stay off drugs or out of prison? Was it classic codependence, one person the caretaker and the other person the advantage-taker? He did provide the house, and she did take advantage of that. But he did not provide emotional support, which is not uncommon in reentry relationships. This was how one recently released woman put it when interviewed for the *On the Outside: Prison Reentry and Reintegration* study:

> Interviewer: Do you feel like your [boyfriend is] supportive for you? Can you talk to him, share issues, concerns, stuff like that?

> What man do that?

> Interviewer: I don't know. Some do.

> Oh. Some you know?

Vicki provided whatever warmth or emotional life there was in the relationship, and he took advantage of that. So they were both caregivers and advantage-takers. He was a quiet, withdrawn man—Vicki thought he was on the spectrum—who may not have wanted or needed a full-time relationship. He had his motorcycle. He had his dirt bike. He had his job. Perhaps that sustained him during those long stretches when Vicki was absent. She had acclimated herself to prison. She was comfortable in that culture, more comfortable inside than out. She had issues. It is entirely possible that neither one of them knew what a healthy relationship was. And that may have been bond enough. That and Jessica, their daughter who lived in a van or on the street and put a needle in her arm every day.

It was Christmas. Among the gift-wrapped boxes under the scrawny tabletop tree on the kitchen counter, there was one big box. Steve said to open that one last. Inside the big box was a smaller box, and inside that a smaller one, and then an even smaller one. The final box was small enough to hold in the palm of her hand. She opened it. Inside was a ring with a little diamond. Vicki was not often speechless. In fact, she talked a lot. And fast. But she just stared at the ring. She knew what it meant, of course, but she never expected this day to happen. Not after three decades. And Steve was neither romantic nor even attentive. He broke the silence. "So," he said, his voice a monotone, "you wanna get married?"

She did. She didn't know how much she did until he asked. Later they would talk about plans. Or rather, she would talk. "I don't care where," she told him. "I just want it to be warm. I want it to be outside, and I want to be barefoot." They could wait for summer. Or they could go to Las Vegas. She liked that idea. Vegas it was.

And then she messed up. Big time.

CHAPTER 16

Vicki tells me everything in a rush, her thoughts tangled, words tripping over each other. And I think to myself, *She's on meth again. This is meth talking.* She says her son got into a car accident on the freeway, got a ticket for reckless driving, had his car impounded, owes hundreds of dollars in fees that he can't afford, and if he doesn't have a car, he can't get to work or go to school. And this is the kid who was doing well. Her daughter is using, she says, either again or still, it's not clear. She was in rehab and now isn't. She is living who knows where. She might be with this guy she was arrested with awhile back, the arrest that landed her in the same prison as her mother. Or maybe she's with someone else now. She is not answering Vicki's texts.

I want to ask about Steve, who seems to be the constant in her chaotic life, but Vicki is already on to something else. She lost her job, she says in a rush. This isn't the job she had when she first got out, a part-time gig organizing racks of vintage costumes in a warehouse. And it isn't the one she had after that, a few shifts a week at a twenty-four-hour convenience store. This is—or was—a job at a bakery that sold gluten-free pies to local grocery stores. She told me about this job before, how she loved the work but hated the "drama:" the run-ins with fellow workers, personality issues, sniping, backstabbing, problems with the boss who she thought didn't know how to run a business. And was a sexist. She had ideas to improve the product, but no one listened. Vicki says she was fired not long ago when business slowed down. But really, she says, she was fired because "I'm not a yes-girl. And I'll never be a yes-girl." This is pre-COVID-19. No one has even heard of COVID-19, although a few months from now it will be the only thing anyone talks about. But at the moment, unemployment rates are at an all-time low. Jobs are plentiful. Or rather, jobs are plentiful elsewhere, but not in the working-class, rural community she lives in—a community that has barely clawed its way out of the 2008 recession. And jobs are never plentiful for an ex-felon. Getting that full-time bakery gig, which actually used a skill she had learned in prison, had been a big win. She was proud of that job.

The story continues. She goes into the local unemployment office to sign up for benefits, and her claim is denied. She hadn't worked at the job long enough. They told her she needed to have worked there a year to get benefits. "But I was in prison," she says, her voice cracking. "How was I supposed to have been working at an outside job when I was in prison?" Now she is out of work, out of money. Her kids are messing up. Her life looks on the brink—and not of something good.

When we talk again a few days later, she tells me she now has a new job, something having to do with the census. I ask her if she'll be going door-to-door. She says no, that this job involves traveling. Where, I ask? She doesn't answer right away, which is odd because she rarely entertains silence in a conversation. Finally she says all she knows is that she'll be "on the road." To do what? I ask. She doesn't seem to know. She says she'll tell me more about it later. She'll get me her schedule in a few days. Maybe she will be traveling up to where I live, and we can get together.

Several weeks go by without a word from Vicki. She's busy with this new job, I think. Good for her. Then another week passes. I text a few times and get no response. Another week passes. And then I forget all about Vicki. There's news of a soon-to-be-named new virus, with people reported sick and dying in China, France, Italy, Iran, Brazil, and then the United States. There's an outbreak, the first of what will be countless others, in Seattle, where I was scheduled to teach. I cancel the trip. The virus spreads. Life changes, at first slowly, then with dizzying speed. People are hoarding toilet paper and baking sourdough bread.

Two months after Vicki told me about her new job with the census, I get an email from the head of the mentorship program at the reentry nonprofit that connected me and Vicki, who writes that Vicki wanted me to know that she has a new phone number. I feel an odd chill. People don't change their phone numbers for no reason. And why wouldn't she just reach out to me directly?

I immediately text the new number: "Is everything okay?"

"Can I call you?" she texts back. I'm in the middle of something. I ask if I can call her in an hour.

"Yes, call me."

When I make the call, the connection is so bad that I can't hear what she is saying. Her voice cuts in and out. But I can hear the tone of her voice. She is scared. She is just holding it together. But I don't know what "it" is. In between the static, I hear her say that she is "in the middle of nowhere." Then we lose the connection. I call again. This time, right before the line goes dead again,

I hear her say that she'll be somewhere with a better connection, a truck stop, in a half hour or so and will call me back.

I am sitting in my car in the rain when the call comes. "I did something very stupid," she says. No preamble. "I did something very, very stupid." There is a catch in her voice. "I made a very bad mistake," she says. I want to know, but I don't want to know. When you reclaim your life after twenty years in and out of prison, when you get clean after a lifetime of drug abuse, it is a fragile life you are living. But Vicki seemed to be doing pretty well. She had a home and a man who stuck by her. She was in the health-care system, getting the right meds for her ADHD and to ease the heroin withdrawal. She had a new job, a government job. It was temporary, like all the new hires for the census, but it was not some minimum-wage sinkhole like her other employment.

"I threw it all away," she says, sobbing. Vicki has told me many things, many sad and bad things, but she has never before sobbed. I've seen her cry. I've seen the tears. I have never *heard* her cry. She cries for a while.

Then she starts to tell me what happened. She was at a friend's house a few weeks ago, and there was, she says, a "quantity of drugs" there. The friend, or maybe it was a friend of that friend—when Vicki tells a story, she goes off on tangents that are hard to follow—says that they needed someone they could trust to sell the drugs. And Vicki says she will.

Just like that.

As far as I know, Vicki had never sold drugs before. She used drugs, but her crimes, at least the ones I know she served time for, were identity theft and forgery, stealing credit cards, paper crimes. But she had just been fired from the bakery job. Her application for unemployment benefits had been denied. Still, she had a home, and her boyfriend, now fiancé, was employed. So she couldn't have been desperate for money. She answers my unasked question. "I don't know why I said yes." Now she is sobbing again, unable to continue. I listen to her weep. After a while she says, "It's like, in a second, I reverted to my criminal way of thinking...without thinking."

———————

Vicki may not know why she said yes in that moment, but the literature of criminology provides clues. What she thought of as a thoughtless split-second decision might well have been the cumulative effect of being triggered. All around her, for months and months, were reminders of her previous life. From the rooms in her house to the streets of her town, the riverbank she walked collecting rocks, the convenience store she stopped in to pick up a cup of coffee—they were all "prompts," conscious or unconscious, to remember and reexperience the past. Each was a temptation, an invitation. Researchers have identified these as environmental stimuli that trigger what they call a "cue-reactivity process." How many times can you be cued before you respond? She could resist, be strong willed, for only so long. And then there were her old friends, her street family, the ones who had long been part of her criminal life. She saw them. They hung out where they always hung out. She didn't really know anyone else, and making new friends, as an ex-felon, was an uncomfortable prospect. She had talked to me about the difficulty of navigating relationships. When do you tell someone who doesn't know you about your past? And how do you tell them? And what do you risk by telling them? Or by not telling them? "I'm not ashamed of where I've come from," she said to me once. "But that doesn't mean I want everyone to know." So those casual get-to-know-you conversations that people have when they are reaching out to others were not so casual for Vicki. It was easier to stick with the people who knew her.

And then there is what prolific researcher and criminologist Shadd Maruna called the "doomed to deviance" narrative. It is the story some ex-offenders tell themselves. In his work tracing the lives of those who had successfully reentered and those who had not, he found that repeat offenders were "not so much committed to a criminal lifestyle as they were resigned to it." Ironically, he found that those who committed new crimes had a realistic view of their prospects and the challenges they faced. He concluded that, in reoffending, they found a kind of psychological shelter. "Intentionally failing may be less stressful on a person's ego than trying to succeed and failing anyway." Did Vicki think she was doomed to deviance?

Her drug addiction had been treated, maybe even successfully. But what caused it had not been. That kind of counseling was unavailable to her, and it took a lifetime. As one of the *On the Outside* researchers who tracked those reentering noted about a subject who seemed to be doing well and then faltered, "under the surface, things were beginning to unravel." For Vicki, the surface was not that smooth anyway. The job loss was a blow. Her children were not doing well.

She took the drugs from her friend and peddled them for a week and a half. Then the cops showed up at her door. She doesn't say that they had a warrant. She says that they "came and kicked in the door." They found "a lot" of drugs in the house. I don't ask what kind. It doesn't matter. This next part of the story, told rapid-fire with Vicki's signature combination of sidetracking and dead-ending, doesn't quite make sense. She says the cops did not arrest her. They did not take her down to the police station and charge her with possession or intent to sell. She thinks it was because she told them she would give up her supplier. But even as she promised, she knew she wouldn't.

"I could never do that," she tells me. For a minute I think it is the "honor among thieves" thing, but then she says, "If I told, these people would go after my family. They would hurt my family." After the cops leave, she begins making plans. All the thinking she should have done before saying yes to selling drugs she does now. She finds out, anonymously, from a local criminal defense attorney's office, how much time she would be facing if convicted. With the quantity and type of drugs found at her house, with her history of criminal convictions and—to top it off—with the proximity of her house to a school, she is told that she would face a mandatory minimum of ten years. "I can't do ten years," she tells me. "I know what I can do, and I cannot do ten years."

I shouldn't say it, but it comes out before I can stop: "And you didn't think about this before you said yes?"

"I know, I know. I blew it. I completely blew it. I ruined my whole life in a split second, that second I said yes. Everything I worked for. It's gone."

I have heard this awful lament before. One of the men in the prison writing group I facilitated lashed out in anger, fueled by alcohol and jealousy, his reptilian brain temporarily in command, and committed a terrible crime more than thirty years ago. In that second, he ended two lives, one of them being his own. Belinda, with no premeditation, had grabbed a knife and stabbed her pimp, changing the trajectory of her life for the next twenty-two years.

Vicki's plan was to skip town. She had not been officially

charged, and she wasn't going to wait to see what happened. She had not yet been contacted to give up the name of her supplier, and she wasn't going to wait for that either. She says there's a statute of limitations on a warrant, should one be issued, of two years. If she can just "disappear" for two years, she will be able to come back home and be clear. She seems certain about this. She tells me that she spent the week after the cops broke in staying out of sight and making plans. As part of those plans, she concocts this fiction about getting a job, one that involves travel.

"What I told you about that census job?" she says. "That was all a lie." There is no job. There never was a job. She made it up to explain, at least temporarily, to friends and family, why she would be taking off. And then she left. She is on the road. She is calling me from some truck stop somewhere. "My family doesn't know. No one knows," she says.

But now I know. And I do not want to know anything more. If I know, I can be asked. If I am asked, I will need to tell.

"You need to go back and turn yourself in," I say, knowing that she won't, but knowing this is what I should say. "If you tell them that you can't make good on your promise to give up the distributor because you are afraid for your safety or your family's safety...they've got to understand that, right? They'll do something." I don't know what I'm talking about, of course. What I know about things like this comes from watching cop shows on television.

"No," she says. "I can't go back. I won't go back. I just have to manage to keep out of sight for two years." I try to dissuade her again, telling her how increasingly difficult it will be to move around now that state after state is instituting stay-at-home edicts, telling people they should leave their homes only for essential purposes, maybe even enforcing restricted movement by patrolling. We are in the first awful rush of the pandemic. But she thinks the pandemic will help her. "I'm not gonna be a priority for anyone," she says. "No one's gonna come looking for me. There's too much else going on." She is probably right.

I can't know where she is or where she is going. But I want to know that she is safe. "You have someplace to be, right?" I ask. "You're not just wandering?"

"Yes, I have someplace."

I tell her to be safe. Then I delete all our text messages from my phone and block her new number. If I am asked, I don't want to have anything to tell.

CHAPTER 17

From the fourth floor of the prison, Sterling stands by the barred window staring at the yellow hydrant. The last time Sterling had been out in the world, on a city street like the one he could see off in the distance, the movie *Shawshank Redemption* was playing in theatres. It was the story of a man sentenced to life in prison for committing two murders, just as Sterling had been that year, 1994.

Sterling would never refer to his cell as his "house," as others did, nor would he think of the penitentiary, the ten acres surrounded by the twenty-five-foot concrete wall, as his "community." To him that would be an act of surrender. It would mean giving up not just his identity as someone other than a prisoner. It would mean giving up a sense of his personal agency, the severely battered but persistent idea he held to that he might have control of his own life someday. That he too might touch the hydrant. He had been working toward that day for almost a decade, his complicated legal case alternately inching forward and plummeting backward. Meanwhile, he continued to live what he could make of the only life he had. Ironically, the work that he did, his prison employment, was in some ways more productive and more meaningful than what many were engaged in outside the walls.

Sterling's job as the chapel clerk was, in the context of the world of the prison, a plum position. He had responsibility. He had some autonomy. His work made a difference. His bosses—the Buddhist chaplain and the rabbi—respected him. But possibly more important than all of that was the fact that he was able to work in a small, private, very quiet office space. This was an extraordinary luxury, and he knew it.

He was in charge of the monthly schedule for all that happened within the prison chapel's domain. Thirty-four different religious groups were recognized inside. All of them had something planned—services, events, meetings, support groups, special projects—maybe not every week but often enough so that Sterling had to juggle as many as 220 different events each month. He scheduled time and space, both of which could be logistical nightmares. There were very few spaces in the entire prison, and only two up in the chapel area, that could accommodate groups of any size. Those spaces, when they were found, needed to accommodate the needs of the event, from chairs, tables, podiums, whiteboards, and microphones to urns of weak prison coffee and stacks of Styrofoam cups for those events fortunate enough to include such extravagance. The events had to be scheduled when there was sufficient staff to monitor and oversee them. Many events, programs, and groups depended on the participation of volunteers from outside the prison, whose visits also had to be arranged so they coincided with staffing and supervision. Sterling acted as the liaison between the institution, the dozens of religious groups, and the scores of volunteers.

One of the most important programs sponsored and supported by the chapel was not associated with any religious group. It was the restorative justice initiative, which had come into the prison via the college class Sterling had taken several years earlier from Nathaline Frener, then a University of Oregon law professor.

Sterling had been an enthusiastic and involved student in that class, a sponge, a thought leader. He knew he could not make amends for his own crime, that no matter how many years or decades or lifetimes he spent behind bars he could not undo the harm he had done. Nothing he could do would bring back the lives of his victims. His time in prison punished him, but it did not heal the wounds of the families of those victims. He held out a sliver of hope that he might, someday, be able to sit in a room with those families and try to speak of his shame and hear their pain. But the restorative justice work Sterling was involved in inside the prison was not about him. It was about exploring, analyzing, and changing both the internal life and the social culture of the two thousand men whose world was that maximum security penitentiary. Under the auspices of the chapel, with Sterling's scheduling assistance, direct participation, and often leadership, study and discussion groups began to form. The men gathered in small groups to talk about the trauma in their own lives and how those experiences had made them who they were. They talked about the work it would take to deal with their pasts, to learn from those experiences and move forward to live healthier lives. They talked about a concept few knew the words for but so many embodied—toxic masculinity—and how the prison environment encouraged and sustained that. Was showing emotions showing weakness? Was the only way to get respect to show force? They talked about nonviolent communication and the intricacies and challenges of conflict resolution. One group called itself Peace on the Inside.

One afternoon Sterling is leading a discussion with a small group of men that includes a young white guy with a swastika tattoo inked on his forearm, two Black men, and a Hispanic guy. Just the fact that they are sitting in a room together is astonishing. They are talking about the chaos of the lives they lived before they landed in prison. "So many things made me who I am," one of them says. Sterling picks up on that immediately. "Right," he says, "but the first thing is..." he leans forward, making eye contact, "the first thing is we have to own the shit that we've done." He has learned that this is how to move forward. This acceptance of responsibility is the place from which to do this work. He moves the conversation to the heart of the issues, the reason they are gathered and will continue to gather.

"How can we shift the paradigm of this place that is full of negativity, hostility, and suspicion?" Sterling asks them. "How can we take what we do right here among us and apply it on a larger scale?"

One of the Black prisoners turns to the man next to him, the Hispanic guy. Out in the yard, things can get bad between groups of men who look like these two men. But these two now know each other. They can sit in the same room next to each other and talk. They can look beyond gang affiliation, beyond race. Is that something they can take out to others?

"A lot of these guys, they want to stay out of trouble, they just don't know how," the Black man says. The other guy listens and nods. Conflict inside hurts everyone, winners and losers. All end up being punished, privileges taken away, maybe sent to the hole, maybe transferred to another prison. And whatever the resolution of that particular altercation was, there is almost always no real resolution, just the intensification of hostility and plans for retribution. Whatever is learned—or reinforced—through this cycle of suspicion, hostility, and violence, this trigger-response way of interacting with others is part of who these men are and will follow them outside the walls when they are released. Unless the work is done here, inside. For Sterling, these intense discussions, these groups he helps organize and sometimes lead, the dramatic "play" that he created for the public event a few months ago, are not just about training others to recognize incendiary situations and douse the embers before they become flames. They are about transforming the self-reinforcing toxicity of prison culture. As long as he is here, which might be, despite the efforts of his legal team, for the rest of his life, he wants to live and work in a healthier, saner environment. "I cannot reduce the harm I've already done," he told me once. "But this is a way, maybe, I can make amends." Then he was silent for a moment, looked down and shook his head. "No matter what I do, it will always be overshadowed by what I did. It is a deficit I can never, ever make up." Still, the chapel work sustains him. Some days, the good days, he allows himself to think that he is making a difference.

And then everything changes. In early March 2020, the prison shuts its gates to all outsiders. Events are cancelled. Teachers cannot come in to continue their classes. Volunteers cannot come in to run programs, give talks, or lead groups. Families cannot come in to visit. It is the beginning of the COVID-19 shutdown, which feels at that moment like it might be temporary. Just a few weeks, maybe a month, maybe two. Up in the chapel, Sterling all of a sudden has almost nothing to do. Small groups of prisoners still meet to continue their transforming trauma and restorative justice discussions, and some religious services are continuing to be held. But mostly the calendar is empty. Sterling tells himself this will free up time to exercise more, to read, to write. Maybe he will finally teach himself how to play the guitar. He wants to play Bob Marley's "Redemption Song." Maybe the shutdown is not such a bad thing. Prison is a place of isolation anyway, a place of quarantine away from society, how bad could this be? Inside the prison, few are masked, and social distancing—then a new phrase, a new concept—is impossible given the six-by-eight-foot, double-man cells, the narrow hallways that run the length of the tiers, the long pill line for meds every morning, the congregate chow hall. And some inside, just as some outside, do not believe the threat is real. Or perhaps some feel that there are so many daily threats already, so many reasons to be on high alert, to be anxious and worried, that this new one hardly registers. At least at first.

A few weeks later COVID-19 officially arrives at the prison when a guard tests positive. He is a guard in cell block A—Sterling's block—who, in the course of his job, has exposed all two hundred men there to the virus. A-Block goes on lockdown, which means no one is allowed to leave his cell. No work. No waiting in line to make a phone call. No going to chow hall. Meals come in paper sacks or plastic trays delivered to each cell. During his decades behind bars, Sterling has lived through many a lockdown, all of them reactions to violence, yard fights, gang threats, or some variety of prisoner unrest. He knows how to handle a lockdown. He knows how to handle isolation. He has experience—too much experience—living months at a time in the hole.

He calls the cell block lockdown layered on top of the institutional shutdown his "COVID-cation." He makes good on his goal to do more writing. He is working on a play, *Austin's Echo*, an ambitious project that had earned him a competitive PEN America fellowship. It was not his first recognition from that organization. A few years earlier a story he had written about his work as a hospice volunteer in the prison's infirmary had earned a national award. But this play presents an extraordinary challenge. He has constructed it as a cross-time dialogue between Austin Reed, a real-life prisoner in the 1830s and the first African American to write a memoir of incarceration, and a twenty-first-century prisoner, a fictional stand-in for himself. He described it in his proposal as a work in which "similarities of prison dynamics, reform debates, and social issues are compared through poetic narration, theatrical elements, and music to demonstrate how prison is virtually the same after 185 years." The concept is complicated. The structure is convoluted. He is trying to create a theatrical work that has narrative force about big, thorny issues. He wants the play to make a point, but he doesn't want it to be preachy. He is struggling. He wishes he could talk to the few people who have helped him with his writing in the past, editors, mentors, teachers—I was and am one of them—but he can't leave the cell to make a phone call. He sits on his iron cot in his cell, stuck.

He spends much of his time reading. One of the stories he comes across is a personal essay written by a correctional officer at a prison in Michigan. She writes about her fear working in the prison, her worry that she could take the virus back to her family. She begins the story, published by The Marshall Project, stating that it is "impossible to practice social distancing when you work in a prison." And Sterling thinks, maybe for the first time during his quarter of a century behind bars, about the similar lives lived by prisoners and guards. Taking a break from the play that is going nowhere, he writes what turns out to be an op-ed that is published in the state's largest newspaper. He writes: "We're all afraid... [W]e are all in this together. Nobody here, prisoner or employee, wants a COVID-19 outbreak. The virus doesn't care whether we're here for punishment or a paycheck. It doesn't discriminate based on social status. COVID-19 is a shared threat because of our shared humanity."

Two weeks later, the first person dies of COVID-19 in the prison, an inmate. As of that day, May 10, one hundred fifteen inmates and twenty-six employees have tested positive in the place Sterling will never call "home." It is the biggest outbreak in the state. As the virus takes hold across the country, prisons are deemed "deadly hot spots" and "petri dishes." The rate of infection for the incarcerated population is estimated at 5.5 times higher than for the general population. The entire prison is now on modified lockdown. The men are allowed out of their cells, but only one block at a time. Aside from yard time, there is nothing to occupy them. All activities are now suspended. Activities are considered "prosocial" because they encourage healthy interaction among a population, many of whom are considered to be *anti*social. The activities give some structure to the days, some variety to the monotony, and they have a momentary, if not a cumulative, calming effect. Visits with family also have that effect. No one has seen family in three months. In the absence of anything to do, with illness in the air, a fight breaks out in the yard. Within minutes, the fight escalates into a riot involving more than two hundred inmates. The media, with no direct access to the prison, dependent on carefully crafted reports from prison officials, reports that the riot was not COVID-19–related. Sterling thinks otherwise. The riot doesn't surprise him. What surprises him is that it took so long for things to explode. He knows that no efforts at conflict resolution would have helped, even if he or any of the RJ-trained men had been out there.

The week following the riot, eighty more prisoners test

positive for COVID-19. Twenty-seven men are sequestered in "medical isolation," which is what the prison was calling the hole. Sterling says the saying going around inside is "if you're tested, you're arrested," meaning if you test positive you are taken to that place in the prison designed to inflict the severest of punishments. No one wants to go to the hole. You can't bring anything with you. The cells down there are even worse than the one you are used to. The isolation is more than many can handle. And so no one wants to be tested. When the guards walk the tiers asking if anyone has a dry cough or a fever, no one admits to feeling sick even if—especially if—they are. Cell mates pledge loyalty to each other. If one were to test positive, the other would be sent to the hole too. They tell each other that if either of them gets sick they'll just ride it out in their cell.

Sterling gets sick, the sickest he'd ever felt in his life. He is a healthy man in his early forties, and he is spiking a high fever, slammed with an intense headache and crushing fatigue, his throat so parched he can barely swallow. No sense of taste. No sense of smell. He doesn't get tested. He rides it out. He stays in his bunk, crawling out once every evening to place a call to Cheryl. The one phone call permitted is the only link he and the other men have to the outside. He doesn't tell her how sick he is, only that he is "not feeling all that well." Maybe he doesn't tell her because he doesn't want to worry her. She doesn't need to know how bad it is. But Sterling is probably keeping silent for another reason as well. Conversations on the prison phones are monitored. If it was overheard by those who monitor the calls that he is sick, he will be tested. And "arrested."

He recovers. Slowly, his strength returns. It is August now, six months into the shutdown, six months since he'd seen Cheryl, six months since he'd been able to meet face-to-face with his legal team. But outside the walls of the prison, negotiations are continuing on his behalf. Sterling's tireless lawyer, Ryan O'Connor, is trying to push the case forward through Zoom and Skype meetings. But in-person negotiations were what he believed the case demanded at this point, and that was not possible. Still, he was hopeful, as was Sterling, that an end was in sight, an end to the years and years of court cases and appeals, judgments, hearings, and more appeals.

O'Connor believes that the state wants to settle. The law is now on Sterling's side. The Supreme Court ruling against life for juveniles along with federal and state cases that had been decided in Sterling's favor have more than paved the way. But it is complicated. The state attorney general's office has made it clear that it is deferring any ruling about release to the local district attorney's office in the county Sterling had been originally sentenced. That local DA, in turn, has made it clear that his office would only agree to what the victims' families agree to. Sterling, student of restorative justice, facilitator of conflict resolution, conceives of a way through this tangle: mediation. What if all parties—Sterling, his lawyer, the victims' families and their lawyer, the DA, someone from the AG's office—what if they all could sit together in a room? What if the RJ principles he has been studying for years and trying to practice in the prison could be applied to his own case? A negotiation. A mediation. If the state won't propose a release date unless the local DA proposes a release date, and the local DA won't propose a release date unless the victims' families agree, then Sterling's future is not so much in the hands of the legal system as it is in the hearts of those he had so grievously harmed. And wasn't that what restorative—transformative—justice was all about?

What he can bring to the negotiation table, or the RJ "circle" he envisions, is his rehabilitated self. He knows—it is always in his mind—that his hope for a better future is offensive to those to whom he should be most accommodating. How can that offense be mitigated in some way? What can he do? What do they want? In his cell he imagines a mediation session in a room at the federal courthouse. If he only had a chance to look them in the eyes, the parents of those two kids. If they could only see who he was now. If the families could be actively involved in forging an agreement, some terms that would both give them closure and Sterling his freedom, he could be out in a matter of months.

When he hears that the families have agreed to a session with an outside mediator, he can't help himself. He is buoyant. This could be it. This could be the breakthrough. Of course it is about his own freedom. But it is also about the chance to show his true contrition, the chance to show the parents of those kids that he is no longer the heartless sixteen-year-old kid who remains frozen in their memory. Even when he learns what really should have been obvious given the pandemic shutdowns—a face-to-face conference is out of the question—this does not diminish his joy. He has learned to celebrate any small victory, any movement forward. That learned attitude comes directly from the work he and Arnoldo did together. *Celebrate that which does not crush you.*

The mediation is set for late August. The prison converts a utility closet into a private space for him to use during the eight-hour session. There is a chair, a table, and a telephone. There is no window. The prison, sections of which date back considerably more than a century, has no air conditioning. The tiny room heats to above ninety degrees very quickly. Sterling sits, sweating. He had thought he could be participating by video—the others are together in a Zoom room—but whether technology is the issue or whether some prison official just nixed the idea, all he has is a phone. The session begins with everyone introducing themselves: the six attorneys, the mediator who is based in the San Francisco Bay area, the victims' parents, and Sterling. When he hears Ian's mother's voice—Ian was the young man he murdered—his throat closes. He forces himself to take a deep breath. He tells himself he must remain calm, that unchecked emotion can sabotage the process, that he must speak from a place of reason and rationality. Sterling is surprised to learn that now, after the introductions, all the statements and discussions between the lawyers, the families, and the mediator will be filtered through the mediator to him. He will hear nothing directly. There will be minutes that turn into hours of silence as he holds the phone and wonders what is being said. When the mediator comes on the line to tell him, Sterling responds to the mediator, who then communicates these thoughts to the others. Sterling again listens to silence on the line. To complicate matters, there's an overlay of technological difficulty on the other end, with malfunctions, loss of connectivity, starting and restarting the Zoom room.

Through all of this, Sterling, via the mediator, tries to communicate as best he can what he wants. He wants to find the terms and conditions that would make the families feel safe and would allow him to live some of his life outside prison. "I am not trying to get away with something," he says to the mediator who will tell the others. "I am taking responsibility. I want closure for us all." It's not just legal closure he wants, not just an end to this tangled, decades-long battle through the courts. It is, he tells the mediator, "moral closure, spiritual closure." He wants the chance to do good in the world, he says. All day he walks this tightrope between advocating for his dreams and hopes while owning his responsibility and shame.

From the mediator, he hears no inkling of compromise from the families, no suggestions of terms they could agree to, restrictions they impose on Sterling that he would promise to adhere to, anything that would budge them from their initial position, the position they have held for a quarter of a century, that Sterling should remain in prison for the rest of his life. The tone of the proceedings is oppositional, adversarial. Sterling can tell from the information the mediator conveys, and even the mediator remarks about the tone. Sterling wonders whether the families had actually been briefed about what a mediation was, the purpose that presumably brought them together this day. Still, they agreed to this session. That must mean something, he tells himself. All day he repeats that he will agree to whatever the families want in exchange for a release date. All day there is no response. The mediation goes nowhere.

Finally, in the last hour of this very long day, the temperature in the tiny room hovering in the high nineties, he makes an offer, his "final offer," he tells the mediator. In exchange for a release date that would be no later than his fiftieth birthday—that would be seven years from now, far longer than he wants or had hoped for—he sets forth these promises: He will not live in the county where the crime was committed. He will wear a surveillance ankle bracelet for five years. (The usual time is one year, and it's often removed in six months). He will agree to any kind of ongoing counseling that the families suggest. He will agree to contractual commitment of social service volunteer activities for the rest of his life. "I don't have to be inside, in custody, to feel responsible for what I did," he tells the mediator. "Please tell them that I don't get to put down this burden of what I did. I will always carry it, for the rest of my life."

If there is no agreement, he and his legal team have already

decided that they will go back to court, where he has already
won three different decisions. He doesn't want to do that. It will
take years, and the continuing challenge of living a life in limbo
is overwhelming. But also, at the end of it all—which he believes
and his lawyers believe will be his release—there will be no closure for the victims' families. Transformative justice will not
have taken place.

Sterling listens to silence as the mediator communicates all
this to the families and their attorney. It is taking a long time.
When the mediator comes back on the line, he tells Sterling that
the family has asked for a few days to consider the offer. They
can reconvene for another session. They don't propose a date
for the next mediation, but "soon," they say. Sterling, who had
been ready to give up hope just a few minutes before, is encouraged. Maybe this is the first time the families have realized that
Sterling's "punishment" could continue after release, that there
were many things that could be done to make them feel safer.

It's time for dinner, but all Sterling can think of is sleep. He
goes back to his cell, drinks the warm can of soda he has saved,
and folds his six-foot-three frame onto a cot made for a much
shorter man.

———————

A week later, with no word back yet about a second mediation
session, Sterling's world suddenly changes again. Unprecedented
wildfires sweep across Oregon, burning more than one million
acres of land, destroying entire towns, and filling the air with
thick, hazardous smoke. More than 40,000 people are evacuated from their homes, including 1,450 inmates evacuated from
prisons in the path of one of the most rapidly spreading fires.

They are transferred to the penitentiary where Sterling is incarcerated. They arrive in buses with nothing. The prison is already at capacity. There is no room for them. They come to a facility that is a hot spot for COVID-19, where 150 inmates have now tested positive. The inmates from the other three facilities may or may not be infected. The evacuated prisoners had been given COVID-19 tests, but none of the results were back yet.

Outside in the yard, the air is literally unbreathable. Inside, the transferred men are sleeping on floors or makeshift cots set up wherever there is a few square feet of room: in the corridors that run the length of the tiers, in the program rooms, the classrooms, on the activities floor—and on the fourth floor in the cramped space that is home to the chapel, where Sterling works. With almost 3,500 men crammed into a space meant to house fewer than 2,000, there is confusion and chaos, long lines for everything, queues to get to the toilet, hours to get into chow hall. Fights break out. The guards use pepper spray to—as a prison spokesperson is later quoted as saying—"gain compliance." The pepper spray mixes with the smoke that has infiltrated the building. Those with existing respiratory ailments and those who have or may have the virus have trouble getting medical attention.

Up in the chapel, two hundred prisoners from evacuated facilities sleep on the floor for seven days. Sterling does what he can to keep them busy. He finds board games and decks of cards, sets up a few of the prison's ancient monitors so they can watch selected programming. He hunts for anything that might provide minimal comfort. He mediates conflict, using all of the de-escalation strategies he has learned. He has no time, no bandwidth, to think about his own future.

CHAPTER 18

Vicki texts me from a new number. It's been three months since I last heard from her. In the interim, as I've tried not to worry too much about what is going on in her life, I have reacquainted myself with the disturbing research about female incarceration and reentry—which, not surprisingly, has caused me to worry more. Since the 1980s, when Vicki first became a returning guest in her local jail, the number of women behind bars has increased more than 750 percent. That's a staggering statistic. The incarceration rate of women is now at an historic and global high with 133 out of 100,000 U.S. women behind bars, according to the Prison Policy Initiative. Vicki has been part of another twenty-first-century trend: the skyrocketing incarceration rate of white women. The Sentencing Project found that in the first two decades of this century, the incarceration of white women increased 41 percent, while the incarceration of Black women actually declined 60 percent. (Despite these trends, African American women continue to be incarcerated at a higher rate: 1.7 times that of white women.)

The research reminds me that when women emerge from prison, they face different—and often tougher—challenges than do men. Most, like Vicki, have children, which can mean anything from engaging in the lengthy and stressful process of reclaiming custody to working the labyrinthine social services system to get benefits to finding family-wage work to, as Vicki has had to do for the entire lives of her two children, facing the guilt over and the damage done by the life you have been leading. Women encounter worse job prospects and make lower wages than men. And because their pathways to prison too often include violence, abuse, and addiction, they are, upon reentry, a "high needs" population that "consistently fares worse than men...for all measures of mental and physical health." That was the conclusion reached by a federally funded study, *Prisoner Reentry Experiences of Adult Females*, that tracked women's post-incarcerated lives at three, six, and fifteen months after release. The home-prison-home cycle had been a part of Vicki's life for pretty much all of her adult life.

Vicki's surprise text—actually a long string of messages—chronicles her problems renting a place to live. As with so many of our interactions in the past, this one feels like I've walked into the middle of an ongoing conversation for which I have no context. She obviously landed somewhere and is trying to settle in. Where is that? I have no idea. How long has she been there, and what is she doing? I have no idea. Are the police after her? I have no idea. But I read the texts. She apparently found a house to rent, and a woman she met said she would share the rent. Vicki must have gotten a job because she had $350 to put toward the deal. Then the woman never came up with her share. Vicki lost her deposit. In the next text she tells me that Steve wired her some money, and she is now renting a trailer.

After that flood of texts, there is silence. I wait fifteen minutes. "Do you want to talk?" I text her at the new number. She calls immediately.

The first thing she tells me, with no preamble, is that she was in jail a few weeks ago. She was pulled over by a local cop. Her car had a cracked windshield and looked "a little sketchy," she says. But she thinks the cop was just looking for an excuse. She thinks he profiled her when he saw her inside a convenience store a few minutes before the traffic stop. "I was a little high-strung," she says. "I bet he thought I was on drugs." I am trying to imagine this scene: Vicki, all five-foot-ten of her, probably carrying her little yappy dog in her arms, jittery, maybe talking too much or too loudly to whoever was behind the counter, fumbling for change. She figures the cop pulled her over expecting to find drugs in the car. Of course the first thing he did was run her plates and her license, both of which were from out of state, through the system.

She sat in the car waiting for him to come back, slap handcuffs on her wrists and take her in. She was sure there was a warrant out for her arrest. That's why she had lied to her family (and me) about finding a "traveling" job with the census, why she had secretly packed up her belongings, stuffed them in the trunk of her car, and driven off to who knew where months before.

The cop came back to inform her that she was driving with a suspended license, which was a criminal offense. Apparently, no arrest warrant had shown up in his search, which confused Vicki. After all, the cops in her hometown had found a large quantity of drugs in her house; she had promised to name her supplier in exchange for the charges being dropped; and she had fled. But she also knew, from long personal experience and acquired street smarts, how unpredictable and idiosyncratic the criminal justice system was. She didn't have time to feel relief, however, because the cop arrested her anyway. Driving with a suspended license was only a misdemeanor, but it carried a fine (which she couldn't afford) and a jail sentence. She spent the next five nights locked up in the county jail sleeping on a tick-infested mattress on the floor. "I ought to sue them," she tells me. Then I hear a bang that sounds like her phone dropping on a hard surface and a yelp. Ziggy, her eleven-year-old dog, is having seizures. She'll call me back. A week goes by.

During the next phone call, and the one after that, supplemented by our on-again, off-again texting, I find out what life has been like since she disappeared—and it is as chaotic as it always has been. First there was that falling out with the woman who was going to pay half the rent on a place Vicki found. The woman agreed, reneged, then changed her mind again and told Vicki to sign the rental agreement, that she was good for the money. She never showed up with a check. She stopped answering Vicki's phone calls. Vicki thinks the women she knew in prison were far more trustworthy than those she meets in the free world. And then there's the job Vicki found at a fast-food franchise. She hates it. She hates her boss. She tells me that she works her ass off but is not appreciated. But in the next breath, she tells me that Steve came to visit, and she missed a week of work. That was followed by a two-week period during which she was late for her shift every day. That's because, she says, she ran out of her meds. She had no renewals left on her prescription, and she didn't have a local doctor. She was pretending to be living in her hometown and trying to work the health-care and social services systems via her phone. Then her phone stopped working. She doesn't have and has never owned—or even sat down in front of—a computer. Her phone is her one and only device.

She tells me with extraordinary pride that her new phone,

the new number she called me from, is on her son's plan. It's the only way she could afford it. "This means he trusts me," she says, "He really trusts me." There's a catch in her voice. She knows she has repeatedly disappointed her children. She has not been reliable, responsible, or for that matter, even *present* for most of their lives. They have learned the hard way, and repeatedly, that they cannot count on her. So this arrangement with her son— she sends him a check to cover her part of the bill—has great significance. It also means (doesn't it?) that her son knows she is not living in her hometown and traveling for this fabricated job. Yes, she says, "both the kids know I live in Oklahoma." And now, with that offhand remark, I know too. I ask her where, and she names a town I've never heard of. I look it up later. It's maybe an hour from the Texas border, population 1,700, median income $22,000, and 90 percent white—a lot smaller, somewhat poorer, and just a little bit whiter than her hometown. She's living in a trailer park with her dog that gets seizures (she can't afford a trip to the vet) and another dog she adopted that has "issues."

She tells me more about the job she hates. She tells me that every week her hours change. One week she worked thirty hours, the next only eleven. The boss is just messing with her. She has been trying to supplement her income by baking and selling cheesecakes. Last week there was money missing in the cash register at work, and she thinks the boss suspects her. She wants to quit. She wants to look for a new job. But it seems like every job requires an online application. "I don't know how to do any of this," she tells me. "And I get frustrated, and then my ADD kicks in." I ask about her daughter. They are apparently texting again. She says her daughter and the boyfriend—the guy with whom she committed the crime that got her sentenced to the same prison as her mother—are saving money to fix up a van to live in. She thinks her daughter is clean. Maybe. She thinks she's maintaining on Suboxone, the same prescription med Vicki takes, which treats opioid addiction. I wonder what "moving forward" even looks like for Vicki, whether her life outside prison walls will always be like this: tenuous, unsettled, one step, or misstep, from disassembling altogether.

The next I hear from Vicki, maybe three weeks later, is that she is back in her hometown. She was fired from the fast-food job. She put a few changes of clothes and her two dogs in her car, the "sketchy" one with the cracked windshield, and drove almost two thousand miles west. She has a plan, sort of. She is keeping a low profile, not seeing friends, not checking in with her street family, still mystified that the cops are not after her for the drug bust. "It seems like no one is concerned about my whereabouts," she says. She sounds slightly disappointed. Meanwhile she is trying to get reconnected with the health-care system so she can find a new doctor and get valid prescriptions for her medications. She is waiting for an appointment at the DMV so she can get her license reinstated. Her cousin borrowed money from her mother so she could pay Vicki for two weeks of work sorting vintage clothes at the warehouse. She has also picked up a part-time job as a weed trimmer, a legitimate gig in those states that have legalized marijuana. For several hours a day she sits at a table pruning away leaves, snipping off stems, and manicuring cannabis flowers without damaging them. The potency of the plant is in the flower, not the leaf. Trimming also gives the product the "bag appeal" needed to compete for customers in the now-booming cannabis industry. Trimmers have to be able to focus on monotonous tasks for long periods of time. I wonder whether Vicki can do this unmedicated, either by legal or illegal means. She says she needs to make $400 so she can buy a new battery for her car and afford the gas back to Oklahoma, where she will, she says, clear out the trailer, pack everything in the car and move somewhere else. "I'm done here," she says about her hometown, the place she has come back to after every stint in prison. "All my negative stuff is here. I am surrounded by it. When I wasn't here, I could breathe differently." Maybe that's true. But two thousand miles away she still found drama in the workplace and in her personal relationships. Two thousand miles away she landed in jail. She got fired from her job.

She is thinking maybe she'll move to Flagstaff. Steve drove through there on his way to see her, and he liked it. He could rent out the house, move there too. Or maybe she could move to Reno. She heard it was easy to find a job there. She is confident she can find one. She is a woman with no special training and a long history of incarceration who was fired from her last three jobs. She is on two medications to treat long-term addiction. She does not know, nor does she have any interest in learning, how to navigate the online world that is job searching. Confidence may be the best, strongest—only—thing she has going for her.

While she tries to earn enough money for gas to make it back to Oklahoma, she has started work on a vision board. This is a collage of images, pictures, and affirmations designed to serve as a source of inspiration and motivation. She learned about vision boards in rehab. One image she knows she'll put on the board is a wedding picture. She and Steve are still planning to get married. She's selected a date based on a numerological calculation she tries to explain to me, but I fail to understand. What I do understand is that she wants to find meaning in her life and the decisions she makes. She wants to start this marriage, now almost thirty years in the making, with some divine help, some mystical support from the world of numbers. Whatever it takes.

CHAPTER 19

Sterling sits with his shoulders hunched, his hands clasped on the table in front of him. The only item on the table is a box of tissues. His prison-issue denim shirt, two sizes too big, billows around his lanky frame. The sleeves are voluminous; the gaping cuffs make his wrists look delicate. He is holding prayer beads, or worry beads, between the fingers of his left hand, the hand with his wedding ring. His head is bowed, his eyes behind the big, serious, black-rimmed glasses fixed on the table, staring, as he tries to gather himself for what is to come. I am studying his face as it appears on my computer screen. Like the other almost seventy people attending Sterling's much-anticipated resentencing hearing, my attendance is remote. It is late October 2020, eight months since the pandemic forced the prison to shut itself off to all outsiders. Since then there have been sixteen COVID-19 deaths inside.

Sterling's lead attorney, Ryan O'Connor, is Skyping in from his law office. The other members of his legal team, a trio from the Criminal Justice Reform Clinic at Lewis & Clark Law School, are gathered, masked, in a distant classroom. They have worked together tirelessly—a clichéd phrase that could not be more apt—these three women and Mr. O'Connor, to prep for this day, developing a strategy, conferring for months with Sterling, collating decades of legal documents and court decisions, gathering more than eighty letters of support, and selecting from those supporters three people to testify at today's hearing. With Sterling's active involvement at every step, they have amassed a 311-page dossier to present to the parole board.

In the three hours it takes me to read through that dossier, my eyes barely leave the page. That's how compelling the documents are, from Sterling's résumé-style introduction that details his achievements—education, publications, honors, workshops and events he has led—to the lawyers' crafted narrative of his life, a tale that extends from his Texas childhood, through troubled adolescence in Arkansas and Oregon, to his terrible crime, to his imprisonment, and twenty-six years later, to his transformation into the tense, earnest man with the worry beads I see on the screen.

I read the story of his childhood with particular care. It is story I know well, a story I learned bit by filtered bit as Sterling trusted me more. Everything included in the lawyers' recounting is factual, but what is not included tells a tale of its own. The lawyers' version, one Sterling told me early on, is of a happy early childhood guided and overseen by a loving "Momma" with all the trappings of a conventional upbringing: school, sports, chores at home; structure, accountability, love. This version sets the stage for the contrast, the shock, that happens when Momma unexpectedly dies and Sterling, age twelve, is farmed out to relatives who are, in turn, uncaring, abusive, and alcoholic. At best, they are feckless; at worst, criminals. What this version of his early childhood omits is a darker, tangled tale. Sterling's Momma, the woman he thought was his mother, was actually his grandmother. His biological mother—a woman he grew up thinking was his sister—the one who gave birth to him while she was serving a prison term, never had custody of him. He was an adult before he knew that she was actually his mother. His father was a Black man about whom he knew nothing. What the young Sterling did know, however, was that he looked different than the white relatives he grew up around, different than the white kids he went to school with.

When Sterling had told me about "Momma," I pictured an older, kindly Black woman. That image fit the stereotype I had of what it meant to grow up in the warm embrace of a single mother in the South. And it made sense to me because Sterling, although light skinned, clearly identifies and presents as African American. I assumed, incorrectly, that his Italian surname was his father's name, that his father was white and his mother was Black. But just a month before today's hearing, Cheryl, Sterling's wife, sent me an image of an old photograph. It was of a ten-year-old boy, reddish-brown afro, café au lait skin dusted with freckles, being hugged by a slender, big-haired, very young-looking white woman. This was Sterling next to his Momma. He was born into pretense. He was born an outsider.

I continue to make my way through the dossier delivered to the parole board. The most compelling section is the extraordinary collection of letters of support, eighty-three of them, arguing for Sterling's release. Dozens are from former university students who were his classmates in restorative justice courses taught inside the prison. They were inspired by him. They learned from him. Now they are in law school, medical school, graduate school. One is working for UNESCO. They write about how he touched their lives. "Sterling is one of the reasons I have decided to pursue a career in the criminal justice system," wrote one young woman, now a doctoral student. "He has dismantled my stereotypes and perceptions of who people behind bars are." There are letters from professors, clergy, business people, attorneys, from one of PEN America's program directors, from Cheryl's mother and sister, from five staffers within the Department of Corrections. There's a letter from Arnoldo, who writes that Sterling was "a mentor to me throughout my personal transformation." That letter highlights the principles of restorative justice—love, trust, care, and humility—that the two men worked together to help propagate throughout the prison, the principles that are part of Arnoldo's reclaimed life. Arnoldo is listening to the hearing this morning from his office at Latino Network.

The sole issue before the board at this morning's hearing is setting a projected parole release date. That means revisiting Sterling's original sentence from 1994, which mandated two life terms to be served consecutively with the earliest release date in 2048. Sterling will be seventy-one then and would have spent fifty-four of those years behind bars. His legal team, backed by Supreme Court and U.S. Circuit Court rulings and state statutes, citing scientific findings about the teen brain, and amassing evidence of Sterling's growth, change, and transformation, is hoping for a restructuring of those sentences that would allow for a much, much earlier release. His attorneys want the board to see Sterling's life as a resounding success story for juvenile rehabilitation.

The hearing is set to begin promptly at 8:30, but clearly that's not going to happen. There are more than the usual technological glitches. Close to seventy people are attempting to join the proceedings, some with video feeds, others audio only, some Skyping in (the DOC deems Zoom a security risk) via computer, others by phone, some veterans of cyberspace, others flummoxed at every click. There are long moments of listening to cross talk and chatter, the rattling of pots and pans, doors closing, street noise, office noise, as people slowly discover the mute button. Sterling remains on screen, almost motionless. In all our many times together, during the close to one hundred writing group sessions we have sat around a table, I have never seen his face so absent of life. I know what he is thinking in this moment because he tells me a few days later when we speak on the phone. He is thinking: *This is a legal case, but I need to show my heart. I am full of emotion, but I can't be emotional. I need to be logical, but I must be my authentic self. I need to be fully present even in this moment when I feel completely disconnected.* And then, working those worry beads, he thinks: *This is it. My future rides on this. This is my best chance. This is the best board will get.*

The four members of board who are Skyping in from different locations this morning face an unenviable task: balancing the evidence meant to show that Sterling is a changed man and should be set free against the deep and unhealed pain suffered by the victims' families who want him to remain imprisoned. Whatever they decide, someone will suffer.

Michael Hsu, the chairperson, a decade younger than Sterling, is a serious, intense man, quiet, measured, thoughtful, a former public defender with a backstory worth repeating. The governor appointed him to the board in mid-2017, three months after he received his green card. He had been living as an undocumented immigrant for twenty-two years. In a magazine profile commending him for winning a Rising Star Award from his law school (coincidentally, Lewis & Clark, home to Sterling's legal trio), he related that his own family's experience with the law had been deeply troubling. His mother had hired an attorney in the hopes of securing a green card for her son. Thousands of dollars and several months later, she discovered he had failed to file any of the necessary paperwork. His office was vacant. She never reported the incident, fearing deportation. When he was admitted to the bar in 2012, he was told he was the first undocumented person in America to have become an attorney.

Vice chair is Greta Lowry, a former assistant district attorney from a mostly rural county along the southern Oregon coast. As a prosecutor she represented the interests of the state at trials, sentencings, probation violation hearings, and release hearings for a wide variety of crimes. Her final duties before she joined the board in mid-2019 focused on determining which individuals could be safely supervised in the community, always a big issue in these board decisions. James Taylor, the third member, is a long-time banking executive, erstwhile sports agent, and chair of an audit committee that oversees the state's youth correctional facilities. A "military brat" who lived in Turkey and Spain before his father settled in California, he attended a small private liberal arts college in the late 1970s. He told a writer for the college's alumni publication that he remembers fellow students telling him he was the first Black person they had ever talked to. The experience, he said, taught him to reach across cultures and backgrounds to connect and communicate. The fourth member of this diverse group gathered to hear Sterling's case is John Bailey, a former parole and probation officer with the state's most populous, most urban county. He holds a bachelor's degree in criminology and a law degree. I look at their faces in the tiles across my screen: Asian, Black, white, male, female. They will determine Sterling's future, Cheryl's future. They come to this moment from such different backgrounds, such different ways of working with and thinking about the criminal justice system. That, I think, is their true diversity. How will that play out today?

Finally the tech issues are settled and, twenty minutes late, the hearing begins. All of us sitting at home or in our offices, in New York, California, Colorado, Indiana, Washington, Oregon, listen as O'Connor, the lead attorney, states the legal case, and a law student from the legal clinic begins questioning Sterling. Her job is to first guide him through a retelling of his youth and then through the crime itself, a necessary part of all these hearings not so much for the details themselves—these are part of the record—but for how the person who committed the crime recounts it: the tone of voice, the emotion or lack thereof. The board is looking for insights into the way the person understands the crime. It is looking, most importantly, for remorse, for evidence that the burden of guilt weighs heavy.

Sterling, looking straight into the camera, his hands clasped tightly, begins this way: "The reason we are here today is that Ian and Bridget are not." That's the young couple Sterling and his friend shot and killed on January 15, 1994. "Anything I share will be difficult and traumatic for their families to hear," he says quietly. "With that awareness I commit to speaking from my heart and being transparent." What follows, under methodical questioning, is first a recounting of his childhood and adolescence, the influences and experiences that made him into a sixteen-year-old who could commit murder, and then a minute-by-minute retelling of the night of the crime. The details of the crime should come as no surprise to me. When he first joined the writers' group years ago, Sterling handed me fifty pages of an autobiography in progress, a part of which focused on the night he and an older friend, a fellow escapee from a group foster home, carjacked a vehicle with a young couple inside, the night that ended in a double murder.

What became clear in this retelling of the crime and what I hadn't realized before, was that the murders themselves were not "just" the result of callous, adrenaline-fueled, pseudo-gangster, teen behavior. They happened by horrible happenstance: a security light came on; a dog barked. They happened because the boys had no plan about what to do with the passengers in the car they had stolen. Sterling and his friend drove around for hours looking for a place to drop off the couple, a location remote enough so that Ian and Bridget could not easily run to a phone and call the police. They stopped at two places—the one with the motion-sensor light and the one with the dog—got scared and drove away. Hearing this made the whole terrible crime even more senseless than it was.

I know Bridget and Ian's parents are watching and listening. I can't see them on the screen right now, and I'm glad of that. Watching their faces as Sterling recounts all of this would be unbearable. "There's nothing a person can do that's worse than killing," Sterling says after the final question about that night. "I did that. This will haunt me to my grave. They had their whole life in front of them."

Sterling is now guided through a recitation of his incarcerated life, his work as a hospice volunteer, his work in the prison chapel with restorative justice and mediation, his education, his writing. All of this must be impressive to the board. Few people, in or out of prison, have accomplished as much as this man. But I also imagine how this extraordinary résumé might sound to the parents of the two murder victims. How they might be replaying Sterling's words of a few minutes ago—*They had their whole life head of them*—and thinking: *That's right. And you took that away. You have had the opportunity to make a life. They did* *not. My child's life could have been one of accomplishment too.* The damned-if-you-do, damned-if-you-don't cliché couldn't be more apt. If the team does not highlight his accomplishments they fail to make the strongest case for his rehabilitation. But when they do highlight these, they are confronting the victims' families with evidence of a life fully lived by the man who robbed their children of a chance to live their lives.

Three carefully selected witnesses then give testimony on Sterling's behalf. One is his wife, Cheryl, for whom being in the public eye does not come naturally. A wife would be expected to support and believe in her husband, but Cheryl does more with her careful, measured words. She does not play on emotions— hers or the board's. She begins by acknowledging the searing pain the victims' families feel and says that her advocacy for Sterling neither excuses nor ignores what he did. She talks about what she knows from her seventeen years as his wife: his transparency, his honesty with himself and others, his ability to communicate, his conscientious decision making, his desire to find common ground and work through thorny issues. She sketches a picture of a mature man living an ethical life. Melissa Michaux, the university professor, speaks briefly about Sterling as a student in her restorative justice class, his contributions, his leadership, his effect on other students, his commitment to conflict mediation and nonviolence.

I have also been asked to speak based on my five-plus years as his editor, writing mentor, and increasingly, his and Cheryl's friend. I spent long hours thinking about and then carefully crafting my testimony, writing it out, editing, revising. I read it to the legal team in a witness-prep Zoom session two weeks ago, feeling anxious but also oddly disconnected, like I was in an episode of a television series. I don't know what weight my words might have. Maybe the board has already made its decision. Maybe they dismiss supporters' testimony as biased. Regardless, I feel an enormous responsibility. When I admit this to O'Connor, the lawyer, he laughs. "Welcome to my world," he says.

I am on camera now, alternately looking down to read from my testimony and staring into the screen of my laptop in an attempt to make eye contact with people I cannot see, with the board, maybe even with the families of the two victims. I conclude with words I hope will stick: "The boy who killed has become a man who heals." I truly believe that. I truly believe that Sterling has remade himself, rewired his brain, redefined his masculinity, that although he can never make up for what he did, he might be able to, as they say, "pay it forward," to do some good in the world. I truly believe he should be released. What would I believe, how would I feel if it had been my daughter, my son whose life he had taken? I don't know. And I hope I never have to find out.

We are now in the final hour or so of what will end up being a six-and-a-half-hour marathon of a hearing. I learn later that this is one of the longest such sessions ever held. I sat in on one other board hearing several years ago, in person. The man in question, who was nearing sixty with bad hips, bad knees, an extra fifty pounds on his frame, and a quarter of a century behind bars, was not deemed "rehabilitatable" enough to be considered for parole. That hearing lasted barely two hours. It turned, I thought at the time, on the testimony of the family members. It was not so much what they said. It was their presence in the room, the palpable pain of it.

It is time for the board to hear from those who do not support Sterling's release. The first, representing the state, is the chief deputy district attorney from the county where the crime was committed. He has been practicing law for almost as long as Sterling has been behind bars. On the screen I see a clean-shaven, square-jawed man dressed as if for court in a conservative business suit. He speaks slowly, deliberately, and without emotion. He is arguing for the board to let stand Sterling's current sentence and far-in-the-future release date. In the face of all the court cases and decisions that are stacked against this, the DA's strategy is not a legal one. As I listen, a biased supporter of Sterling's release, I bristle at his words. But I also admire his tactics. He is using Sterling's accomplishments against him. He is reiterating what Sterling's supporters—and Sterling's proven record—said, that he is a talented and award-winning writer, a persuasive speaker, an artist. But here's the twist. Sterling, the DA tells the board, is "an actor" and a "storyteller" who has "regaled people with tales of his troubled upbringing...convincing many people that he is a reformed man." But he is not a reformed man. His rehabilitation is not sincere, not real. He is a guy making up a story. This story is motivated only by his desire to get out of prison. The DA is making the case that because Sterling is such a good storyteller, he should not be trusted. Part of me thinks that's brilliant. The DA also says, several times, in that same near monotone, that "the sentence needs to be proportional to the crime" and that "the only way justice can be served is if Sterling spends the rest of his life in prison." I don't know if that's true. I don't think any of us do. Short of "an eye for an eye," what is a life "worth"? How much punishment is enough? Is any punishment enough?

Bridget and Ian's families are being represented by the executive director of a nonprofit victims' rights center, a former prosecutor and one-time newspaper reporter. She sets the stage for the families' testimony by focusing on their ongoing trauma and loss, the pain they suffered and continue to suffer. Like the DA, she reiterates the seriousness of the crimes and the appropriateness of the life sentences. She then introduces the fear—a fear that every victim or victim's family must feel and that the board itself must always consider in every case it hears—that Sterling, if released, could commit additional crimes. Of all the reasons to argue against release, this seems to me to be the weakest. I wonder if she believes it herself.

The families' testimony is the hardest to hear, the most searing. On-screen they look haggard, careworn, old. Ian's mother wants to make the point that her son's murder a quarter of a century ago affected and continues to affect the entire family. His older brother still struggles with the loss, she says. The lives of her subsequent children, "born into a living nightmare," have forever been affected. About Sterling's many accomplishments, she has this to say: "Of course you now claim to be a fine upstanding citizen. You have had time and resources that the average person does not have," that her son did not have. She does not believe Sterling has changed. She begs—"beg" is the word she uses, her voice catching—the board to not order an early release. There is a long silence after she stops speaking. I cannot see Sterling on the screen, but I can imagine his face.

Bridget's father is now on-screen, a seventy-ish man with thinning white hair and a bony face. His wife, shoulders hunched, eyes trained on the screen, sits next to him, immobile. He begins by reminiscing, talking about his daughter and Ian as a couple, how they met, what they did together, the fun they had, snowball fights in the driveway. His memories are specific and vivid, as if all this happened last week. He recounts the night of the murder, how when Bridget didn't return from work at the usual time—she had a part-time job at a local pizza parlor while taking community college classes—he and his wife joked that maybe the couple had decided to elope. He remembers where he was, what he was wearing, when the police came to tell him they had found his daughter. He puts his face in his hands and begins to sob. His wife, frozen, looks forward. He tries several times to collect himself, apologizes, starts again. Finally, he says to the board, to Ian's parents, maybe to Sterling: "Don't forget about these two young kids." Another long pause. "We thought we would be planning a wedding, not a funeral."

It is clear that the twenty-six years Sterling has spent in a maximum security prison has not eased the pain of these families. Will more time—another decade, two decades, the rest of his life—alleviate any of their suffering? Is there such a thing as "restitution" for the crime of murder? If Sterling is released and goes out into the world and does good, will that help balance the karmic score? Bridget's mother talked about how kind and compassionate her daughter was. Ian's father talked about Ian as a peacemaker. What would those two kids want from Sterling?

Hsu, the chairman, sitting alone, masked, looking weary, closes the proceedings by saying that the members will not make a decision today. Apparently it is common in these resentencing hearings to offer same-day decisions. But there are too many documents to read, too much testimony to consider, and the statutes and legal rulings underlying the case are complex. There is also so much emotion in this moment that it is impossible to imagine making and then announcing such a momentous decision right now. It may take the board up to a month to decide, he says.

Back six and a half hours ago, when the hearing first began, someone walked into the room reserved for Sterling at the prison and placed a sealed envelope on the table in front of him.

When he went to reach for it, a voice instructed him not to open it until there was a break in the proceedings. He pushed it away, off-screen, but not before he glanced at the return address. It was from one of Bridget's cousins. He learned later that it had arrived just minutes before the hearing started. He read it during one of the short breaks that long morning. Two days later, when we spoke on the phone, he read it to me. "My family wants Mr. Cunio to suffer," it read. "But all we can do, separately and together, is heal." She wrote that the notion of exacting "payment" for the murder of her cousin was "nonsensical." It is not a debt that can be repaid. "Bridget would have wanted to sit down and talk about it." Sterling thought the letter was one of the bravest things he'd ever read.

CHAPTER 20

Vicki's quick visit home stretched into a two-and-a-half-month stay. Navigating multiple government bureaucracies is tough work for anyone. But if you are someone with ADHD and minimal computer skills, battling addiction, enmeshed in the daily complications of a life poorly lived, the work is harder still. Finally, she did whatever it was she needed to do, including staying out of trouble, and earned enough money to finance her trip back to the trailer park in Oklahoma. She got in her car once again and headed east.

———

Trevor bought himself a new motorcycle. He had three now. Harleys were his passion. He rode one into work in the early morning, even when it was cold, sometimes when it was raining. He commuted into the office all through the pandemic year, working alone at his desk, staring at a screen all day. He was glad to be employed when so many others weren't. But his job organizing materials for defense attorneys kept him anchored in the world of criminal justice, and riding was his escape from that, his therapy. The short morning and evening commutes were often his favorite part of the long day. He loved the bikes as much as his fiancée, Loraine, loved cats. Right now he was "winning" this tug-of-war in their relationship, and she was losing. She wanted a houseful of cats. Trevor was not a fan of felines, and he didn't want any extra responsibilities. Maybe when they found a place with some land. Maybe after they got married. For now it was enough to work, to live this quiet life—except for the thrum of the bikes—to feel at ease in the world.

———————

Dave grew tulips in pots on the tiny balcony off his bedroom. He created craft projects, which he mounted, framed, and hung on the walls of his room. But mostly, when he wasn't at work behind the deli counter, he was in his car, the 2011 Mitsubishi Eclipse Spyder convertible he bought for himself just days after his release. It was, as *Car and Driver* might have put it, a "sporty roadster." The color was a semi-showy sort of burnt orange, officially "Sunset Pearlescent." At least twice a month, maybe more, he drove, often with the top down in decidedly nonconvertible weather, to the ocean. He spent a lot of time looking at the ocean. Sometimes the sunset was the same color as his car. Once a month he drove an hour to visit a retired prison volunteer who had befriended him long ago. One day, on a whim, he drove to a casino where he played the machines and won $121. But mostly he reported for his shifts and kept to himself. He thought about applying for a job one of his "prisonville" buddies had mentioned, factory work on the line at a planing mill. It paid $18 an hour, $5 more than he was making working the deli counter. He considered what that extra money would mean—$200 more a week, almost $1,000 more a month. He could save for that apartment he wanted to move into. But that meant change. And stability is what he craved.

———

Catherine's advocacy and outreach job at the nonprofit changed from travel and public appearances and sit-down committee meetings to virtual everything. The work didn't stop. It Zoomified. Catherine, a true extrovert, was energized by being around other people. Now, like so many millions of others during the pandemic, she sat at home and stared at her screen, meeting after meeting, planning sessions, brainstorming sessions, strategy calls, one-on-ones. Like single working mothers everywhere, she struggled with childcare. Her toddlers were as high energy as their mother. "Rambunctious" would be the best word. They ran from room to room, jumped on couches, shrieked at each other. Damon, their father, was helping out. But the day care facilities had been shut down by governor's orders, and her family was three thousand miles away. Her energy was not limitless. As challenging as her pandemic work life was, though, she was learning something very important. She could do this job from anywhere. She didn't have to be a continent away from her family, especially from her brother Curtis. If she thought it all through, if she strategized the details, if she saved a little money, if the nonprofit agreed—so many ifs—she could move back to Florida. She could continue remaking her life in the place she was born. She could reclaim her place in the state where she had spent seventeen years behind bars.

―――――――

Arnoldo got a promotion. It was a recognition not just of his importance to the organization but also of his particular skills as a manager, the way he could listen with intensity and take his time to respond, the combination of self-confidence and humility he brought to every encounter. Working remotely, which is what everyone at Latino Network was doing in COVID-19 times, was more stressful than he imagined—and for what struck him as an odd reason. It wasn't so much the hour after hour staring at the screen. It was that he missed the downtime he used to have in the car in between meetings. Now the meetings were scheduled back-to-back, with not a moment to decompress. He didn't complain. He worked.

Although he could not visit Sterling—the prison had been closed to outsiders for a year now—he thought about his friend often. "Sterling was the one who reeled me in," he told the almost one hundred people who had joined an online "Transformative Justice 101" conference organized by Professor Michaux. Arnoldo and Sterling had been the first two prison facilitators in Michaux's restorative justice class. It was because of that class and the long conversations with Sterling out in the yard and those small study groups focused on transforming trauma that Arnoldo was where he was today—not just on the screen sharing his work at this conference, but where he was in life. Sterling believed, and had said so many times to so many people, that "you have to own the shit you did." But that despite the harm you caused in the past—maybe *because* of the harm you caused in the past—you had the ability and the responsibility to do good in the future. Those words, that attitude, had set Arnoldo on the path he was on: understanding and using his past to pay it forward.

Arnoldo told the Zoom audience about that path, about the work the Latino Network was engaged in with at-risk youth. Just a few minutes before his on-screen time, Nicole, his wife, had held center stage (or, in the Zoom world, center tile) as a featured speaker focusing on the principles of and research behind restorative justice. Before she launched into her talk, she shared a photograph that helped explain why she was so deeply involved in this movement to, as she put it, "support healing and accountability over punishment." The image on the screen was of her and Arnoldo, sitting on a stone hearth shoulder to shoulder, with Sol, now two-and-a-half, tucked between them. At first glance, it was a typical smile-for-the-camera family portrait. But unlike other such portraits, the smiles did not look forced. The faces had not frozen in a pose. And then there was how Sol had rested his head against Arnoldo's neck while flinging one leg over Nicole's thigh. This new life connected their two very different lives. Nicole had taught classes in San Quentin, spent years studying and researching the issues surrounding incarceration, earned a doctorate in jurisprudence and social policy, all many years before she ever met Arnoldo. It was Arnoldo who had brought it all home, literally.

The two-hour conference had begun with a clip from a documentary-in-the-making by Lydia Smith, who had been allowed access to the prison pre-COVID-19 to film Melissa Michaux's RJ class as well as one of the peer mentoring sessions Sterling facilitated inside. And so Nicole and Arnoldo and Melissa, and dozens of students who had sat in those RJ classes, and volunteers and community advocates who had seen Sterling in action when he moderated events inside the prison, and the scores of other people who joined via Zoom that afternoon saw Sterling on screen. Dressed in his baggy prison blues, his long dreadlocks draped over his shoulders, the lenses of his big, black plastic-framed glasses reflecting the key light Lydia brought in to illuminate the room, he sat on a folding chair in a semicircle with five other men. "We did what we did," he told them. "But we have the ability to do good in the present."

———————

Sterling had waited to hear back from the parole board after that six-and-a-half-hour hearing. He had been buoyed by all the letters of support, by the testimony. The board chairperson, Michael Hsu, had said that, even though decisions on hearings like this one were usually made the same day, this one would take a while. Sterling waited. One week, two weeks, a month. He and Cheryl spoke briefly by phone most nights, their calls, monitored, rarely discussed legal issues. He told her what music he was listening to, and after they hung up, she would find it, stream it, and listen. It was a way of connecting. They had so few these days. Another week went by. He worked to maintain his optimism. That resentencing hearing was his best chance for release. That's what Sterling thought, and that's what his lawyers thought. The current board members, they all thought, were more likely than other panels that had been convened to rule in Sterling's favor. Another week went by.

A month and a half after the hearing, the board issued its Action Form:

> Cunio, Sterling Ray
> Original Admit: 08/30/94
> Parole release is 09/14/2032.
> The new projected parole release date is 11/27/2028.

The "action" of the board was, essentially, no action at all. The five years the board had shaved off the adjusted parole date was five years of earned "good behavior" time, time the board was obligated to subtract from the original sentence because of the years of honor points Sterling had accrued. The board had decided that Sterling did not deserve early release. The resentencing hearing did not result in resentencing.

During that long hearing, members of the board had acknowledged the extraordinary level of community support for Sterling and commended the positive changes in his life. In the weeks after the hearing, the members of the board had presumably read at least some of the more than seven dozen letters of support submitted as part of his packet. It would be hard to imagine a more profoundly changed, more deeply transformed person than the man whose case was before them. Was there a better example of what prison was supposed to do—create a repentant, law-abiding citizen out of a criminal?

The decision blindsided both Sterling and his attorneys. At his most optimistic, Sterling had imagined a release date within a year. The more cautious estimate from one of his attorneys was two to three years. Now, if this decision stood, he would be serving out thirty-four years, imprisoned from age seventeen to age fifty-one. The Board's decision had nothing to do with the overwhelming documentation of Sterling's rehabilitation. It flew in the face of the Supreme Court's ruling that sentencing a minor to life in prison was unconstitutional. It seemed to be, Sterling said, and his lawyer privately speculated, a decision based on the likelihood that a ruling in his favor would inflame vocal victims' rights groups, garner media attention, and could lead to political repercussions. The attorney general—one of the highest-profile elected offices in the state and the person who oversaw the Department of Justice—had just won an election. She was an incumbent, a Democrat in a bluer-than-blue state. Her challenger, who had no legal credentials or background, had gotten 41 percent of the vote. It was, perhaps, a time for her to be cautious.

The mediation session had gone nowhere. Now the resentencing hearing had gone nowhere. Meanwhile, the complications surrounding the case kept piling up. Sterling's legal team had won an important decision in federal district court when the court issued a mandate that he must get a "*Miller* hearing," so-called after the *Miller v. Alabama* Supreme Court case. If, at such a hearing, the applicant was deemed rehabilitated, he must be released. The Department of Justice had resisted (and appealed) a lower court ruling in his favor on this issue. Now the federal court *mandated* the hearing. "Mandated" meant the decision could not be appealed.

Suddenly, everything looked promising again. He would *have* to get that hearing. The evidence of his rehabilitation would be incontrovertible. He might be out in a matter of months. The elation lasted not even a week. With the possibility of any appeal cut off by the mandate, the DOJ countered by insisting that the resentencing hearing that had taken place months ago was, in fact, a *Miller* hearing. But, by the state's own rules and policies, it was not. The move meant the case was stalled, as the lawyers on both sides considered how to proceed, jockeying for position, playing on this chessboard that was Sterling's life. His fight for parole was a legal quagmire. The complexity was almost breathtaking. It seemed that the twisted knots of the legal fabric could never be untangled.

Sterling, who had become an expert on his own case, wrote about this in a 2,700-word, fully footnoted (using the

Bluebook-style citations lawyers used) document, which he titled "Cyclical Denial: A Legal Perspective." It was an impressive piece of research that could have been published in a law review. He wrote it sitting on his bunk at night and, whenever he had a moment during the day, at his desk up on the chapel floor. He submitted it to his legal team, conferred with them, edited and reedited. He deeply respected their expertise. He wasn't trying to be a "jailhouse lawyer." But the truth was, no one knew more about his case than he did. His lawyers were involved in other litigations, lawsuits, and disputes. Sterling was his own sole client.

"Cyclical Denial" provided an erudite and dispassionate map through the labyrinth that was his case, from the "legal void" he fell into when he was sentenced during a time when there was no release mechanism for juvenile lifers through the ten state and federal cases addressing this issue, to the landmark Supreme Court case—and all of the maneuverings that followed. The document would be part of a new packet he was putting together, yet another approach to try to gain his freedom. "I might lose all the time," Sterling told me during one of our many phone calls, "but I ain't defeated." While his legal team, as indefatigable as the man they represented, pressed the point that Sterling was entitled to—and had not gotten—a *Miller* hearing, while they filed a request for an administrative review of the board's decision after the resentencing hearing, while they mounted a challenge to the rules the board used, Sterling was busy putting together a clemency package to put before the governor. In the midst of all this, the roller coaster that was Sterling's legal battle and Sterling's life took a nosedive. The now ultra-conservative Supreme Court undercut the *Miller* decision, which had been the foundation of Sterling's case for a decade. The entire architecture of the case, the many lower court cases he had won, the appeals successfully mounted—everything was in jeopardy. The appeal for clemency appeared to be the only play left for Sterling.

"Executive clemency is an extraordinary remedy of last resort." That's how the published guide to the application process put it. It was, in other words, a Hail Mary pass. During the previous three years, the governor had received 391 petitions for clemency and had granted a total of nine pardons and four commutations. Sterling was not after a pardon. He was guilty. He was not asking the governor—or anyone—to forgive him for what he had done. He was asking for a commutation, a second category under "clemency." A commutation was different. A commutation was not an exoneration or an absolution. It was a partial reduction in a prison sentence. If the governor commutated Sterling's sentence, she could rule that the time he had already spent incarcerated—twenty-seven going on twenty-eight years—was sufficient punishment.

She had other choices, or so Sterling calculated. She could commute the five-year "age tax," a parole board add-on that had been appended to his original sentence, termed ironically—in the jargon of the legal world—an "enhancement." Back when he had been convicted in the 1990s, the collective wisdom of the criminal justice system went like this: Statistics show that the older a person is when released, the less their chance of reoffending. So let's keep juveniles incarcerated longer. Let's tack on an extra five years to their sentence. Meanwhile, the collective wisdom from the world of neuroscience and adolescent development pointed in the opposite direction. Juveniles, the research showed, were far less capable of controlling impulsive behavior and far more susceptible to peer pressure than were adults. This developmental immaturity, this "neurological deficit," as the medical literature termed it, "renders them less culpable for their actions," in the words of Harvard-trained psychiatrist and legal ethicist Paul Appelbaum. Shaving off this five-year "enhancement" as part of commutation would not be that much of a controversial move for the governor. Alternately, she could reduce or eliminate the seventy-month sentence Sterling had gotten long ago, in the early days of his incarceration, for assault. Or she could do both. It might be that Sterling could go before a parole board within a year or at least in less than two.

"Do not expect a prompt response," warned the material concerning the clemency process. It might take up to six months. For Sterling, six months *was* prompt. He had waited years between mounting a case and hearing a decision, years between mounting an appeal and hearing a verdict. On the other hand, "it might take up to six months" could be an absurdly optimistic statement. Previous governors had sat on clemency appeals for years until their terms in office were just about to end and then off-loaded the decision to the next governor.

Sterling tried not to think about that as he edited his clemency statement. His motto had long been "Dare to struggle / Dare to win." That's how he signed all his letters. If he was a model of rehabilitation, he was also an exemplar of resilience.

CHAPTER 21

What is successful reentry?

The most common measure is how many of the hundreds of thousands of men and women released from custody every year end up back in prison after a few months, or a year or two. Those who, in the parlance of the criminal justice world, "recidivate," are reentry failures. They have not made the transition to life in the free world. By this calculation, successful reentry is elusive. Nearly half of all who are released are rearrested within the first year, and two-thirds are rearrested within the first three years. This is according to the Department of Justice. But that distressing statistic doesn't necessarily mean what we think it does. It doesn't mean that within just a few years 65 percent of ex-felons go out and commit another crime. It doesn't mean *once a criminal, always a criminal.* In fact, technical or administrative parole violations account for a significant percent of these rearrests. The Marshall Project, a nonprofit that focuses on criminal justice issues, calls this the "misleading math of recidivism." Technical parole violations might be serious—or might signal a serious problem—but many are not and do not. Breaking curfew, traveling without permission, changing a residence without informing a parole officer, failure to report to a parole officer, failure to pay mandated fines or fees, and failure to take or pass a drug test are all violations that can result in being sent back to prison. In many states, these arrests are lumped with arrests for the commission of new crimes.

In a report on rearrests and reconvictions conducted by the University of California Irvine's Center for Evidence-Based Corrections, 60 percent of those rearrested in California during the period under study were arrested for technical violations. In New York, 51 percent were technical parole violators; in Texas, it was 42 percent. Those who go back to prison (the majority of those we incarcerate) *have* failed to reenter successfully. But that failure is more complicated and more nuanced than the recidivism statistics indicate. Many failed not because they continued to live a life of crime but rather because the road to reentry was—is—steep and rocky, full of potholes, a winding path with unmarked detours.

When researchers survey ex-felons to evaluate their post-incarceration lives, they ask: Have you found a place to live? Have you found a job? Are you clean and sober? They might ask about family. But they very rarely ask about the way life is being lived day to day, about ordinary activities, the simple ways of being and doing that most of us take for granted: The scores of small decisions we make every day, choices we face with relative ease; our casual interactions with others; our fluency in reading body language; the way we effortlessly navigate space; our composure in crowds; our curiosity about the new and novel. These are behaviors we have learned and honed and internalized as citizens of the free world. They do not come naturally to those who have spent decades behind bars, where they have learned and honed and internalized a completely different set of behaviors. The success of those who do not recidivate is most often measured by the metrics most easy to measure—housing and employment—and not by the subtler and often far more difficult to accomplish feats of psychological and psychosocial reintegration.

A constellation of learned behaviors behind bars, the cumulative effect of what social psychologist Craig Haney has called "prisonization," makes truly successful reentry challenging in ways that are not easily computable but are deeply felt. During those decades behind bars, prisoners become accustomed to and then dependent on the structure and regimentation of the institution, the control it has over every aspect of their lives, and consequently, the lack of control they have over their own lives. In a place where there are almost no opportunities to make meaningful decisions and few opportunities to make even trivial choices, it is easy to forget how. Learned helplessness is not so easily unlearned. It is also not easy to unlearn the masking of emotions or hypervigilance, a protective strategy in a potentially violent and toxic place, but a disabling, psychologically damaging one in the free world. Nor is it easy to override an acquired and reinforced attitude of suspicion and distrust, an "us versus them" default. It is not easy to overcome—or even recognize— the cumulative trauma of witnessing or being the victim of the violent or demeaning behavior that can be the norm behind the walls. The chronic stress of life in prison can, not surprisingly, lead to PTSD, not often diagnosed and even less often treated.

The Norwegian model of incarceration is in direct contrast to all this, with decision making, community building, self-efficacy, and mutual respect at its core. Prisoners live in small units. They plan and cook their own meals. Prisoners and guards are together in activities all day, interacting and forming bonds. The director of one prison in Norway, a trained clinical psychologist, explained to a journalist from *The Guardian*: "If we treat people like animals when they are in prison they are likely to behave as animals. Here we pay attention to you as human beings." Are Hoidal, another prison director, put it this way: "Every inmate in a Norwegian prison is going back to the society. Do we want people who are angry—or people who are rehabilitated?" Norway has the lowest recidivism rate in the world.

Despite its success, the Norwegian model is not likely to make inroads in the U.S. "carceral state," as it has been called, where philosophically, politically, and economically, punishment trumps rehabilitation. The punishment of imprisonment is not just loss of freedom and separation from family, which is how the Norwegian system defines it. It is, in this country, the creation of facilities that make life as unpleasant as possible, that inflict psychological and emotional—and too often physical— harm. We want those who have done harm to us to suffer, to pay for what they did. But in making them suffer, we create the kind of human beings we do not want back in our communities.

———

Trevor was a success inside prison. He created that for himself. He sought out challenges. He learned organizational and management skills. He took on responsibilities. He learned how to navigate an environment that was rigid and rule bound but could, occasionally and with no warning, shift the ground like an earthquake and rattle the (literal) cages. He learned to survive and adapt. He learned patience. This set him up for success upon reentry. He was also young and healthy. And perhaps most important, he had the unwavering and unconditional support of his mother. So he was primed for success. Out in the free world, he found a job that made use of his organizational skills and kept him close—sometimes he thought too close—to the world of criminal justice. Still, he took every opportunity to work for change within the system, sitting on panels, giving talks, visiting youth facilities, being as much of an activist as he felt he could be. What held him back from doing more was the knowledge that, however well-intentioned his motives were, his public persona could trigger pain and cause trauma for the family and friends of his victim. Although he was learning how to live well—his relationship with Loraine was stable and mutually supportive; they had bought a house together—his past was never that far from his present. He was preternaturally observant to his surroundings. Whenever he heard a siren or saw a flashing light, his first thought was *they're coming to get me*. He had to take a breath and remember who he was, where he was. One time, he and a friend were standing on a downtown sidewalk waiting to cross the street. There were no cars in either direction. His friend stepped off the sidewalk and made his way across the street. Trevor hesitated, then walked a half block to the corner where there was a signal light and a crosswalk. Suppose a cop saw me jaywalking, he thought. Suppose that could be counted as a parole violation. Suppose I got sent back to prison.

His past lived inside him in a more profound way, preventing the creation of what the culture would consider a "normal" life for a thirty-something man in a long-term, loving relationship: he and Loraine would never have their own family. When he first told me that he didn't want children, he said he didn't want the responsibility. "There was so much I missed out on during those years of incarceration. I want to be able to do those things," he said. Then he added, maybe realizing that he sounded too selfish, "The planet doesn't need another person." The real reason came out later, after we talked for a while. "I have a lot of shame around the fact that I was raised well and still made a terrible mistake, a terrible choice. I do not want to be responsible for a child who does something terrible."

———————

Catherine, on the other hand, put herself on the fast track to be a mother. She had her daughter with her first real boyfriend, a man she met at her first job out of prison. She gave birth to her son barely a year later. It was a headlong rush into creating the childhood she never had, a way to experience, by proxy, the simplicity and innocence of those years. She would be the protective, caring mother she never had, showering them with love, cocooning them in safety. And they would love her unconditionally. They would always see her first as Mommy, not the way others saw her, through the lens of her crime, her conviction, her years inside.

Children were at the center of her new life. But they were not everything. After dead-end fast-food jobs and a minimum-wage night shift job that left her exhausted, she now had what she called her "dream job" working for a nonprofit on a mission to help juvenile offenders. As a program director she helped shape strategy. She reached out to corporations and potential donors who could be enlisted in the cause. Like Trevor, she gave talks and sat on panels. She was the public face of her organization, Campaign for the Fair Sentencing of Youth. Her job was to change the narrative. "When they see me, when they hear me, they begin to think differently about kids who spend decades behind bars," she told me. Behind the scenes, she led a group called Heart to Heart, a network of formerly incarcerated women who supported each other.

It had been a long haul. She thought of her post-incarceration life in five phases. First was the "time of reckoning" when the reality of freedom slapped her in the face. She hit the ground running and got little traction. Employment was a struggle. Entire occupations were permanently out of reach. Phase two began, again, with optimism: new life, a baby, a new city. But phase three—she termed this "survival mode"—and phase four, "sick and tired," quickly followed. The reality was she was a single mother with two toddlers and a job that didn't pay enough to afford childcare, let alone reliably cover the rent. She was a Black woman and an ex-felon, a combination that did not get you anywhere good. Unless, like Catherine, against so many odds, you believed in yourself. Did it help that she was young and smart and had no history of substance abuse? Yes. Catherine would say God had something to do with it. Perhaps that's why she named the fifth phase, her current phase, "redemption." This was when—*is* when—she learned she did not need a man, or a romantic relationship, to feel complete. It is when she changed the taillight of her car by herself. When she made a loud noise and was heard.

She had saved and planned for a week's vacation with the kids. Work at the nonprofit was going well. Finally, there was some stability. What a treat, after all this time, to even think the word *vacation*, let alone plan for one. She booked an apartment through Airbnb. A few days later she received an email, which read in part: "We regret to inform you at this time Airbnb, Inc., has made the determination to permanently deactivate your

account due, at least in part, to the following information...
Criminal Records Match." Catherine went into high gear, post-
ing the Airbnb response on social media. She texted a friend, a
cop who ran a nonprofit, who contacted his friend, who happened to be a nationally prominent social justice advocate with
29.6K Twitter followers. Suddenly, her post caught the attention
of thousands. And Airbnb. At first, the company sent her an
email stating that its decision was final. Then, a few hours later,
she was advised that her account had been reactivated. She had
advocated for herself—and won. "I would love to say that I felt a
sense of victory, but I don't," she posted. "When we are judged
based on who we are and not what we've done, then and only
then have we won."

This powerful "redemption" phase also included the hard
work of forgiving her father, the man who failed to protect her
from the sexual abuse that marked her childhood, the abuse that
triggered her crime, the crime that put her in prison for sixteen
years. Where does that kind of forgiveness come from? Catherine
explained it this way: "To receive forgiveness, forgiveness must
be extended." It would be, she thought, hypocritical to want forgiveness for herself if she were not willing to extend it to others.

She spent months preparing for a move back to Florida. It
was difficult logistically and economically. Everyone at work had
to be on board. There were intense negotiations with Damon,
the father of her two children. They wanted to coparent even
though they had not been a couple for quite a while. Would he
move across the country to continue that relationship with his
kids? There was searching long distance to find an affordable
place that would rent to her. But the biggest challenge was emotional. This key element to her "redemption" phase was, in large
part, sparked by her father's failing health and her need to be

a good daughter, her need to show her own children the transcendent importance of family. But it was exhausting. He suffered from congestive heart failure. His lungs filled with fluid. He was always a (literal) heartbeat away from being rushed to the ER. Which is where Catherine found herself, too often, as she juggled the life she was finally, fully—and most of the time, joyfully—inhabiting.

Dave's post-prison life was the least complicated and, it seemed, the least satisfying. He was successful by the reentry metrics: housed, employed, no brushes with the law. But was that all his life was going to be? A checking of boxes? He would be sixty-two soon. He was still living in supported housing, the kind of setup designed for college students. His quad mates, with whom he had almost no contact, checked all the boxes too. The wrong boxes. One was a drug addict; another had alcohol problems; the third had what Dave described as "girlfriend issues" and was never around. He was still working the same job, the deli counter at a chain grocery store, still making just over minimum wage. Even without a three-decades-long, violent offender prison record, a man in his sixties with no real-world job references was not likely to get anything much better than what Dave had. He didn't apply for the factory job his friend told him about or for any other job. It's not that the deli counter work fulfilled him in any way, not that he saw a promotion in his future, or anticipated more than a small raise every six months or so. It was that any change would be a risk. He would have to answer questions about himself, his past. He would have to figure out—"negotiate" is the word he always used—new relationships. How to act, what to say. At his current job, his boss knew him and, Dave thought, liked him. He had achieved a kind of anonymity.

What made his post-prison world uncomplicated is also what made it lonely. He had no family. His crime had been against his family. His older brother had testified against him at his trial. And he had few friends. He had been behind bars far too long to maintain any friendships that had existed back in his twenties. And he had been in prison more than long enough to forget what a casual, uncomplicated relationship looked like. The learning curve for that was a steep one. In his new life, he had two men he thought of as friends, both of whom were left-overs from his incarcerated life. One was more than a friend. Or so Dave had thought. They had made big plans for a com-bined future. Dave harbored that dream, or some small part of it, during his first year out. They were in close contact, mostly by phone. In fact, they shared a phone plan. But Kevin now had a "girlfriend"—Dave used the quotation marks when he referred to that relationship—and he was, Dave thought, going nowhere, living what turned out to be an unstable life. Nine years out and Kevin had nothing to show for it. Finally, Dave broke off the relationship by getting his own phone. He said he had been too close to see "the really bad negatives." Whatever traits had been attractive inside did not translate to this reentered life.

Dave worked hard to maintain a friendship with the second man, but the effort was one-sided. Either Dave was blind to that, or he read the signals wrong. The nuances of facial expressions, of body language, of tone and demeanor continued to elude him. One brilliantly sunny spring day, a midweek day off for Dave, he packed up a gourmet sandwich from the deli and a slab of chocolate cake and set off in his car to surprise his friend with lunch. He related the story this way: "I knew I was sideswiping him at his workplace, but I thought lunch would be the ticket to see each other and have a quick bite." Dave texted this to me when he got home. "Well, not only was he not happy to see me, but he also refused the lunch I brought." The text was followed by a surprise-face emoji. Then he sent a selfie of him sitting on his couch in his room eating the cake. He had driven two hours, more than one hundred miles, to surprise the man who was clearly not his friend.

This friendship thing, even casual contact, was a continuing mystery to him. On one of his many trips out to the ocean, he had just parked his car in a visitors' lot and was walking to a lookout point to enjoy the sunset. A guy came up to him who had parked a few spaces away and made a casual, complimentary remark about Dave's car. And Dave immediately thought: Why would this guy start a conversation with me? What does he want? How am I supposed to respond? His thoughts were racing. If he didn't say something friendly back, would that be rude? If he did say something friendly back, would he be "encouraging" this stranger? This is how he overthinks even chance encounters. He forced himself to be, in his words, "prosocial." They talked for a moment about cars, which Dave deemed a safe subject for two men.

A few minutes later, as Dave was standing on the promontory staring out over the ocean, the man arrived to take in the view. Should Dave say something? Would that be too forward? He stood there momentarily paralyzed. The man nodded and smiled. Okay, Dave thought, taking a breath. This is harmless. He is just a nice guy. They watched the setting sun. When they started walking back down the path to their cars, Dave, now interested in being friendly but not sure how to do that, mentioned that he worked at the deli counter. "Stop by sometime and say hello," he said. A week later, the man came into the store, greeted Dave behind the counter, and bought a sandwich. Dave watched him walk away and wondered, "Should I have invited him out for coffee?"

———————

Vicki was the only one who "fell"—that is, in prison parlance, she was rearrested, albeit for a misdemeanor—and the only one who still, two years out, seemed to be living an only modestly sanitized version of the life that had landed her behind bars so many times. She was the only one with a long history of drug addiction. She was also the only one who, upon release, went back to the community, the street, the house, the domestic relationship that formed the foundation of her criminal life. These all seem related, although exactly how it is hard to tell.

Vicki should have been the biggest reentry success story. She was not a violent offender, so she did not have to carry the weight of that psychological burden. Although she had spent cumulative decades behind bars, none of her individual sentences took her away from the free world for longer than five years at a time. Her reentry shock would be blunted. She did not have to struggle to find—or even think about finding—a safe and comfortable place to live. She found employment. The jobs were mostly menial and low wage, but she was never in danger of not being able to pay the bills. Someone else was paying the bills. That "someone else" was a person who had been in her life for thirty years. Stability like that is seen as a good thing. Add to this that, despite her drug use, she was in decent health, and (although this should not make any difference, we are now very aware that it does) she is white. So the reentry deck was stacked in her favor. But she was the one—she is the one—holding those cards. She is the one playing the game. Even with good cards, a player who doesn't know how to win won't win.

Vicki returned to Oklahoma to find that her trailer had been burglarized. When she had hit the road a month before, she told a "friend" he could stay at her place. He was a recent acquaintance, a guy she'd met in town. He was an ex-felon, a drug user who was staying clean. They bonded over that. He was trying to save money working construction so he could travel to another state to look for his son. It was a twisted story that got weirder with every detail. Vicki said that the man's children had been "stolen" by his mother-in-law. The son, a minor and the eldest of five kids, had run away. The mother, this man's wife, was currently serving time for conspiracy to commit murder. The man was staying in her trailer, but he left town for a few days to work on a job site. When he came back, he found that the trailer had been broken into. His carpentry tools were stolen along with $1,800 in cash from unemployment benefits. He had no bank account. He cashed his checks and hid the money in his clothing. Whoever burglarized the trailer knew this guy, knew he'd be out of town, undoubtedly knew about the stashed cash.

That burglary made some sense. What didn't make sense was that the trailer was targeted a second time. This time Vicki's stuff—"everything I own," she told me during a teary phone call—was taken, and the place was trashed. The "everything" that Vicki had in the trailer did not include expensive or new electronics. No jewelry. No drugs, she insisted. What the burglar took was clothing and craft supplies, nothing remotely worth the risk of the serious crime of breaking and entering. Presumably, the trailer had been cased during the previous break-in, or so Vicki thought. But what was the motive? And why ransack the place? And, to add to the mystery, why did none of Vicki's very nearby trailer park neighbors report either break-in? Vicki knew the answers, not the specific answers but the general outline. She was living the life. She was mixing with people who were living the life. She was living amid people who were living the life. This was what happened.

Vicki looked at the mess that was her trailer, that was her life, and thought about the rush of relief she'd feel if she could just shoot up. It took so much strength for her to tell herself, remind herself, that drugs were the problem, not the solution. She was very proud of herself for that, *very* proud. I told her, speaking as her mentor, as a person who had come to care about her, how very proud I was too. The decision not to use gave her the energy to clean out the trailer and pack up her car. She headed back west with vague plans to move "somewhere big where no one knows me" and "somewhere hot because I love wearing shorts and a tank top." She would find some kind of job. Steve would follow her there. Maybe.

———

And then there was Arnoldo, perhaps the biggest success of them all, and the least likely: poor, brown, the son of a violent alcoholic father who gave him his first drink when he was six, a father who abused him and his mother, who beat up people on the street. A loner, an introvert, a gun-toting gangbanger who went into the system at fifteen and spent nineteen years behind bars, many of them in the hole as punishment for yard fights, for gang activities. He had to unlearn not just a way of life but a way to *be*. He had to remake himself from the ground up, learning how to respond rather than react, understanding the power of composure, discovering that strength comes from the opposite place he thought strength came from—vulnerability—redefining what it meant to be a man.

Today he is a positive force in the Latinx community, an emerging leader in the nonprofit that employs (and has consistently promoted) him. He is making an impact, every day, on kids who look and talk and act a lot like he did. He and Nicole have ever so carefully built an honest, thoughtful, and transparent marriage, and they work hard to keep it that way. He is a loving father who moved beyond his own rage and anger to forgive his own father. That's what he learned in deep conversations with himself in the hole: that the not-forgiving was hurting and haunting him; that he could not move forward unless he let go.

He had—inside, alone in the hole, in long conversations with Sterling, and in small groups of men struggling to make sense of their past—achieved what Karuna, the chaplain who married him, Melissa, the professor who taught restorative justice, and most of all Sterling, his friend and his mentor, believed could happen. He had transformed trauma. "Who I am now is completely unrecognizable from who I was twenty years ago," he told me in his deep, quiet voice, his son Sol squirming on his lap. "Even for me it is shocking how different I am."

———

It is 6:00 a.m., dark and raining. Cheryl, Sterling's wife, is sitting in her truck in a prison parking lot waiting for Ivan to walk through the gate. Ivan and Sterling have been friends for twenty-five years, cellmates, brothers. They are a matched set. Almost exactly two years apart in age—both Aries warriors—and two inches apart in height, Ivan's six feet five inches edging out

Sterling's six feet three inches, they came to prison within two years of each other. Both are the sons of Black fathers and white mothers. Cheryl isn't waiting outside the prison that housed Ivan for a quarter of a century, the prison that still houses Sterling. As often happens in the system, Ivan was transferred from that maximum security facility about a year ago to this nearby minimum security prison as part of "step-down" preparation for release.

The heater is on in the truck. The sky has lightened to a steely gray. Now it is 7:00 a.m., and he is still not out the gate. She watches as several other men—nine are set for release today—make their way across the asphalt. Finally, she sees him, a tall, lanky man hefting two enormous plastic bags that contain all his belongings. He is dressed in the black sweatpants, black hoodie, and gray T-shirt she delivered to the prison gate an hour ago, the "tall man" clothes she had to special order online. He is calm. He is always calm. Like Sterling. He gets into the truck and asks for something to wipe his hands with. The guard touched his hand. She starts driving out of the parking lot, down a little road. He is staring out the window. "This is wild," he says, transfixed by the movement but unruffled. He hasn't been in a private vehicle for a quarter of a century.

She drives to a nearby city park and drops him off by a trail that follows the river. He has his earbuds in, plugged into his old MP3 player. She waits in the car, stressed with the details of orchestrating this morning. Ivan was late getting out. Now he's out walking. She wants him to enjoy this moment, but Sterling will be waiting.

They arrive at the penitentiary at 7:40 a.m. Ivan doesn't want her to pull into the prison's parking lot. He doesn't want to be on prison grounds again. But they are late, and it's the closest place to their destination. They get out of the car and start walking through the lot to State Street, to the hydrant. Ivan puts up his hood. "I don't want anyone to see me," he says, only half kidding. Then he realizes what he looks like to the cars passing by—a big Black man in a dark hoodie skirting the perimeter of the twenty-five-foot-high walls of a prison. "This isn't cool, this isn't cool," he says, not kidding now, but still calm.

They get to the yellow hydrant. Cheryl is videoing this on her phone. They both look up at the windows on the fourth floor. It's too far away to see Sterling's face, but they can see an outline. Ivan bends down to touch the hydrant, and Cheryl captures the moment. Sterling watches. How many men has he seen walk into their new lives from this window? Will it ever be him out there? He waves. He turns the lights on and off, on and off. Ivan stands there in the rain. Then he asks to borrow Cheryl's phone, and she shows him how to take his first selfie.

CHAPTER 22

It is Tuesday, September 28. Another workday for Sterling. He leaves his cell on A-Block, walks down the tier, out across the control floor, and up four flights of stairs to the chapel. He is settling in when his friend, Anthony, rushes in, grinning, to tell him the news: The governor has commuted his sentence. He will be getting out within weeks. Like Sterling, he had been in prison for murder since he was a teen. Sterling had befriended and mentored Anthony, as he had so many other men, had introduced him to RJ, had brought him into the study groups.

Sterling is genuinely, deeply happy for his friend. But he is also scared. Karuna is there in the office watching the two men. Sterling is way more than scared, she thinks. He is panicked. He is distraught. He knew that his and Anthony's commutation packages had reached the governor's office on the very same day.

It was back in mid-May, almost four and a half months ago, that Aliza Kaplan and her legal team at the Criminal Justice Reform Clinic had submitted the packages for both men. Sterling had been working on his personal statement not just since the dispiriting news from the resentencing hearing many months before that, but really for years, for decades, as he struggled to make sense of what he had done and how to explain his hard-won transformation. That statement, along with a number of the letters that had been part of the resentencing package and five new letters written by state legislators, made up the one-hundred-plus page submission.

Sterling had won cases and appeals and judgments. He had tried mediation. Little had come of it. He knew, his lawyers knew, that commutation was not just his best shot. It was his only shot. And so he waited. He was accustomed to long stretches of silence. But now, today, Anthony had heard, and Sterling had not. That can't be good news, he thinks. He keeps his head down, finishes up work, goes back to his cell.

A while later he is told to report back to the chapel. There, in Karuna's office, he sees Nathaline Frener, the former law professor who had taught restorative justice classes inside and was now an administrator at the prison. Next to her is an inmate assigned to take photographs and videos of prison events. They are here, he is told, to interview Anthony. Now Karuna and Nathaline have their heads together, whispering, in the corner. Sterling, taught by his years of incarceration to be hyperalert, to read body language, to parse nuance, is confused. Something is going on. But what?

Nathaline asks him to walk down the hall to the library with her. There she pulls out her phone and starts scrolling, begins to say something, pauses, doesn't finish the sentence, fumbles. Sterling has known Nathaline for a decade. He knows her as organized, focused, to the point. She doesn't fumble. And here she is fumbling. In retrospect, he sees that she was just stalling for time.

Then Nathaline looks up from her phone. She smiles at Sterling. Her smile is radiant. "You've got a phone call," she tells him. They walk back to Karuna's office. Aliza Kaplan and two members from the Criminal Justice Reform Clinic legal team are on the line, on speakerphone.

"Will you go out to breakfast with us on November 1st?" That's what Aliza says, no preamble.

And then it hits him. *He's getting out.* He too, like Anthony, has had his sentence commuted. "I do the manly cry thing," he tells me on the phone the next morning, recounting a blow-by-blow. "I cover my face. Cry into my hands. Then I suck it up." And the whole rest of the day, he walks around saying yes to everything. He doesn't know what he's said yes to. But "yes" is the word of the moment.

———

A little more than a month later, thirty-three days to be exact, Cheryl and I are texting each other near midnight. She is camped out on a cot in her living room surrounded by her three cats. Her mother, sister, aunt, and nephews fill her small house. We know we need to get up at 4:30 the next morning, but neither of us wants to break off the connection. We have been friends through Sterling for only a few years, but sometimes there is a way people connect that has nothing to do with time spent. "Maybe you don't know this," she tells me, "but you have been my rock." It's 6:30 the next morning, Monday, November 1. Dawn is another forty-five minutes away. Serious rain is maybe fifteen minutes away, coming in fast from the coast. A small crowd is gathered across from the gate, illuminated not by the moon—it is overcast—but by the glare of the prison tower spotlight. There are close to thirty people here to welcome Sterling back into the world he left behind more than a quarter of a century ago as a sixteen-year-old kid. There's Anthony, released a week ago, Arnoldo—with Sol on his shoulders—Ivan, Jabari, and a few other prison friends who were freed before him. Trevor is here too. There are a handful of students who were in the RJ class with Sterling. There's Melissa, the quiet activist and professor from Willamette, who keeps RJ going inside, along with a few community activists. And Karuna, of course. And Steven Finster, the man responsible for the writing group that brought Sterling and me together. There are the women from Sterling's legal team. There's the film crew, Lydia the documentarian whose film about RJ had been on hold since the pandemic, along with a cameraman, lighting guy, and sound guy. And there is Cheryl, her sister who looks so much like her as to be her twin, her mother—a tiny woman next to her almost six-foot tall daughter—and a lively, smiling nephew.

A few minutes after seven, Sterling walks out the gate holding a huge, impossibly leggy plant that he nurtured from nothing in his cell over years and years. He strides. He always strides. He looks both relaxed and stunned. I don't know how that is possible, but that's what it is. He makes his way through the crowd, calling out people's names, hugging, moving on to the next. Everyone wants a piece of him. Big body hugs with audible backslapping when he sees one of the guys from inside; gentler, longer hugs for the others. Cheryl stands off to the side and watches the Sterling show. "I don't own him," she told me last week when we were texting about how public this event will be. "He's everybody's." He hugs two more guys, grabs Anthony, whose head comes up to Sterling's shoulder, and pulls him close. The film crew is maneuvering around looking for the shots.

"Where's Cheryl?" Sterling asks, moving from public persona

to private. She is right there, behind him, watching, waiting. They embrace. They stay locked like that with the mist starting to come down and the prison tower spotlight illuminating them.

Sterling is in control, which is astonishing—and yet somehow not surprising. This first moment out, this first breath of free air, is, for many, paralyzing. Not Sterling. He addresses the crowd. He relates the story about the plant he grew. He tells the crowd about the books that sustained him. About the writing he did that nurtured him. About the music that kept his soul alive. He tells everyone about the hydrant and its meaning, about how many times he's watched other guys touch it and walk off to freedom. Now it is his turn.

It's raining hard. Maybe two dozen of us follow him down the sidewalk and out of the prison grounds. The hydrant, on a grassy strip sandwiched between a sidewalk and a busy street, is just steps away. He stands in front of it, staring at it, the cars on State Street zipping by, the rain sheeting down. No one speaks. Then he kneels down, extends his long arm, and touches it. His hand does not linger. We clap and whoop and take pictures with our phones.

What happens next takes your breath away. It makes you question how a moment can be so real, so authentic, and so cheesy all at once. If this were a film, and this was the ending, you would groan. If this were a novel, and it was the final paragraph, you would dismiss it as overwrought. But let me tell you: this moment is real, and this moment is pure magic.

Sterling stands up to his full height, turns his back to the hydrant and the street now crowded with early morning traffic. He is facing the prison, visible behind its twenty-five-foot concrete perimeter. He lifts his fist in the air, holds it there. In the distance, up on the fourth floor, he can see—we all can see—the outlines of maybe a dozen people, inmates inside, inmates watching. Sterling punches the sky with his fist and calls out to them. And then, at that very moment, a murmuration of starlings—Mary Oliver calls them "acrobats in the theatre of the air"—swoops across the gray sky over the prison. They dive and soar, loop in the air, switch direction, and fly overhead again. Starlings are Sterling's favorite bird.

RESILIENCE
Sterling Cunio

Resilience is picking yourself up when no one sees you fall.
It's ten deep breaths after a devastating phone call.
It's learning how to make something out of nothing.
It's knowing that your own mind is all you need in an empty
   room.
Resilience is a bird in a tree glimpsed over concrete walls.

ACKNOWLEDGMENTS

Writing—the act itself—is solitary, but almost nothing else about the creation of a book is. That's what acknowledgments are all about.

I would not have been halfway smart enough to even think about pursuing this project had it not been for the foundation laid by a generation of criminologists, sociologists, historians, and others who illuminated the path with their careful and clear-eyed inquiries. Their research is referenced in the source notes and bibliography, but I want to single out just a few whose work opened my eyes, questioned my assumptions, and prompted me to look, listen—and think—in new ways: Joan Petersilia for her pioneering studies; Bruce Western and Marieke Liem for their meticulous chronicling of post-incarceration lives; Caleb Smith for his stunning work on the ideology of the prison; Megan Comfort for her game-changer of a book about women who love and marry men behind bars.

Those who work in the reentry field, juggling the busiest of schedules and shouldering commitments that can sometimes, literally, be life or death, were extraordinarily generous with their time, sharing their professional (and sometimes personal) experiences about the long road from prison to home. I thank Paul Solomon, Brett Bray, Nick Crapser, Kristie Mamac, Amy Myers, Maxwell Morris, Summer Robinson, Brandon Chrostowski, and Jackie Austin. You were not just sources of information. You were (and are) sources of inspiration. And that goes for attorney Ryan O'Connor, who, over many hours of conversation and many emails, helped me understand the tangled legalities of sentencing laws, court cases, and appeals while he worked tirelessly to help gain release for the man who gazed out at the yellow hydrant.

I thank Melissa Michaux, Taryn VanderPyl, and Michelle Inderbitzen for helping me explore the restorative justice terrain and for the extraordinary work they do in their classrooms, both those on campus and those in prison. And, close to home, I am deeply indebted to my son Zane, who first introduced me to the theory and history of restorative justice as he studied it and completed several internships.

Because it is impossible to understand the winding, rock-strewn path that leads from caged to free without understanding the culture inside prisons, I have spent years—for this book and for my previous work, *A Grip of Time*—learning about what life is like for those who spend decades of it behind bars, especially those who come of age inside. I have gotten so much help here. I thank Steven Finster, a long-time prison staffer, whose optimism, energy, and tenacious support made it possible for me to start and run a writing group inside the walls for those serving life sentences. The men in that group—every one of them in very different ways, but all of them with honesty, humor, and great patience—taught me about incarcerated life and the kind of person one becomes to survive inside. I owe an enormous debt to Michael, M2, Wil, James, Jimmie, Kaz, Don, Jann, Lee, and Eric. Karuna Thompson, prison chaplain, tough and tender, sister-from-another-mother, I cannot adequately express my gratitude not merely for all you have done to help me understand incarcerated life but for all you continue to do, inside, for those living it.

When people are sources of information, you thank them for their help. When people open up their lives to you, let you see their vulnerabilities, trust you with their stories, there is no way to thank them. There is only the responsibility to do right by them. I hope I have done that. I owe this book—and very much more—to Arnoldo Ruiz, Catherine Jones, Trevor Walraven, "Dave," "Vicki," and most especially to Sterling Cunio. He thinks I have taught him a lot. It is nothing compared to what he has taught me.

I thank (and so greatly admire) the extraordinary women who stand not *behind* their men but beside them, and often in front of them, for their candor, their honesty, their trust in me, and for the many hours, virtual and otherwise, we spent together: Cheryl Cunio, Karen Cain, Nicole Lindahl-Ruiz, Loraine McLeod, and Tricia McGilliard Hedlin. As Cornel West said, "Tenderness is what love looks like in private. Justice is what love looks like in public."

Thanks to my friend and former editor, Julia Serebrinsky, for introducing me to Heather Jackson, the smartest, savviest, most supportive, passionate, and persistent agent in the known universe. This book happened because she cared deeply about it and because she believed in me. I am overwhelmed with gratitude.

Sourcebooks, my publisher, embraces books that change lives. A big thank you to founder Dominique Raccah for her vision and her creative and entrepreneurial energy. I am honored to be a Sourcebooks author. It has been a pleasure to work with my editor, Anna Michels, who is insightful, thoughtful, and sensitive. The book is better because of her. I thank the rest of the team at Sourcebooks (Sarah Otterness, Heather VenHuizen, and Liz Kelsch) for their work on my behalf.

Everyone who shared their stories with me to make the story that is this book believes in the power of stories to change lives. I hope you do too.

READING GROUP GUIDE

1. How much did you know about the prison system in the United States before reading this book? What was the most surprising thing you learned?

2. Of the primary characters, whom do you think was most affected by asynchronicity? Who was released into a world most similar to the one they had left? If you were imprisoned today, which aspect of your life would make you feel most "left behind"?

3. Compare Vicki's short but frequent incarcerations to a long sentence like Arnoldo's or Dave's. How does recidivism impact someone's support system?

4. In your opinion, which character had the most successful transition from prisoner to citizen? What were the most important resources they used to achieve that success?

5. Arnoldo and Sterling are both deeply involved with restorative justice (RJ). Discuss the ways they apply RJ and conflict resolution. How do these practices shape their ongoing experiences? How would you use RJ to help someone like Trevor, who faced extreme community backlash after his release?

6. Vicki's reentry has been especially complicated, and Kessler specifically avoids learning some details as a sign of support. If you followed your first impulse, what would you have done in Kessler's position? Do you think your strategy would change any of Vicki's outcomes?

7. Kessler describes each character's outfit upon release. How do your clothes communicate your identity? How do each ex-prisoner's clothes reflect the conditions they will meet out in the world?

8. Some of the characters were tried as adults for crimes they committed as teenagers. Should children under eighteen ever be tried as adults? How does that practice influence long-term rehabilitation outcomes?

9. In your opinion, what is the biggest obstacle to successful reentry? Can you think of a solution?

10. There is some debate about the purpose of imprisonment. What purpose do you think prisons are currently serving? What purpose *should* they serve? Name three changes you would make to enact the purpose you've identified.

A CONVERSATION WITH THE AUTHOR

How did you first get involved with the prison community? What motivated you to write this book?

I believe in the power of stories to change lives. And I believe that "owning" your own narrative is the key to both self-awareness and self-empowerment. That's why I was initially interested in going into a prison to launch and facilitate a writers' group, especially for those who had been behind bars for a long time. They lived lives we knew nothing about. They were invisible, and their voices were unheard. I wanted to help them tell their own stories. The book that emerged from that experience, *A Grip of Time: When Prison Is Your Life*, catapulted me into this one. In doing the background research for *Grip*, I discovered what to me was an astounding fact: 95 percent of all those we imprison will be released one day. I knew the life they had been living behind bars would make the transition from caged to free an enormous challenge. I knew the journey must be so much more nuanced than the (few) reentry stories we had already heard: the astonishing successes, the abject failures. I had to find out. I wanted their stories to help us—force us—to think about rehabilitation, transformation, and hope.

How did you select the six characters that we follow through-out the book? What were the biggest challenges of following their stories?

It was a Process with a capital P. I began thinking that I would embed myself in a reentry nonprofit, Margaret Mead style, watching, listening, learning from people remaking their lives. Unfortunately, after many months and countless conversations, I could not arrange the access I needed. I then pivoted—but still held onto my idea of finding a group situation. I applied for, was hired, and trained for a bottom-rung job at a women's reentry halfway house. But privacy concerns, despite everyone's best efforts (and my pledge of transparency), could not be overcome.

And so I networked. I started with people I knew and built from there, conscious at every step that I wanted a diverse cast of characters. "Diverse" means a lot of things: gender, race, age, backstory, family, time inside. It was a juggling act. I knew Sterling from the writers' group. He introduced me to Arnoldo. A university professor put Trevor on my radar, and Trevor, in turn, introduced me to Catherine. I volunteered at a wrap-around services reentry and trained as a mentor. Vicki was assigned as my mentee. Dave was also from my prison writers' group. He was such a mystery to me, and he was older than the others when he went inside, had spent more time incarcerated than the others, and was the oldest of the group upon reentry.

The biggest challenges? Earning the trust of people who have spent decades in environments where few could be trusted. Confronting and challenging my own biases. Shifting from in-the-trenches fieldwork to working in virtual spaces without losing intimacy. Honoring these stories.

What is your writing process? Is there a time and place you prefer?

Writing is my passion, yes. But it is also my job. I do my job. Every day. I have a room lined with bookcases that is my writing room. I go there and shut the door. I have (and have had for five years) a standing desk. It is not an up-and-down desk. There is no down. I stand. Period. I look out over a weedy meadow to a tree line. Often (too often) there are marauding deer. Not lovable Bambis. Deer that eat everything including deer resistant plants. Sometimes there are families of turkeys. Occasionally, a cougar saunters by.

When I am involved in the writing part of a book project, as opposed to the immersion reporting, or the sitting-on-the-floor-organizing-file-cards part, I work from about ten to three. Before work, I run, bike, work out, take an online class. After three, my writing brain is dead. I will do chores—laundry, shopping, meal prep, email. Maybe gardening or lawn mowing if it's that time of year. Maybe go for a walk with a friend. Too often I answer the siren call of social media. I am active on Facebook and Instagram. I have a blog.

What did your writing process look like for *Free*? What are some of the bright spots in your writing life?

I see the creation of a book as a kind of three-act play, only one of which is the writing. All acts present ongoing challenges. If they don't, then I'm doing something wrong. I never want to be in a comfort zone with my work. I always want the bar to be higher—I want to set the bar higher—so I can continue to learn and grow.

The first "act" is conceptualizing the book. How do I approach a big social issue in a compelling narrative fashion? Where are the small stories that will illuminate the big theme? I burn a lot of brain cells figuring this out. But it mostly looks like I'm just staring out the window. The in-the-trenches research, the fieldwork, is the next act. I love everything about this. It is an alive time, a time when I must be alert to everything, when I learn the most, when I feel the most porous, when I need to stay the most transparent. Before the pandemic, when I first started the fieldwork for *Free*, I spent a lot of face-to-face time with all the characters in the book. We got to know each other. We met for coffee. We talked and walked. I met girlfriends and wives, dogs and cats. After COVID made that at first impossible and then just very challenging, we Zoomed and phoned and texted, exchanged videos, used Marco Polo to send brief, in-the-moment messages. The writing is the final act, and everything about it is challenging: Making characters come alive on the page; crafting scenes that bring the reader into the moment; interweaving background, backstory, and context with ongoing narrative; making it hard for a reader to put down the book; staying true to the people who have let me into their lives.

The bright spots? I GET TO DO THIS. It is daily privilege of which I am acutely and deliciously aware.

If you could pick one thing for every reader to take away from *Free*, what would it be?

People are capable of transforming their lives.

What do you read in your free time?

As both a reader and a writer, I am attracted to deeply researched, true stories told as compellingly as any great novel,

so I mostly read narrative nonfiction. Lately I find myself reread-
ing the classics for inspiration and grounding—John McPhee,
Joan Didion, Tom Wolfe, Annie Dillard, Tracy Kidder. I reread
A River Runs Through It every year. Yes, every year. If there is
a wiser, more lyrical book out there, I have yet to discover it. I
think Katherine Boo and Stacy Schiff are brilliant and will read
anything they write. Ditto for Geraldine Brooks, who so very
gracefully weaves fact and fiction into something that is both and
neither. My favorite novels of late are Lily King's *Euphoria* and (a
reread) Louise Erdrich's *Love Medicine*. On my nightstand right
now: Paul Kalanithi's *When Breath Becomes Air* and Roxane Gay's
Hunger. Oh, I also read Raymond Chandler. And cookbooks.

SOURCE NOTES

CHAPTER 1

To clarify how I work: I immerse myself in the lives of the characters you will meet as much as possible and as much as they will permit. I have spent considerable time with them over the course of at least two years and in the case of Sterling for much longer. That time is not spent conducting traditional interviews, although of course I ask questions. It is time immersed in the dailiness of their lives and in deep and wide-ranging conversation. Prior to the pandemic, we met in person, on their turf. Since then, we have shifted to phone, Skype and Zoom conversations, and text exchanges. Some of these people live more public lives than others, and I learn about them through the work they do, their social media presence, and articles written about them. About the scenes that I recount, here and in the chapters that follow: Many I have witnessed. Others were captured on video or in photographs that were shared with me. Such is the case with the extended scene in this chapter, which is based on many hours of interviews and conversations with

Sterling, Arnoldo, Karuna, and Cheryl; photographs and video captured by Cheryl; and my own extensive, personal knowledge of the prison, its layout, and its procedures. In the chapters that follow where you learn about these characters and are experiencing what they encounter, hearing them speak, seeing them in action, know this is how that material was gathered.

CHAPTER 2

For reliable statistics about U.S. (and global) incarceration, see data gathered (and updated) by Prison Policy Initiative, Vera Institute of Justice, U.S. Bureau of Justice Statistics, and The Sentencing Project. For a succinct discussion of the evolution and causes of the incarceration boom, see the introduction to *On the Outside*. The statistics concerning inmates released after serving their sentences comes from the U.S. Bureau of Justice Statistics. Martin Seligman's work on learned helplessness, referred to here and elsewhere in the book, is essential reading when trying to understand the difficulty of transitioning from prison to home. In addition to the two journal articles under his name cited in the source section, also note one for which he is second author (Steven Maier is first author). *When Prisoners Come Home*, *Homeward*, and *After Life Imprisonment* all discuss what successful reentry looks like. For more about Ann Jacobs and the work of the John Jay College's Prisoner Reentry Institute and Institute for Justice and Opportunity, see: https://justiceandopportunity.org/. Nick Crapser presents his "Three Es" in the TEDx presentation on YouTube cited in the source section. The U.S. Department of Justice's Roadmap to Reentry is here: https://www.justice.gov/archives/reentry. An Overview of Offender Reentry is here: https://www.ojp.gov/pdffiles1/nij/251554.pdf. This report from Harvard University Institute

of Politics is also helpful: https://iop.harvard.edu/sites/default
/files/sources/program/IOP_Policy_Program_2019_Reentry
_Policy.pdf.

CHAPTER 3

I owe the in-the-moment details of the Madison, Wisconsin, reentry simulation exercise to Jackie Austin, Program and Editorial Assistant at JustDane (formerly Madison-area Urban Ministry), who spent hours talking with me and even more hours answering my follow-up questions. Here is the Urban Institute study referenced in this chapter: https://www.urban .org/policy-centers/justice-policy-center/projects/returning -home-study-understanding-challenges-prisoner-reentry.

Bright writes about "the corrected life" in *The Powers That Punish*. For details on gate money, see: www.themarshallproject .org/2019/09/10. Much has been written about what is—and is not—offered in and outside of prison to help with reentry. See this summary report from Vera Institute of Justice: https://www .vera.org/state-of-justice-reform/2017/the-state-of-reentry. This National Institute of Justice–funded report is also enlightening: https://nij.ojp.gov/topics/articles/nij-funded-research -examines-what-works-successful-reentry, as is the introductory chapter in *On the Outside*. Here is the link to the National Institute of Justice report that (surprisingly) finds the Second Chance Act a failure: https://nij.ojp.gov/topics/articles/lessons -learned-second-chance-act-moving-forward-strengthen -offender-reentry. Here is what the Department of Justice has to say about the effects of money spent on education within prisons: https://www.justice.gov/archives/prison-reform. For Lewis Conway's entire statement about the continuing punishment of life after release see https://www.aclu.org/news

/smart-justice/recidivism-will-only-decrease-if-successful
-reentry-is-embraced-as-an-antidote-for-mass-incarceration/.
See this extensive report on collateral consequences prepared
by the U.S. Commission on Civil Rights: https://www.usccr.gov
/pubs/2019/06-13-Collateral-Consequence. See also this extensive report by Michael Pinard, who is quoted in this chapter:
https://www.bu.edu/law/journals-archive/bulr/volume86n3
/documents/PINARDv2.pdf.

Much has been written (and researched) about the challenges
of cognitive change upon reentry. See especially the conclud-
ing chapter in *On the Outside* and the work of Peggy Giordano:
https://scholarworks.bgsu.edu/cgi/viewcontent.cgi?article
=1012&context=soc_pub.

I first heard about PICS (post-incarceration syndrome) from
Maxwell Morris, a counselor at Sponsors. Here is a much-cited
research paper on the subject https://www.researchgate.net
/profile/Marieke-Liem/publication/236636420_Is_there_a
_recognizable_post-incarceration_syndrome_among_released
_lifers/links/5b17d95fa6fdcca67b5d90aa/Is-there-a
-recognizable-post-incarceration-syndrome-among-released
-lifers.pdf.

CHAPTER 4

Vicki says she self-medicates with meth for her ADHD. The
research is interesting on this subject, suggesting that substance
abuse and ADHD co-occur. See: https://www.ncbi.nlm.nih.gov
/pmc/articles/PMC2676785/.

Here is where you can learn more about Sponsors, Inc., the
nonprofit wraparound reentry services agency that connected
me and Vicki (and offered temporary housing to Dave) see:
https://sponsorsinc.org/.

CHAPTER 5

If the notion of "mitigating narrative" in the law (and sentencing) is new to you, here are two law review articles that help explain: https://scholarlycommons.law.hofstra.edu/cgi/viewcontent .cgi?article=2620&context=hlr and https://scholarlycommons .law.hofstra.edu/cgi/viewcontent.cgi?article=2812&context=hlr.

Quick primers on the teen brain: https://www.aacap.org /AACAP/Families_and_Youth/Facts_for_Families /FFF-Guide/The-Teen-Brain-Behavior-Problem-Solving-and -Decision-Making-095.aspxandhttps://www.urmc.rochester.edu /encyclopedia/content.aspx?ContentTypeID=1&ContentID= 3051.

CHAPTER 6

Here is the Second Look statute that made it possible for Trevor's early release: https://www.oregonlaws.org/ors/420A.203.

Trevor's success as a worker in the prison's laundry is touted here: https://oce.oregon.gov/content/showcasing_success _trevor_walraven.asp.

And here is a summary of his background, his crime, his release (and a photo of Trevor and Loraine): https://psuvanguard .com/growing-up-behind-bars/.

CHAPTER 7

Catherine on challenges after prison for the Campaign for the Fair Sentencing of Youth: https://www.youtube.com /watch?v=2pol3r64qS0.

Catherine and her brother are America's youngest convicted murderers: https://www.nbcnews.com/news/us-news /americas-youngest-convicted-murderers-held-1999-slaying-be -released-n398311.

CHAPTER 8

This well-informed Wikipedia article on prison sexuality offers three dozen references to research and media coverage on the subject: https://en.wikipedia.org/wiki/Prison_sexuality.

If you want to know more about the history of Pell Grants in prison and what helping to fund education inside means to prisoners, this *The Atlantic* article is a good read: https://www .theatlantic.com/ideas/archive/2021/03/restoring-pell -grantsand-possibilitiesfor-prisoners/618256/.

Also this from Inside Higher Ed: https://www.insidehighered .com/news/2021/01/27/pell-grants-restored-people-prison-eyes-turn-assuring-quality.

CHAPTER 9

Gangs, like the one Arnoldo joined as a youth and the one he closely associated with in prison, may be sources of violence and criminal activity, but they serve other purposes as well: https:// family.jrank.org/pages/674/Gangs-Family-Gangs-Gang-Family. html; https://tarrant.tx.networkofcare.org/kids/library/article. aspx?id=1814.

There is significant—and damning—research about the effects of isolation on prisoners. https://www.apa.org/monitor /2012/05/solitary.

Here is a primer on restorative justice for those who want to read more: http://restorativejustice.org/restorative-justice /about-restorative-justice/#sthash.WXY4Rxn1.dpbs.

CHAPTER 10

After Life Imprisonment, Homeward, and *On the Outside* all offer insight into the experience of those first days after release. Here you can read short responses to "What does the first day of prison feel like?" from prisoners themselves: https://www.quora.com/What-does-the-first-day-out-of-prison-feel-like. The increase in reentry services organizations is detailed in Ortiz and Jackey. The Urban Institute study is here: https://www.urban.org/research/publication/prison-home-dimensions-and-consequences-prisoner-reentry.

Here is the portal to the Boston Reentry Study, which includes research briefs and working papers: https://scholar.harvard.edu/brucewestern/boston-reentry-study. DeAngelo, quoted in this chapter, was a participant in the Michigan Study chronicled in *On the Outside*. His comments are on p. 61. Here are some stats on drug abuse among the incarcerated population from the Bureau of Justice Statistics, U.S. Department of Justice: https://www.bjs.gov/content/pub/pdf/dudaspji0709.pdf. NIH's National Institute on Drug Abuse also has credible figures: https://www.drugabuse.gov/publications/drugfacts/criminal-justice. Trevor's parole restrictions were extreme, but in fact, the parole system in general has shifted from casework, treatment, and integration to surveillance. See this analysis: https://www.uscourts.gov/sites/default/files/fed_probation_dec_2006.pdf. Catherine's *Florida Today* interview is here: https://www.floridatoday.com/story/news/local/john-a-torres/2015/11/20/after-prison-catherine-jones-now-gazes-stars/75931226/.

CHAPTER 11

Restorative justice, which has had such a significant impact on Sterling and Arnoldo, traces its history to the late 1970s and the pioneering work of Howard Zehr. Please take a look here: https://zehr-institute.org/staff/howard-zehr/. Karuna Thompson, one of the prison's chaplains and a passionate advocate for restorative justice, appears in this chapter (and elsewhere). Her work is

extraordinary. She is one of the chaplains featured in this documentary: http://chaplainsmovie.com/. I was—as is probably obvious—a participant in both the events chronicled in
this chapter. For the restorative justice event orchestrated by
Sterling, my middle son, Zane, who had just earned his master's
degree in restorative justice and conflict resolution, came into
the prison with me. His astute observations greatly enhanced
my own. Sterling's incredibly complicated legal case is mentioned here and elsewhere in the book. Ryan O'Connor, his lead
lawyer, was both generous with his time and very patient with
me. The tangled web of case law, state statutes, and Supreme
Court rulings is, well, tangled. I have tried to simplify. Here
is a thorough explanation of the Supreme Court *Miller* ruling:
https://www.oyez.org/cases/2011/10-9646.

CHAPTER 12

To read the entire Prison Policy Initiative report on homelessness and those released from prison, go here: https://www
.prisonpolicy.org/reports/housing.html. Stable housing is viewed
as the foundation for successful reentry. See especially the work
of Gunnison and Helfgott; Rodriguez and Brown; also Lutze, pp.
472–3; Baptiste, p. 2. Here is that Harvard study on the decline
of low-cost rentals: https://www.jchs.harvard.edu/blog/the
-continuing-decline-of-low-cost-rentals. You can find Patricia
McKernan's story about Darryl at www.voa.org/homelessness
-and-prisoner-reentry. Concerning sexual abuse in Catherine's
home: the abuse was revealed during an interview with *Florida
Today* and verified in confidential documents revealed to *Florida
Today* by an attorney working to gain the children clemency:
https://www.floridatoday.com/story/news/local/2015/07/31
/catherine-jones-free-woman-florida-brevard-county-curtis

-jones/30935093/. Here is the housing page from the Sponsors website. You can see how attractive the facilities are where Dave spent his first ninety days. https://sponsorsinc.org/housing/.

CHAPTER 13

Employment is a much-studied aspect of reentry. The research I read and present in this chapter on employment/unemployment rates, and the difficulties and obstacles encountered by ex-offenders come from Baptiste; Couloute and Kopf; LeBel and Maruna; Vishner, et. al. The race and gender specific out-of-work statistics come from Couloute and Kopf's report. Here is a link to that Center for Economic and Policy Research study on ex-offender employment rates: https://www.prisonlegalnews.org/news/2011/dec/15/study-shows-ex-offenders-have-greatly-reduced-employment-rates/. The data on educational levels of prisoners comes from https://www.prisonpolicy.org/reports/education.html. Discussion about and research on the "collateral consequences" of incarceration can be found in Baptiste and Petersilia, and in the lives and stories recounted in *On the Outside* and *After Life Imprisonment*. Here is an overview comparing all fifty states on policies and legislation concerning the licensing of ex-offenders: https://ccresourcecenter.org/state-restoration-profiles/50-state-comparisoncomparison-of-criminal-records-in-licensing-and-employment/. For background on and research about Ban the Box, see Agan, and Doleas and Hansen.

CHAPTER 14

This is not an easy read, but if you have never heard of life-course criminology and want to understand its theory and development, go here: https://doi.org/10.1111/j.1745-9125.2003.tb00987.x.

On the Outside devotes an entire chapter to marital

relationships, pp. 107–39. In *After Life Imprisonment*, Liem states that marriage and employment are the two most meaningful turning points in an ex-offender's reentry. See pp. 139–45 for details from the lives of the participants she tracked. Also see the extensive research conducted by Wallace, et. al., on the role of marital relationships. Megan Comfort's book on women who marry, and stand by, incarcerated men, is a revelation. Everyone should read it. For more on "assortative mating," see https://pubmed .ncbi.nlm.nih.gov/5441731/.

This *Psychology Today* article is a good primer on hybristophilia: https://www.psychologytoday.com/us/blog/in-excess/201310 /passion-victim.

CHAPTER 15

The ACLU's summary of data on women in prison is here: https:// www.aclu.org/other/words-prison-did-you-know and here: https://www.aclu.org/other/facts-about-over-incarceration -women-united-states. The Bureau of Justice Statistics's report on incarcerated mothers is here: https://www.bjs.gov/content /pub/pdf/pptmc.pdf

The interchange between the interviewer and the study participant is on p. 130 of *On the Outside*.

CHAPTER 16

The cue reactivity process with drug, alcohol, and nicotine addictions has been widely studied: https://psycnet.apa.org/ record/2013-04651-014. Maruna's work on "doomed to deviance" is explained in his book, *Making Good*. This summary is very helpful as well. http://dx.doi.org/10.4135/9781412959193.n159

CHAPTER 17

This article will help explain toxic masculinity in prison: https://www.psychologytoday.com/us/blog/prisons-and -prisms/201904/toxic-masculinity-in-and-outside-prison. As the pandemic took hold, local and national news media covered COVID-19 outbreaks in prisons. This research in the *Journal of the American Medical Association* discusses the conditions in prisons that made these places hotspots. The 5.5 times elevated rate in prisons is part of these research findings: https:// jamanetwork.com/journals/jama/fullarticle/2768249. Here is Sterling's April 2020 COVID-19 op-ed in *The Oregonian*: https:// www.oregonlive.com/opinion/2020/04/opinion-to-those -behind-bars-or-patrolling-them-covid-19-represents-a-shared -threat.html. The evacuation of prisoners from Oregon facilities due to the wildfires was such big news that *The Guardian* covered it: https://www.theguardian.com/us-news/2020/sep/14 /oregon-prison-evacuations-pepper-spray-wildfires

CHAPTER 18

Again, most accurate data on incarcerated women can be found here: https://www.aclu.org/other/words-prison-did-you-know and here https://www.aclu.org/other/facts-about-over- incarceration-women-united-states.

The study on the reentry experiences of women is here: https://www.ojp.gov/pdffiles1/nij/grants/230420.pdf.

CHAPTER 19

Sterling's legal case is very complicated, and reading the case law is confusing. This overview, written for laypeople helps clarify: https://www.prisonlegalnews.org/news/2020/jul/1/oregon -federal-court-8th-and-14th-amendments-mandate-miller-hearing/

That said, here is the U.S. district court's ruling in its entirety: https://www.documentcloud.org/documents/6784170- sterlingcuniorulingfeb2020.html, which includes the legal cita- tions to all the various cases.

CHAPTER 20

See source notes above (Chapter 19) for Sterling's legal battle and many cases.

CHAPTER 21

The Marshall Project's data on the "misleading math of recidivism" is here: https://www.themarshallproject.org/ search?q=misleading+math+of+recidivism

This is the portal to a variety of publications and research findings concerning recidivism gathered by the Bureau of Justice Statistics: https://www.bjs.gov/index.cfm?ty=tp&tid=17. The UC Irvine report on recidivism as a consequence of parole viola- tions (not because of another crime): https://cpb-us-e2.wpmucdn .com/sites.uci.edu/dist/0/1149/files/2013/06/bulletin _2005_vol-1_is-1.pdf. Haney's work on "prisonization" is much cited. Here is an abstract. The entire paper is download- able from the site. https://www.ojp.gov/ncjrs/virtual-library /abstracts/psychological-impact-incarceration-implications -post-prison. Read about the Norway model here, with the quotes from the prison officials: https://norwaytoday.info/ culture/what-are-prisons-in-norway-like-really/.

SOURCES

Abramson, L.Y; Martin Seligman and J. Teasdale. "Learned Helplessness in Humans." *Journal of Abnormal Psychology* 87, no. 1 (1978) (1): 49–74.

Aerten, Ivo and Brunilda Pali, eds. *Critical Restorative Justice*. London: Bloomsbury, 2020.

Agan, Amanda. "Increasing Employment of People with Records: Policy Changes in the Era of Ban the Box." *Criminology and Public Policy* 16, no. 1 (Feb. 2017): 177–85.

Ames, Blair. "NIJ-Funded Research Examines What Works for Successful Reentry.. *National Institute of Justice Journal* 281 (November 2019).

Baer, Demelza, et. al. "Understanding the Challenges of Prisoner Reentry: Research Findings from the Urban Institute's Prisoner Reentry Portfolio." Washington, DC: Justice Policy Center, Urban Institute, 2006.

Baptiste, Nathalie. "After Incarceration, What Next?" *American Prospect*, Jan. 26, 2016. http://prospect.org/article/after-incarceration-what-next.

Barnard, Jeff. "Seemingly Sheltered from Evil, Oregon Teens Face Murder Charges." *Associated Press*, June 6, 1999.

Blumstein, Alfred and Kiminori Nakamura. "Redemption in the Presence of Widespread Criminal Background Checks." *Criminology* 47, no. 2 (May 2019): 327–59.

Bright, Charles. *The Powers That Punish: Prison and Politics in the Era of the "Big House," 1920-1955*. Ann Arbor, MI: University of Michigan Press, 1996.

Bushway, Shawn, Michael Stoll, and David Weiman. *Barriers to Reentry? The Labor Market for Released Prisoners in Post-Industrial America*. NY: Russell Sage, 2007.

Casella, Jean, James Ridgeway, and Sarah Shourd, eds. *Hell is a Very Small Place*. NY: New Press, 2016.

Christian, Johnna, Jeff Mellow, and Shenique Thomas. "Social and Economic Implications of Family Connections to Prisoners." *Journal of Criminal Justice* 34 (4): 443–52.

Ciavaglia, Jo. "Barriers to Betterment: How Occupational Restrictions Hurt Ex-Offenders' Economy." *Bucks County Courier Times*, Feb. 22, 2019.

Clifford, Stephanie. "The First Year Out." *Marie Claire*, June 8, 2020. www .marieclaire.com/politics/a32630854/prison-release-recidivism.

"Collateral Consequences: The Crossroads of Punishment, Redemption and the Effects on Communities." U.S. Commission on Civil Rights Briefing Report. Washington, DC: U.S. Commission on Civil Rights, June 2019.

Comfort, Megan. *Doing Time Together: Love and Family in the Shadow of Prison*. Chicago: University of Chicago Press, 2008.

Couloute, Lucius. "Getting Back on Course: Educational Exclusion and Attainment among Formerly Incarcerated People." Prison Policy Initiative Report, Oct. 2018. https://www.prisonpolicy.org/reports/education.html.

Couloute, Lucius and Daniel Kopf. "Unemployment Among Formerly Incarcerated People." Prison Policy Initiative Report, July 2018. www.prisonpolicy.org /reports/outofwork.html.

Covington, Stephanie. "A Woman's Journey Home: Challenges for Female Offenders and Their Children." Paper presented to From Prison to Home Conference, Jan. 2002. www.urban.org/research/publication /womans-journey-home.

Crapser, Nick. "Three Es of Reentry." TEDx Humboldt Bay. www.youtube.com /watch?v=aEWUg1zeUsg.

Crawley, Elaine and Richard Sparks. "Is There Life After Imprisonment? How Elderly Men Talk about Imprisonment and Release." *Criminology and Criminal Justice* 6 (1): 62–82.

Doleac, Jennifer L. and Benjamin Hansen. "Does 'Ban the Box' Help or Hurt Low -Skilled Workers? Statistical Discrimination and Employment Outcomes When Criminal Histories Are Hidden." National Bureau of Economics Research working paper no. 22469 (July 2016). https://www.nber.org /system/files/working_papers/w22469/w22469.pdf.

Evans, Jeff, ed. *Undoing Time: American Prisoners in their Own Words*. Boston: Northeastern University Press, 2001.

Fellner, Jamie and Marc Mauer. "Losing the Vote: The Impact of Felony Disenfranchisement Laws in the U.S." Washington, DC: The Sentencing Project, 1998. https://www.sentencingproject.org/publications/losing-the -vote-the-impact-of-felony-disenfranchisement-laws-in-the-united-states/.

Ferner, Matt. "These Programs are Helping Prisoners Live Again on the Outside." *Huffington Post*, July 28, 2016.

Gunnison, Elaine and Jacqueline B. Helfgott. "Factors That Hinder Offender Reentry Success: A View from Community Corrections Officers." *International Journal of Offender Therapy and Comparative Criminology* 55, no. 2 (March 2010): 287–304.

Harding, David, Jeffrey Morenoff, and Jessica Wyse. *On the Outside: Prisoner Reentry and Reintegration*. Chicago: The University of Chicago Press, 2019.

Harvard Kennedy School. "The Boston Reentry Study: Finding Work After Prison." Rappaport Institute, June 2015. https://scholar.harvard.edu/files /brucewestern/files/employmentvfinal.pdf.

Human Rights Watch. "Prison Conditions in the U.S." New York: Human Rights Watch, 1991. https://www.hrw.org/reports/1995/WR95/HRWGEN-04 .htm.

Hunter, Brownwyn, et. al. "A Strength-Based Approach to Prisoner Reentry: The Fresh Start Prisoner Reentry Program." *International Journal of Offender Therapy and Comparative Criminology* 60 (11): 1298–1314.

Ignatieff, Michael. *The Needs of Strangers*. NY: Penguin Books, 1986.

LeBel, Thomas, Matt Richie, and Shadd Maruna. "Can Released Prisoners 'Make It'? Examining Formerly Incarcerated Persons' Belief in Upward Mobility and the 'American Dream.'" In Stan Stojkovic, ed. *Prisoner Reentry: Critical Issues and Policy Directions*. New York: Palgrave Macmillan U.S., 2017, pp. 245–305.

Li, Melissa. "From Prisons to Communities: Confronting Reentry Challenges and Social Inequality." The SES Indicator (March 2018). www.apa.org/pi/ses /resources/indicator/2018/03/prisons-to-communities.aspx.

Liem, Marieke. *After Life Imprisonment: Reentry in the Era of Mass Incarceration*. NY: New York University Press, 2016.

Liem, Marieke and Maarten Kunst. "Is There a Recognizable Post-Incarceration Syndrome among Released 'Lifers'?" *International Journal of Law and Psychiatry* 36, no. 3-4 (April 2013): 333–7. doi.org/10.1016 /j.ijlp.2013.04.012. Epub 2013 Apr. 30.

Lindquist, Christine, et. al. "Prisoner Reentry Experiences of Adult Females: Characteristics, Service Receipt and Outcomes of Participants in the SVORI Multi-Site Evaluation." U.S. Department of Justice Report Dec. 2009.

Loeffler, Charles. "Does Imprisonment Alter the Life Course?" *Criminology* 51, no. 1 (Feb. 2013): 137–66.

Lutze, Faith, Jeffrey Rosky, and Zachary Hamilton. "A Multisite Outcome Evaluation of Washington State's Reentry Housing Program for High-Risk Offenders." *Criminal Justice and Behavior* 41, no. 4 (April 2014): 471–91.

Maier, Steven and Martin Seligman. "Learned Helplessness: Theory and Evidence," *Journal of Experimental Psychology: General*, 105, no. 1 (1976): 3–46. doi.org/10.1037/0096-3445.105.1.3.

Manza, Jeff and Christopher Uggen. *Locked Out: Felon Disenfranchisement and American Democracy*. NY: Oxford University Press, 2008.

Maruna, Shadd. *Making Good: How Ex-Convicts Reform and Rebuild Their Lives*. Washington, DC: American Psychology Association Press, 2001.

Mauer, Marc and Meda Chesney-Lind, eds. *Invisible Punishment: The Collateral Consequences of Mass Incarceration.* NY: New Press, 2002.

McCollough, Michael. *Beyond Revenge: The Evolution of the Forgiveness Instinct.* San Francisco: Jossey-Bass, 2008.

McKernan, Patricia. "Evidence-Based Strategies that Promote Improved Outcomes." www.voa.org/homelessness-and-prisoner-reentry.

Metraux, Stephen, Dana Hunt, and Will Yetvin. "Criminal Justice Reentry and Homelessness." Center for Evidence-Based Solutions, Feb. 2020. http://evidenceonhomelessness.com/wp-content/uploads/2020/04/Reentry-and-Homelessness_Synthesis-of-the-Evidence.pdf.

Mooallem, Jon. "You Just Got Out of Prison. Now What?" *New York Times Magazine,* July 19, 2015.

Morris, Norval and David Rotham. *Oxford History of the Prison.* NY: Oxford University Press, 1995.

Mowen, Thomas and John Boman. "Do We Have It All Wrong? The Protective Roles of Peers and Criminogenic Risks from Family During Prison Reentry." *Crime Delinquency* 65, no. 5 (2019): 681–704.

Mumola, C.J. "Incarcerated Children and their Parents." Bureau of Justice Statistics Special Report. Washington, DC: Department of Justice, Bureau of Justice Statistics, Aug. 2000. https://www.bjs.gov/content/pub/pdf/iptc.pdf.

Ortiz, Jennifer. "Gangs and Environment: A Comparative Analysis of Prison and Street Gangs." *American Journal of Qualitative Research* 2, no. 1 (2018): 97–117.

Ortiz, Jennifer and Hayley Jackey. "The System Is Not Broken, It Is Intentional: The Prison Reentry Industry as Deliberate Structural Violence." *The Prison Journal* 99, no. 4 (2019): 484–503.

Pager, Devah. "The Mark of a Criminal Record." *American Journal of Sociology* 108, no. 5 (2003): 937–75.

Petersilia, Joan. *When Prisoners Come Home: Parole and Prisoner Reentry.* NY: Oxford University Press, 2003.

Rhodes, Lorna. *Total Confinement: Madness and Reason in the Maximum Security Prison.* Berkeley: University of California Press, 2004.

Rodriguez, Nino and Brenner Brown. "Preventing Homelessness Among People Leaving Prison." Vera Institute of Justice Issues in Brief, Dec. 2003. https://www.prisonpolicy.org/scans/vera/209_407.pdf.

Roman, Caterina and Jeremy Travis. "Where Will I Sleep Tomorrow? Housing, Homelessness and the Returning Prisoner." *Housing Policy Debate* 17, no. 2 (Jan. 2006): 389–418.

Ross, Jeffrey and Stephen Richards. *Beyond Bars: Rejoining Society After Prison.* NY: Alpha, 2009.

Saloner, Brendon, Kalind Parish, and Julie Ward. "COVID-19 Cases and Deaths in Federal and State Prisons." *Journal of the American Medical Association,* July 8, 2020. www.jamanetwork.com/journals/jama/fullarticle/2768249.

Schnittker, Jason and Michael Massoglia. "A Sociocognitive Approach to Studying the Effects of Incarceration." *Wisconsin Law Review* 2 (2015): 349–79.

Seligman, Martin. "Learned Helplessness." *Annual Review of Medicine* 23, no. 1 (1972): 407–12.

Seligman, Martin, et. al. "Coping Behavior: Learned Helplessness, Physiological Change and Learned Inactivity." *Behavioral Research Therapy* 18, no. 5 (1980): 459–61.

Sered, Danielle. *Until We Reckon: Violence, Mass Incarceration and A Road to Repair.* NY: The New Press, 2019.

Smith, Caleb. *The Prison and the American Imagination.* New Haven: Yale University Press, 2009.

Stevenson, Bryan. *Just Mercy: A Story of Justice and Redemption.* NY: Random House, 2014.

Thacher, David. "The Rise of Criminal Background Screening in Rental Housing." *Law and Social Inquiry* 33, no. 1 (2008): 5–30.

Toch, Hans. *Corrections: A Humanistic Approach.* Albany, NY: Criminal Justice Press, 1997.

Travis, Jeremy. "But They All Come Back: Rethinking Prisoner Reentry." Sentencing and Corrections Issues for the 21st Century. U.S. Department of Justice, National Institute of Justice, May 2000. https://www.ojp.gov /pdffiles1/nij/181413.pdf.

Travis, Jeremy and Caterina Roman. "Taking Stock: Housing, Homelessness and Prisoner Reentry." The Urban Institute, March 8, 2004. http://dx.doi .org/10.13140/RG.2.1.4698.5203.

Travis, Jeremy, Amy Solomon, and Michelle Waul. "From Prison to Home: The dimension and consequences of prisoner reentry." Washington, DC: Justice Policy Center, Urban Institute, June 2001. https://www.ojp.gov/ncjrs /virtual-library/abstracts/prison-home-dimensions-and-consequences -prisoner-reentry.

Travis, Jeremy and Christy Visher, eds. *Prisoner Reentry and Crime in America.* New York: Cambridge University Press, 2005.

Veysey, Bonita, Johnna Christian, and Damian Martinez, eds. *How Offenders Transform their Lives.* Portland, OR: Willan Publishers, 2009.

Vishner, Christy, Sara Debus-Sherill, and Jennifer Yahner. "Employment After Prison: A Longitudinal Study of Former Prisoners." *Justice Quarterly* 28, no. 5 (Oct. 2011): 698–718. doi.org/10.1080/07418825.2010.535553.

Vishner, Christy, Nancy LaVigne, and Jeremy Travis. "Returning Home: Understanding the Challenges of Prisoner Reentry." Research Report, Justice Policy Center, Urban Institute, Jan. 2004. http://webarchive.urban .org/publications/410974.html.

Vishner, Christy and Jeremy Travis. "Transitions from Prison to Community: Understanding Individual Pathways." *Annual Review of Sociology* 29 (2003): 89–113.

Wallace, Danielle, et.al. "Recidivism and Relationships: Examining the Role of Relationship Quality in Reincarceration." *Journal of Developmental and Life-Course Criminology* 6 (May 2020): 321-352. doi.org/10.1007 /s40865-020-00144-6.

Wasilewski, Louise. "New Way to Help Ex-Inmates Reenter Society and Stay Out of Prison." TEDxTalks, Nov. 14, 2017. https://www.youtube.com /watch?v=1gTNgijhKzw.

Western, Bruce. *Homeward: Life in the Year After Prison*. NY: Russell Sage, 2018.

Western, Bruce, et. al. "Stress and Hardship After Prison." *American Journal of Sociology* 120 (5): 1512–47.

Wyse, Jessica, David Harding and Jeffrey Morenoff. "Romantic Relationships and Criminal Desistance: Pathways and Processes." *Sociological Forum* 29, no. 2 (June 2014): 365–85.

Yeager, David. "Older Inmates Adjust to Life Outside Prison." *Social Work Today* 12, no. 1 (Jan./Feb. 2012): 28.

Zehr, Howard. *Changing Lenses: Restorative Justice for Our Times*. Harrisonburg, VA: Herald Press, 2015.

ABOUT THE AUTHOR

Lauren Kessler is an award-winning immersion reporter and narrative nonfiction writer who specializes in exploring invisible subcultures in our midst. Combining lively storytelling with deep research, she has written about everything, from the gritty world of a maximum security prison (*A Grip of Time*) to the grueling world of ballet (*Raising the Barre*) to the surprisingly vibrant world of those with Alzheimer's (*Dancing with Rose*). She ran a writing group for lifers inside a maximum security penitentiary and volunteers as a mentor and résumé-writing coach at a prison reentry services nonprofit. Founder of two graduate programs in narrative journalism, she currently teaches storytelling for social change at the University of Washington and for the Forum of Journalism and Media in Vienna. She is, by nature if not by birth, an Oregonian.

laurenkessler.com